M000273718

Getting Results from Software Development Teams

Lawrence J. Peters

PUBLISHED BY
Microsoft Press
A Division of Microsoft Corporation
One Microsoft Way
Redmond, Washington 98052-6399

Copyright © 2008 by Lawrence Peters

All rights reserved. No part of the contents of this book may be reproduced or transmitted in any form or by any means without the written permission of the publisher.

Library of Congress Control Number: 2007928772

Printed and bound in the United States of America.

1 2 3 4 5 6 7 8 9   QWT   3 2 1 0 9 8

Distributed in Canada by H.B. Fenn and Company Ltd.

A CIP catalogue record for this book is available from the British Library.

Microsoft Press books are available through booksellers and distributors worldwide. For further information about international editions, contact your local Microsoft Corporation office or contact Microsoft Press International directly at fax (425) 936-7329. Visit our Web site at www.microsoft.com/mspress. Send comments to mspinput@microsoft.com.

Microsoft and Microsoft Press are either registered trademarks or trademarks of Microsoft Corporation in the United States and/or other countries. Other product and company names mentioned herein may be the trademarks of their respective owners.

The example companies, organizations, products, domain names, e-mail addresses, logos, people, places, and events depicted herein are fictitious. No association with any real company, organization, product, domain name, e-mail address, logo, person, place, or event is intended or should be inferred.

This book expresses the author's views and opinions. The information contained in this book is provided without any express, statutory, or implied warranties. Neither the authors, Microsoft Corporation, nor its resellers, or distributors will be held liable for any damages caused or alleged to be caused either directly or indirectly by this book.

Acquisitions Editor: Ben Ryan
Developmental Editor: Devon Musgrave
Project Editor: Kathleen Atkins
Editorial Production: Waypoint Press
Technical Reviewer: Michael Deutsch; Technical Review services provided by Content Master, a
                     member of CM Group, Ltd.
Copy Editors: Jennifer Harris and Christina Yeager
Cover Illustration: John Hersey

Body Part No. X13-23796

For my grandsons, Jacob and Joseph

Contents at a Glance

Table of Contents

Part I The Preliminaries

Part II Software Development as a Process

What do you think of this book? We want to hear from you!

Microsoft is interested in hearing your feedback so we can continually improve our books and learning resources for you. To participate in a brief online survey, please visit:

www.microsoft.com/learning/booksurvey

What do you think of this book? We want to hear from you!

Microsoft is interested in hearing your feedback so we can continually improve our books and learning resources for you. To participate in a brief online survey, please visit:

www.microsoft.com/learning/booksurvey

Acknowledgments

Anyone who has written a book of any kind knows that it takes a bunch of people, not machines, to create, perfect (to some extent) and produce the content the reader sees. In this regard, a bunch of people whom I have never met are due a great debt of thanks: Steve Sagman and his editors at Waypoint Press, Jennifer Harris and Christina Yeager, who demonstrated a high pain threshold and waded through this author's meandering, helping to shape it into something coherent. The Waypoint Press art staff who took drawings that were done in an engineering format and turned them into something palatable. The editors at Microsoft Press who saw this production through three major overhauls, reorganizations and revisions. Ben Ryan at Microsoft Press for his patience and understanding. Devon Musgrave at Microsoft Press, for his patience and valuable organizational and content suggestions. John Zumsteg, Mike Deutsch, Ray McKenzie, and Ron Schultz for their insights, honesty, and sharing of experiences.

To all the project managers I have had the privilege of working with, thank you for providing dozens of examples and counterexamples, some of which were described in this text. Last, but not least, to Cathy, my wife, who is the best project manager I know, and who calls them like she sees them, even if it means a re-write, thank you. After almost 42 years, I love you more than ever.

Finally, the Acknowledgments section of a book of this type always reminds me of a quote from G.K. Chesterton: "I would maintain that thanks are the highest form of thought, and that gratitude is happiness doubled by wonder."

Preface

In my 40 years of experience in the software industry, I have worked on dozens of projects, seen successes and failures, and constantly strived to understand how projects and project managers achieve success. I have been incredibly fortunate in having worked with some of the best systems engineers, software developers, and project managers one could ever imagine, as well as some of the worst, and everything in between. During that time, I witnessed accomplished software engineers, who were competent in the software developer domain, struggle and frequently fail as software project managers. All too often, their software projects failed as well.

I was one of those software engineers who struggled to achieve some success in software project management, but somehow, I successfully brought projects in on time, on budget, and meeting or exceeding requirements. Those successes and my work as a software project management consultant led me to conclude that it would have been helpful to me and my colleagues if there existed a resource that covered the spectrum of management methods and techniques needed for success, without promoting a specific agenda or "method du jour." Such a resource also had to address how to achieve the maximum performance from software development teams who determine one's success as a software project manager. This is an essential issue in this book because I have seen software projects fail that were staffed with highly qualified people who availed themselves of consulting support, and that were supported by software tools and environments, but that were poorly managed. The main thesis of this book is that you and I, the software project managers, are the keys to project success. This book is a resource that can help ensure such success. Use it in good health. Now get out there and be successful!

—Larry Peters, Kent, Washington, March 31, 2008

Part I
The Preliminaries

Chapter 1
On Software Engineering and Management

All men can sustain adversity. If you want to test a man, give him power.

—Abraham Lincoln

Software project management might be the most widely ignored, least formalized part of the software profession. But the concept of what software project management is and is not has begun to evolve. Software project management is not software development and all that development involves. It is all about coordinating and directing software development activities by applying proven engineering management methods and principles that have been adapted to software engineering. Understanding how software engineering and project management interrelate is fundamental to the remainder of this book.

But first, a few preliminaries are in order. Project management involves leadership. Some see a distinction between management and leadership, but effective software project managers must both manage and lead. Leadership in the software project management domain is not about giving orders and expecting people to obey them; it is about formulating a plan of action to do what needs to be done, altering that plan over time to accommodate reality (all the while encouraging others to engage in developing the plan further), and achieving success via the plan. Leadership also involves listening and addressing all opinions, especially those contrary to our own, fairly, with respect, and recognizing their merit. Leadership means creating and maintaining an environment wherein everyone from the best and brightest to the most challenged does not avoid questioning a decision, reporting bad news, or experimenting with some new concept for fear of failure. Last, leadership involves hard work to achieve and maintain all of these goals and more over the course of a software project. In my career, I have watched arrogant software project managers stifle creativity, muffle dissent, and "shoot the messenger" bearing bad news. These behaviors tend not to lead to success. I have also seen firsthand software project managers who have performed what appear to be miracles by succeeding under the most trying circumstances with less than adequate teams. The difference between these two outcomes has always intrigued me. The difference is leadership. If you are willing to work at it, relinquish some autonomy, and entertain opinions contrary to your own, being a software project manager can be a rewarding and fulfilling profession. Let's look at how software engineering and management principles are related.

We'll begin with a few terminology conventions. Although they are often used interchangeably, the terms *plan* and *schedule* have separate and distinct meanings. A schedule is a list of dates and events directed at achieving a goal or goals, whereas a plan is a logically ordered set of tasks that will result in achieving those goals. For example, "design complete" is an event, while a time-ordered list of tasks with durations and resource assignments needed to achieve this goal constitutes a major part of a plan.

The reason these terms are so frequently interchanged is that the software project managers' success is based on hitting both the key target dates (the schedule) and the cost/feature/task targets. The need to successfully manage both of these critical aspects of a project is often overlooked by those who have decided to go into software project management. In this text, I will use the term *plan* to include schedule and the term *schedule* to refer only to the key dates and events associated with the project.

The Path to Management

Does your company have a clearly defined career path to get into software project management? If not, the absence probably seems odd, since generally companies have clearly defined paths to move from a junior-level engineer to a more senior position. These paths often involve obtaining an advanced degree and/or demonstrating exemplary techni- cal skills and so forth. But project management is another story. Either companies do not understand what is needed to be a project manager or they do not understand just what project managers do. In any case, this situation exists in spite of the fact that not having a defined means of moving from one place in the company to another has been cited as reducing job satisfaction and productivity (Linberg, 1999). One "casual" way into manage- ment is to become a group leader. Depending on the company, a group leader might also be referred to as a lead, lead programmer, software engineering lead, or senior software engi- neer. The job title will depend on the company involved and how that company has defined these roles. Once you achieve this leadership status, perform well, and indicate a desire to manage other leaders as a true manager, things might happen, but not with any degree of certainty. In many firms, you will go into management with little or no training, no assess- ment or refinement of your interpersonal skills, no introductory training in labor law, no training in motivation theory, and no knowledge of estimating, accounting, or status metrics reporting—all skills and knowledge needed to be effective at management. This greatly re- duces the potential effectiveness of software project managers and their chances of success.

The perception that a manager is a "company person" is largely a true one. The company envisions managers as putting the company first and everybody else (including themselves) second. The higher one goes within the firm, the stronger this view and the accompanying expectations that can become more and more intrusive into one's personal life. This percep- tion is exemplified during periods of high unemployment. Companies will lay off nonman- agers quickly in a high ratio to managers. In other words, managers would be the last people laid off. But for the manager who has been laid off, getting a job with another firm can be extremely difficult, because firms tend to promote managers from within the company. This means that the manager has a company-centric viewpoint, with some skills that might not transfer readily to another firm. The recent downturn in the software business has wreaked havoc on just about all of these and other "common wisdom" views. The loyalty that managers had to their firms was reciprocated by the loyalty and, in a manner of speaking, "protection" that firms showered on their managers. It used to be that managers were the last to be laid off. Now they often are among the first to go, in order to reduce payroll costs more quickly by laying off the more expensive workers.

Managing must be something that you want to do and do well because it will have a greater potential impact on the outcome of a project than programming, testing, or other project-related duties. But be forewarned: it does not hold the type of loyalty from the company or the monetary rewards it once did. However, the satisfaction of putting together a team, having the team members mature and grow as a group, and successfully bringing in a new system or making alterations to an existing system will always be there.

The Smart People Got It Wrong

Throughout its history, the field of software engineering has been marked by famous successes, infamous failures, and mounting pressure to find that magic elixir that will make the problems go away. The people who founded this industry and invented the term *software engineering* were bright people. They might even have been geniuses. But like most people, they had their shortcomings. Based on their writings and the direction that software engineering as a profession has taken for more than 40 years, the problems associated with software engineering have been seen as technical in nature. The conclusion this viewpoint presents us with is that if a problem exists, it is because a technical solution has not been found or an ineffective technical solution is being used and needs to be abandoned. The data we now have indicates that the problems encountered by most software projects are not technical in nature but relate instead to management (and to its use of power or, at least, authority).

Consider the pace with which we have been improving software engineering productivity over the period 1970 to 2000. We have seen a steady growth in software engineering productivity of about one source line of code per person-month per year over the reporting period (Jensen, 2000). Regardless of the new concepts introduced since, this progression implies that technical approaches alone will have, at best, only a minor impact on productivity. In his technically oriented book on software cost estimation, *Software Engineering Economics* (Prentice-Hall, 1981), Barry Boehm did not address project management factors with the assumed implication that software project management was uniform, constant, and good. As observed by Jensen, it has been uniform, not good, and unchanging. Take a look at Figure 1-1.

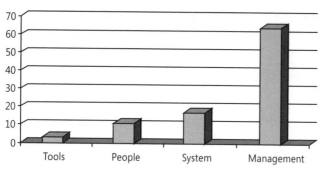

FIGURE 1-1 Relative percentage (vertical axis) of cost factors per the Constructive Cost Model (COCOMO).

The relative impact of the software project manager on the successful outcome of the project far exceeds the combined total of the other factors. Yet in spite of this and other evidence, the emphasis in the industry is still on technology as a solution to everything. Otherwise, how could one explain the disappearance of the IEEE Special Interest Group on Software Personnel, the relatively few tools and methods available to software engineering managers as compared with software engineers or developers, and the relatively recent "discovery" by the Software Engineering Institute (SEI) that people's capabilities might be important to success (Software Engineering Institute, 2003)? All of this is consistent with an assumption that software engineering project issues are technical in nature and are not management problems and that software project management is consistent, good, and effective.

At the risk of incurring the wrath of some gurus of the software industry, we can conclude that the founders of the software engineering profession got it wrong. In fact, they got it wrong for a long time. The issues can still be addressed with what we now know using the strategies and methods suggested in this book. These are presented as elements from which you can choose to create and tailor a system of methods and techniques appropriate to your organization and projects.

The Rest of Us Are Still Getting It Wrong

The Standish Group publishes an annual report on the state of health of software technology. The report is generally regarded as objective since their business is to acquire data and publish accurate analyses not directed at advertising some method or software tool. One recent report gives us a snapshot of where the state of the art of software engineering was at the beginning of this decade (Standish Group, 2001). Their top-ten list of factors leading to success in software engineering weighted according to their relative importance, shown in Table 1-1, reveals why software projects continue to fail.

TABLE 1-1 Relative Importance of Software Project Success Factors

Success Factor	Relative Importance (%)
Executive support (senior management commitment)	18
User involvement (continuous interaction with client)	16
Experienced project manager (manager has a record of success)	14
Clear business objectives (criteria for project success established)	12
Minimized scope (avoiding "feature creep")	10
Standard software infrastructure (existence of a defined process)	8
Firm basic requirements (low number of requirements changes)	6
Formal methodology (defined method exists for conducting project)	6
Reliable estimates (easier said than done)	5
Other criteria (everything else not thought of earlier)	5
Total	**100**

Notice the position of executive support. This support involves more than tacit approval of the software project manager's approach; it requires an unwavering belief in the software project manager's approach even if some software engineers and, perhaps, other managers are resisting the changes being instituted by the software project manager. The significance of this factor will become more obvious later in this book, but for now, its presence indicates that there are systemic problems within organizations that drive software projects to failure. When we introduce new methods and processes into an organization, success is highly dependent on support at the highest levels. What is being attempted is a culture change to improve software project results. Unless everyone knows that support for this change emanates from the highest levels of the firm, the change is unlikely to become permanent.

As part of the Standish Group's *CHAOS Report* for 2004 (Standish, 2004), a survey of executive managers found that in spite of the fact that various methods and techniques have now matured, executive managers believe that there are now more project failures than five and ten years ago, as shown in Table 1-2.

TABLE 1-2 Executive Managers' Perceptions of Project Failures

Category	Number of Failures Today Compared with 5 Years Ago	Number of Failures Today Compared with 10 Years Ago
Significantly more failure	27%	17%
Somewhat more failures	21%	29%
No change	11%	23%
Somewhat fewer failures	19%	23%
Significantly fewer failures	22%	8%

Clearly, Table 1-2 indicates that there is still a lot of room for improvement and, more important, that the approaches used in the past (for example, programming languages, new methods, and programming schemes) do not appear to be working as well as one would hope.

If the software engineering literature had been responsive to the information in Table 1-1, the number of articles published regarding the importance of project management would reflect its relative importance. The report indicates that the correlation is not positive, as shown in Table 1-3. A blank for an item in Table 1-3 indicates that the number of articles for that factor is negligible. Notice that the top six success factors (executive support through standard software infrastructure) constitute 70 percent of the weighted success factors but that their discussion in the literature is only 30 percent. In other words, the focus of software engineering in academia and the literature is on those areas with the least impact on project success.

TABLE 1-3 Relative Occurrence of Articles by Success Factor

Success Factor	Relative Occurrence (%)
Executive support	—
User involvement	20
Experienced project manager	—
Clear business objectives	—
Minimized scope	—
Standard software infrastructure	10
Firm basic requirements	25
Formal methodology	20
Reliable estimates	25
Other criteria	—
Total	**100**

It is certainly not helpful or encouraging to read that a panel of experts at the annual International Conference on Software Engineering who have extensive experience in the industry and who have studied this issue over the years concluded that the software industry has "failed to produce a cadre of competent Software Engineering Managers" (Schlumberger, 1991). Considering its source and the fact that these experts noted that this situation had existed for some time, this is quite a condemnation. Does this mean that there are no competent managers in the industry? No, certainly not. What it does mean is that "good," or effective, managers are a rare commodity in this industry. The reasons for this are somewhat evident already but will become clearer as this book unfolds.

A more important question to ask might be, "Why are there so few competent software engineering managers?" The answer to this question has several parts. First, there is the issue of how the executives of major corporations view managers in their respective software engineering organizations. They are not usually viewed favorably. Why? Because the problem with a product or some new service the company is launching always seems to be the software. It tends to be ready late, to overrun budget, and to be not as feature rich as originally envisioned. Such a track record rarely endears one to one's division manager or CEO (chief executive officer).

Second, in my experience, most executives understand neither software nor software people. Part of the reason for this, again in my experience, is that few high-level executives came out of the software development or information technology arena. This lack of understanding leads to the third reason: the lack of appropriate training. Most software engineering managers have had no training in management or the more specialized training needed to successfully manage software professionals (for example, motivational methods, project controls and metrics, and estimating). This is exacerbated by a serious perception difference between higher-level managers and project managers (Thanhaim, 1986). Table 1-4 illustrates how each group has identified its perception of the primary causes of overruns. I have highlighted the top three causes in each group. Notice that higher-level management sees the cause of overruns as being related to early planning, the project plan, and underestimating the project's scope, whereas project managers see overruns as being caused by the customer, technical complexity, and the project plan. They do at least agree that the project plan is among the top three causes. Other than that, we have some serious communications issues to overcome—specifically, identifying and agreeing on just what is causing the overruns.

TABLE 1-4 Perceptual Differences Regarding the Cause(s) of Overruns

As Ranked by General Managers	As Ranked by Project Managers	Problem/Issue
1	10	Insufficient front-end planning
2	3	Unrealistic project plan
3	8	Project scope underestimated
4	1	Customer and/or management changes

As Ranked by General Managers	As Ranked by Project Managers	Problem/Issue
5	14	Insufficient contingency planning
6	13	Inability to track progress
7	5	Inability to track problems early on
8	9	Insufficient number of checkpoints
9	4	Staffing problems
10	2	Technical complexity
11	6	Priority shifts
12	10	No commitment by personnel to plan
13	12	Uncooperative support groups
14	7	Sinking team spirit
15	15	Unqualified project personnel

Fourth, most companies do not publish how their employees might become software project managers. This is in spite of the fact that not having a defined means of moving from one position within a company to preferably a higher position has been identified as reducing job satisfaction and productivity (Linberg, 1999). One informal means of getting into management is to take on a leadership role such as a programming lead or senior software engineer. Once you achieve this leadership status and are reasonably successful, you might be offered the opportunity to move into a management slot. But no specific timetable or process is followed. Regardless of the company or circumstances, managing must be something that you want to do and do well, because it will have a greater impact on the success or failure of the project than any other factor. Building, motivating, and leading a team of software professionals to a successful outcome can be extremely rewarding personally and professionally for the software project manager.

The Functions of Management

Although the details are not widely agreed upon, all managers must perform a few basic functions:

- Planning
- Scheduling
- Controlling
- Staffing
- Motivating

I will expand on each of these functions later in this book, as well as cover some other functions of management that have been proposed by various authors. For now, keep in mind that the different viewpoints among management experts are exemplified by the fact that the *IEEE Software Engineering Series* does not mention motivation in its list of functions, whereas motivation is a standard topic for discussion in all management texts in the business community (Thayer and Dorfman, 2002). Even the *Software Engineering Body of Knowledge (SWEBOK)* gives it very little space (Abran and Moore, 2001). This is only one of many areas within the software engineering project management arena that finds itself at odds with the more accepted and successful management practices of the business community.

Some Data of Interest

One can make all the excuses in the world or question opinions, but it's pretty hard to argue with actual data. As an aphorism attributed to the Swiss Army goes, "When the map and the terrain disagree, trust the terrain." Here are some "terrain"-oriented numbers that should help put the importance of software engineering project management into perspective:

- Up to 60 percent of project costs can be attributed to personnel turnover (Cone, 1998).

- The number-one reason people leave a project or a company is the management (Linberg, 1999).

- Management is the most important factor in project success (Standish Group, 2001).

If the preceding list was a bit of a surprise, here is some more information that further emphasizes the scope of the problem (Standish Group, 2001):

- The average cost overrun in software projects is 189 percent.

- The average schedule overrun is 222 percent.

- On average, 61 percent of systems fail to meet expectations.

If the software industry wants to improve its success rate, we must find a way to improve the way software projects are managed.

Hope on the Horizon

Lest I approach the end of this first chapter without offering insight into how and where things can get better, consider the following from a talk given by Steve McConnell (McConnell, 2003). McConnell was discussing a firm that had achieved Capability Maturity Model (CMM) Level 5. For now, CMM can be described as a means of evaluating a software development organization's maturity and, by implication, its ability to produce quality software. It is a system for assessing the relative software engineering capability of an organization. The approach was developed by the SEI (Software Engineering Institute, 1993). The CMM levels range from Level 1 (chaos, no repeatability) to Level 5 (systematic, repeatable, controlled). McConnell related an incident that occurred at a CMM Level 5 firm, Telcordia. They had a 1-million-plus-source-line system that had to be modified due to a decision by the Federal Communications Commission (FCC). The change required about 3,000 lines of code to be created or modified. The changes were made, and no errors were reported in the first year of use. While this is remarkable by itself, there's more to the story. The company had undergone growth of about 40 percent, to 3,500 management and technical personnel, within the 18 months prior to the changes having to be made in the code. The most impressive part of the story is that the changes cited were made in just one 9-hour day. That's right, less than one flow day. So the next time someone remarks that this process improvement stuff is OK when things are going well but not in an emergency, just remember Telcordia. None of this would have been possible without a significant commitment of time and money as well as an act of faith by management. They had to believe that the CMM approach had merit, and they had to convey that belief through their actions to the software engineering team over a period of several years. In order to put the preceding discussion into perspective, it should be noted that Telcordia had a complete and thorough understanding of the application problem domain. Conversely, there have been many other firms who possessed such understanding within their own domain of interest but failed miserably in similar circumstances. In this case, we cannot overlook Telcordia's commitment to adhering to practices that had worked for them in the past and using them in what amounts to an emergency situation. All too often, software project managers have abandoned processes in an emergency. As you'll see later in this text, this is precisely the opposite of what they should do.

Perhaps one of the greatest benefits of institutionalizing processes within an organization is its effect on morale and productivity. The common wisdom among most managers is that instituting such measures will have a detrimental impact on the productivity of the organization. After all, these are creative people, and creative people "need some room to work in." Here the common wisdom is wrong again. Too many software project managers forget that people who deal with computer programming languages to create a product are inundated with syntactic and semantic rules. They thrive in this restrictive environment. Is it any wonder then that results like this are possible given the right environment? Remember, management sets the environment. As shown in Figure 1-2, a survey of 50 companies reveals the impact of CMM level achieved on morale (McConnell, 2003). With CMM Level 1 being the lowest and CMM Level 5 bordering on management nirvana, CMM Level 3 is a happy medium. I treat it this way because Level 3 is considerably easier to achieve than Level 5, and it represents, I believe, the best value for the investment made in change. Notice that the morale shift (and productivity shift) takes a significant jump in going from Level 1 to Level 3, with less added benefit from Level 2 to Level 3. This and other studies are showing a consistent pattern of people being more productive in structured and defined situations in which they know what is expected of them and can find ways to provide it.

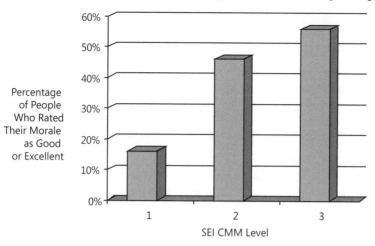

FIGURE 1-2 Impact of CMM level on morale through Level 3.

Summary

The evidence is quite clear that success in software engineering involves more than technical breakthroughs and is heavily dependent on project managers. These managers must possess and employ appropriate skills and attitudes about software projects and the people who populate them. They employ both tactical thinking (that is, rapid response to a potentially catastrophic event) and strategic thinking (long-range planning to prevent potentially catastrophic events). This thinking is most often actualized by means of some published method or technique, sometimes modified to suit the individual manager's preferences.

In the remainder of this book, I'll focus on methods and techniques that enable software engineering project managers to control three primary assets:

- **Scope**   This is what the project hopes to accomplish. Scope is more than just the requirements statement—it includes quality issues, customer expectations, marketing issues, corporate strategy, and more.

- **Resources**   These include cost, the reputation of the development manager, ultimately the company's reputation, possibly the company's existence, and most of all, the company's people, the most important resource to be managed.

- **Schedule (and plan)**   This relates to the flow time during which the software will move from a concept to a viable product or service.

The functions of management I mentioned earlier—planning, scheduling, controlling, staffing, and motivating—of course relate to management control of these assets and will be covered in greater detail in the coming chapters.

References

(Linberg, 1999)   Linberg, K. R. "Job Satisfaction Among Software Developers," doctoral dissertation. Walden University, St. Paul, MN, 1999.

(Jensen, 2000)   Jensen, R. W. "Don't Forget About Good Management." *CrossTalk*, p. 30, August 2000.

(Boehm, 1981)   Boehm, B. *Software Engineering Economics*. New York: Prentice-Hall, 1981.

(Software Engineering Institute, 2003)   Curtis, B., B. Hefley, and S. Miller. "SEI People Capability Maturity Model." Technical Report CMU/SEI-2001-MM-001. Pittsburgh, PA: Software Engineering Institute, Carnegie Mellon University, 2003.

(Standish Group, 2001)   The Standish Group. *The CHAOS Report*. West Yarmouth, MA, 2001.

(Standish Group, 2004)   The Standish Group. *The CHAOS Report*. West Yarmouth, MA, 2004.

(Schlumberger, 1991)   Schlumberger, M. "Software Engineering Management," in *Proceedings of the 13th International Conference on Software Engineering*. Los Angeles: IEEE, pp. 152–153, 1991.

(Thanhaim, 1986)   Thanhaim, H. J., and D. C. Wileman. "Criteria for Controlling Projects According to Plan," *Project Management Journal*, **17**(2), pp. 75–81, 1986.

(Thayer and Dorfman, 2002)   Thayer, R., and M. Dorfman, Eds. *Software Engineering*, vols. 1 and 2. Los Alamitos, CA: IEEE Computer Society, 2002.

(Abran and Moore, 2001)   Abran, A. and J. Moore, Eds. *Software Engineering Body of Knowledge (SWEBOK)*, Trial Version 1.00. Los Alamitos, CA: IEEE Computer Society, May 2001.

(Cone, 1998)   Cone, E. "Managing That Churning Sensation," *Information Week*, **680**, pp. 50–67, 1998.

(McConnell, 2003)   McConnell, S. "10 Myths of Rapid Development," lecture presented at Construx, Inc., Bellevue, WA, January 2003.

(Software Engineering Institute, 1993)   Paulk, M., B. Curtis, M. Chrissis, and C. Weber. "Capability Maturity Model for Software, Version 1.1." Technical Report CMU/SEI-93-TR-024, ESC-TR-93-177. Pittsburgh, PA: Software Engineering Institute, Carnegie Mellon University, February 1993.

Chapter 2
Why Is Software So Difficult?

Nearly all of project management is some form of risk management.

—Michael Deutsch, Texas A&M University

In the last sixty or so years, stories have proliferated about an area of the Atlantic Ocean bounded by Bermuda, Puerto Rico, and the east coast of Florida—the "Bermuda Triangle"—stories with just enough mystery and semi-fact to encourage their acceptance. The concept is that something in that region has caused many plane crashes, ship disappearances, and any manner of unexplainable phenomena. In this chapter, I'll examine the software industry's equivalent of the Bermuda Triangle, the balancing act that software engineering project managers must perform in executing a project plan while trying to meet all the demands and constraints that have changed and been placed upon it.

Not the least of these unreasonable constraints are the practices of setting a delivery schedule and budget without having developed a detailed design, estimating without input from the development team, and a lack of cognizance regarding the relationships among cost, schedule, and metrics. The triangle is composed of the three elements mentioned at the end of the previous chapter: scope, resources, and plan or schedule. Many software projects have "disappeared" (that is, failed) when they've encountered the interrelated problems that compose software's Bermuda Triangle. Let's look at how to recognize and effectively deal with the issues that the "triangle" presents.

The Nature of the Beast

A lot of software engineering project managers have looked longingly at other fields where life seems simpler and more predictable. The industry most often looked at is construction—both home building and large building construction (skyscrapers, sports arenas, and so on). It seems relatively straightforward: you have a set of requirements, the customer's expectations are set early on and are relatively easy to manage, a blueprint is developed before firm estimates and schedules are committed to, you are dealing with physical principles and construction practices developed over thousands of years, subcontractors do their thing, you finish close to the deadline promised and within cost, and you make a profit. What could be simpler?

Well, anyone in the construction business will tell you that it's almost never that simple. When a construction firm bids a fixed price on a job, it's often to build something that no one else has built. When this is the case, estimating becomes something of an art. Experience and intuition hold sway over science and engineering. Bids are set up in such a way that if there are no changes to the original blueprints, the contractor will make no profit, since the original bid covers only costs and labor. This strategy is based on the fact that there are almost always changes in requirements and blueprints. It is in making and charging for those changes that profits lie. Many contractors will openly admit this practice, since they foresee great risk in bidding a fixed price on a job that they have never done before—at least not one identical to this new one—and they do not know what to expect.

In software, it seems we are always building something new and different. It might not seem so when you're working on your nth order entry and inventory control system or Internet-based customer response system, but they are all new and different in some way from their predecessors. Not unlike ancient Roman architects, who built new cities on top of old ones, you might be building these "new" software systems on the ruins of preceding ones or at least making use of some of the lessons learned with the old system. But there are some real and significant differences between building in the physical world and building in the software world. One significant difference lies in our comprehension of the problems faced in successfully completing the software project. In complex software systems (somehow, they always seems to be complex), the problems we face are understood only in broad terms. This is partly due to the complexity we face but also due to our meager understanding of the interactions among the various elements of the future software system. The full ramifications of what has to be done are not revealed until later, when the details are addressed. The complexity, the newness, and the opportunity for the software development team to "do it right" (or at least better) this time motivates the team but obscures the level of complexity we will have to deal with.

Objects in the physical world have attributes that we experience with our senses. One problem with software is that it is an abstraction. It resides in a domain we cannot experience with our senses. It has properties that make it different from what we experience in the physical world, as described in Table 2-1. Not having other experiences to guide them, the software project manager and the team members most often revert to what they have experienced in the physical world. It is as though our learning takes place in one domain, while our work takes place in another.

TABLE 2-1 **Comparison of Hardware and Software Properties**

Phenomenon	Hardware	Software
Manufacture of exact duplicates	A challenge	Not a problem
Wearing out with use or passage of time	A major issue	Not a problem
Experienced physically	Not a problem	Not experienced
Progress measured during construction	Observable	Observable only via a baseline process
Cost, schedule, and planning	Experienced physically	Requires speculation and relatively high risk

In the physical world, whether we are building an aircraft or a house, we can go out and see, touch, and experience the results of the process. If we're satisfied that progress is sufficient, our anxiety goes down. For example, the digging of the foundation for a home, setting forms, pouring concrete, and so forth indicate steps in a process that will lead to a complete home. These steps happen sequentially. Their completion indicates real progress that a customer can experience and evaluate. But in the case of software development, all we end up with at the early stages are (hopefully) some documents stating what the requirements are, an assessment of the cost and schedule, an architectural design, and so on. Until some form of the system is available to try out, the customer has little to experience. Sometimes this early "trial system" is a prototype. Software requires something of a leap of faith for the customer, the manager of the project, and those involved in developing it. They must mutually believe that the process being used, the means of documentation, and the content of regularly scheduled reviews and status reports can be trusted and that proper progress is being made. But as we know, there's nothing like reality to ruin a great theory or illusion!

In general, engineering in the physical world has a better track record of foreseeing problems and planning for them. For instance, the engineers of the new international airport in Hong Kong and, more recently, the newest international airport in Japan both had foreseen serious settling problems because the airports were built on fill material. They took this into account and maintained the slope of the runways through elaborately constructed systems. Why is this sort of planning difficult in software? One major reason is physics. Engineers dealing with the physical world are working with the immutable laws of physics. For example, a colleague of mine frequently notes, "Gravity wins—it always wins." These laws of physics have not changed since the earth was formed. So it is predictable that, in the case of a runway built over fill material, there will be settling. This can be experimented with, measured, documented, and planned for. It is more difficult to deal with the future in the software domain, where unforeseen problems or changes in the business climate can often cause major setbacks. In software, there is a lack of similar principles with which to plan for and prevent problems.

There isn't a software project manager running a nontrivial project who hasn't been faced with a scheduling, cost, or feature problem at some point. The project has spent well above the expenditure projections, the project is behind the timeline established for it, or not all the features are going to be present in the production system. In many instances, the project manager has to deal with all three of these problems—the Bermuda Triangle of software, shown in Figure 2-1—at the same time.

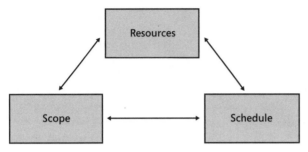

FIGURE 2-1 The Bermuda Triangle of software.

Far too many software project managers have wandered into this set of issues and, essentially, never found their way back out:

- **Scope**   The requirements (for example, functional, performance, strategic, and legal) that the system must fulfill.

- **Resources**   The money, people, and skills brought to bear on completing the project.

- **Schedule**   The flow time allocated to the project, at the end of which a product or service will be usable or commercially viable.

Consider these truths about the triangle as it relates to software projects:

- All three aspects of the triangle are interrelated. For example, one cannot change the scope of a project without having to address changes in resources and schedule. Failure to do so relegates the project to the scrapheap.

- Adding people to a software project does not help as much as you might think and might actually make a project that is behind schedule even later (Brooks, 1995). Given our experience with deterministic problems, this one needs some explanation. For example, doubling the number of people working on a project originally estimated to take one year will only knock down the flow time to about nine months. There is a law of diminishing returns here. If we tripled the size of the team, we might get completion time closer to six months, but then other issues such as cost, synchronization, availability of computing resources, and so forth come into play. Some efforts just can't be crunched or reduced beyond a certain point. Finding that point can be a risky and expensive undertaking.

- It is not possible to make the calendar go more slowly.

- The feature list often increases (a phenomenon called *feature creep*) during the course of the project rather than decreasing as the project becomes better understood.

All of these truths have a negative impact on team morale because what the team experiences is a growth in the size of the job without a corresponding change in schedule, while people keep being hired who need help to become effective in the software development environment.

Now take a look in Table 2-2 at how issues related to scope, resources, and schedule are remedied in the hardware and software contexts.

TABLE 2-2 Remedies in Hardware and Software Projects

Situation	Remedy/Repercussions in the Hardware World	Remedy in the Software World
Behind schedule.	Add people and/or equipment, and balance expense elsewhere.	Adding people makes matters worse, so cut features, which impacts customer and morale. Alternatively, go into death march mode.
Over budget.	Stretch out delivery time; you might lose incentive fees.	Cut features, which impacts customer and morale. Alternatively, go into death march mode.
Budget and schedule are OK, but not all features will be delivered.	Renegotiate the contract; customer might get another vendor to finish the job.	Reassess, focusing on customer's "must have" features; customer expectations might impact opinion of results. Alternatively, go into death march mode.

The term *death march mode* refers to the practice of going all out on a project to finish it, resulting in 18-to-20-hour workdays, 7 days a week. Death march mode results when the project manager's experience of the physical world causes the manager to treat the problem of system development as a deterministic one. Here's an example of a deterministic problem: We need to haul a large pile of dirt from point A to point B by using wheelbarrows. Points A and B are within easy walking distance of each other. If we add more people with wheelbarrows or work the people we have for longer hours, the job will get done more quickly. This scaling even in such simple problems has its limitations due to fatigue, having so many workers that they get in each other's way, and so forth. Similarly, in software, mental fatigue sets in quickly in death march mode, productivity plummets, and error rates usually increase. More importantly, in software, the problems are not deterministic. For example, tracking down a bug and correcting it is definitely not deterministic—there is no assurance as to how long it will take or whether it will be successful.

One viable strategy to overcome cost and schedule overruns is to cut features (reduce requirements), but this has some negative side effects, as you'll soon see. Unlike building construction, in which a team of people address a number of features, in software, it's often the case that only one or two people (or a small team) are responsible for a feature. Cutting that feature can have a serious impact on the morale of those individuals and the team. In software, the situation is such that the persons responsible for a particular feature will identify with what they have built. Having it deleted from the delivery, even if it will be incorporated into the second or subsequent release, is disheartening for the developers involved and might actually cause them to leave the project. Assuming that the features work, if you are the software project manager on an effort that has to cut features, it is advisable to meet with the key team members who authored the features to be cut and assure them that their work was appreciated and that the cuts are due to scheduling reasons and do not reflect on their skill level or the quality of what they produced.

Software Development as a "Wicked" Problem

Some years ago, Horst Rittel proposed the existence of a class of particularly troublesome problems that he labeled "wicked" problems (Rittel and Weber, 1972). He further proposed certain properties of wicked problems so that we could recognize members of that class when we encountered them. Basically, a *wicked problem* is one that is particularly elusive. When we attempt to solve it, other problems or previously unknown aspects of the wicked problem become known, presenting an impediment to the solution.

In the context of software development, wicked problems have all or many of these properties:

- **A wicked problem cannot be definitively stated.**   Whenever we attempt to bound a project using something like a specification, the requirements change, often in unpredictable ways.

- **There is no rule or guideline to determine when a wicked problem is solved.**   In the physical world, we usually have a reasonable stopping point for generating solutions. For example, a mechanical engineering problem associated with determining the flexure (to the nearest tenth of an inch) at the midpoint of a bridge under stated dynamic or static conditions can be computed. That answer can be independently verified, and the problem is solved. But in software development, there is no stopping point other than to run out of money or time.

- **Wicked problems have only good or bad solutions, not right or wrong ones.**   Getting back to our mechanical engineering example, there is a range of answers that are correct, and anything outside that range is wrong. As compared with software, that range of correct answers is very narrow. But in software, there can be many solutions that meet the specification that by that standard are good. Presumably, those that do not meet the specification are bad.

- **A wicked problem cannot be definitively tested.** This seems reasonable. If there are no right or wrong answers in the wicked problem space, there shouldn't be any way to accept or reject the solution in an analytic or a scientific way. One exception in software is whether the solution meets the specification. However, even specification issues tend to be arguable and not clearly right or wrong.

- **Solutions to wicked problems are too significant to be experimented with.** Although the defense establishment occasionally has aircraft companies create prototypes for a "fly off" competition before a contract is awarded, building multiple software systems and selecting the best from among them is usually prohibitively expensive in both monetary and temporal terms.

- **Neither the number of possible solutions nor the means of distinguishing among them is limited.** Software development is at least this wide open.

- **Each wicked problem is unique.** If you don't think so, try to determine how many order entry and inventory control systems have been built worldwide.

- **Wicked problems are often symptoms of higher-level problems.** If, in an embedded real-time system, we are having serious timing issues (that is, the system is too slow), it might mean that we are using too slow a processor. The processor might have been picked to keep the cost down. Hence, the timing problem could actually have been a symptom of a lack of funding for the effort.

So is software development a wicked problem? It definitely is from many standpoints. Coping with these problems is not strictly a technical endeavor; it requires more of an empirical approach from management. Successfully coping with software's Bermuda Triangle involves using what we now know, employing the data that has been gathered, and having the faith in these results to use them in spite of the conventional "wisdom" some managers employ.

Myths Associated with Software

The non-physics-based and therefore almost mythological nature of software's Bermuda Triangle represents one danger zone that all software projects must pass through, but a number of self-generated myths also conspire to threaten software projects. These myths are conceptual in nature and, unfortunately, are often held to be self-evident truths by many software managers.

Myth #1: Software is easier to change than hardware. This myth is more common and more counterintuitive than most managers would care to admit. At first glance, changing software looks a lot easier than changing hardware. For example, how easy would it be to change Hoover Dam? Not very. That is exactly why so much effort went into designing, analyzing, redesigning, and reanalyzing that structure before a single yard of concrete was mixed and poured. Not surprisingly, that project finished ahead of schedule and under budget and is still considered to be one of the greatest feats of engineering in the history of the world!

So what about software? The problem is that we take the ease-of-change issue for granted; we "see" solutions early on and often begin programming without really understanding the problem we are trying to solve and without looking to the future. The Year 2000 problem was a perfect example. People just did not realize that what they built in 1980 might still be in use in the year 2000. Furthermore, they took great pride at that time in achieving storage savings by storing only a two-digit number rather than a four-digit number to represent the year. A simple analysis or survey would have shown that a lot of software used in 1980 had been written much earlier, and it would be too expensive to replace it all every 20 or so years.

Myth #2: We're in maintenance mode, and it's rare that we write something new, so we don't need to measure what we're doing, gather statistics, or define processes.   This statement was made to me by the director of software engineering for a multibillion-dollar hardware and software vendor. Such a lack of knowledge of the software business is, unfortunately, not unusual. Is it any wonder that the software the firm produces is notoriously of poor quality? This attitude is a tough one to overcome since it has so many "obvious" cost-saving aspects. After all, why do something you don't have to do? This approach fails to learn valuable lessons from the hardware world.

If you know people in the aircraft maintenance business, you'll find that they have processes for doing what they do. Consistent with Federal Aviation Administration (FAA) requirements, they gather statistics on every aircraft maintained, including who worked on the aircraft, what they did, what they did it with (for example, what lubricant was used, who manufactured it, and so forth), and if there was a failure, who worked on that aircraft last and touched that system. Using this information, they can go over the processes involved and make appropriate changes to prevent future problems. In this way, the organization is always improving the quality of its results, reducing failures, and reducing costs.

Believers in this myth really represent major stumbling blocks to bringing about change within an organization and/or improving the quality of the results of maintenance. The director of software engineering mentioned earlier ran a shop in which there was almost no accountability, serious bugs would go unfixed for months and years, and everyone did their own thing. It is the equivalent of *laissez faire* programming. The problem is that without measurements, processes, and methods, costs rise, quality suffers, and everyone loses—especially the company's customers.

Myth #3: We don't need to document the code by including comments, because any proficient programmer can tell what the code does by looking at it.   Really? How about trying to understand Fortran code whose integer variables all have names in the form $n1$, $n2$, $n3$ and whose real variables have names in the form $X1$, $X2$, $X3$? This practice burns up a lot of resources, thereby affecting the other points of software's Bermuda Triangle. In the variable naming example just mentioned, it turns out that the programmer was mad about having to document, so he took out his aggression on all succeeding maintainers of this code. What he did was use this incomprehensible naming convention and not provide a table that told the reader what each variable was. He left the company shortly thereafter, leaving his replacement to do the job of deciphering the meaning of each variable and explaining what formulas the various portions of the code were implementing.

This myth is so closely held by some that they actively pursue removing the comments from any code they work on. One programmer who actually does this was confronted by her colleagues and questioned about this practice. Her response was, "Why bother putting in comments when they will be out of date very soon anyway? By removing them, I am saving everybody a lot of effort since they will not be misled by what they find." Both arguments fall by the wayside when you consider that turnover can cause tremendous communication and productivity problems. A simple requirement that the programmer certify that the comments have been updated and are correct when the code is checked in has often prevented this problem. But some programmers and managers assume that this will result in longer, more expensive development time. Nothing could be further from the truth. Besides, following such practices ensures not only maintainability but also flexibility in job assignments. Of course, someone in quality assurance has to spot-check to ensure that people are making a good faith effort to keep the comments accurate.

Myth #4: Quality can be tested into the system—what we should do is get it coded as rapidly as possible and then test it as thoroughly as possible.   Henry Ford is thought to be the first person in the United States to direct the creation of a modern-day production line. He got the idea from observing a meat-packing plant. The concept of quality might have occurred to him as well, in that breaking down the process into small steps and then executing those steps efficiently and perfectly with quality inspections at key points along the way produces a high-quality result at lower cost.

Another aspect of this myth can be seen in how Japanese industry operated before and after World War II. Before and during that war, the attitude in Japanese industry was that labor is cheap, so simply build as many items as you can, and then test them and ship the ones that work. Once Japanese industry underwent a makeover, due in part to W. Edwards Deming's concepts, their products became revered for their quality worldwide (Deming, 1986). The correct concept with respect to testing is that testing reveals only what quality is present or absent; it does not assist in increasing the quality of a product. In today's marketplace, quality products at least have a chance of being successful, whereas those lacking quality are doomed to the scrap heap.

Myth #5: Why bother performing analysis and design? After all, the code, not these preliminary documents, results in a marketable product.   Subscribers to this myth really don't understand the roles that analysis and design have played in engineering for more than two thousand years. There is evidence that the Romans built models, drew the equivalent of blueprints, and otherwise labored over a project before executing it. That is, rather than simply building an aqueduct based on a few observations and the availability of slave labor, they ensured success by doing the mathematics, measuring, estimating, analyzing, and otherwise working the project through in many ways before committing to laying the first stone. What analysis and design actually do for the development team is get them synchronized with what will be built and why it will take a particular form or architecture and, essentially, preprogram them for success. With a well-thought-out design in hand that has been walked through and agreed to by the development team, a successful execution of that design is nearly certain.

Myth #6: We don't need a quality assurance group—we hire smart people, and they don't make mistakes.   Most of you (well, maybe not all of you) would be surprised at who is being quoted here. Let's just say that this person is the head of a large software company whose products have often been cited for their lack of quality. The quality assurance group's function is not simply that of testing software. More accurately, its primary function is to ensure that errors do not find their way into the software to start with. It is this group's job to establish a system of processes, checkpoints, procedures, standards, guidelines—whatever it takes—to reduce the number of bugs in the code being put into the build to something that is controlled and traceable enough to find where they came from. This will enable the quality assurance team to make the adjustments to the processes and so forth that are deemed necessary to prevent bugs in the future.

Myth #7: Increasing their compensation gets software professionals to perform at a higher level.   This is not always the case. It might actually encourage them to leave the company. According to the latest research, there is a better than 50/50 chance that a person will leave the firm within three months after receiving a raise. I do not want to give the impression that outstanding performance should not be rewarded—quite the contrary. But some clarification is in order. When people are putting in long hours, frequently informing their manager that they need additional help or some relief in the schedule or something to get their life outside of work back, they are often ignored. When this situation occurs and the person involved then gets a raise, the message sent is that the company is pleased with how things are going. The raise implies that the situation is not going to change. So that person feels that he or she has no choice but to leave the company. On the other hand, if the person sees that this is a short-term situation, the outcome might be very different.

Myth #8: The way to encourage people to get into management is to give them special perquisites.   Definitely the wrong incentive scheme (Townsend, 1970). If people go into management for the money and perquisites, we end up with what we have today—a cadre of managers who would rather be programming, are uncomfortable dealing with personnel issues, do not understand what they are supposed to do, and are, in a word, miserable. This myth also requires some changes in thinking from companies. A person's pay should be a reflection of the company's perception of that person's value to the firm. Position within the hierarchy of the firm and pay won't necessarily correlate when using the preceding guideline. Instead, a few forward-looking firms have a policy that it is possible for a manager to be paid less than the people who report to her or him.

Myth #9: Software processes are great, but when the project is behind schedule, we don't have time for such things.   It has been my experience that projects fall behind schedule precisely because the development team either did not follow some predefined process or they took following it to the extreme. The issue is a delicate one. What is involved is a matter of balance. Often one finds that the technology gatekeeper in an organization is enthusiastic about a development process he learned in a course that the company spent thousands on and that he follows the process to the letter, without regard for whether the process makes sense for the project, the company, or its customers. This is how teams get into trouble. Remember, the author of the process book is not going to have his career hurt by a failure— you are.

An alternative way to look at this is that "a process is not worth using if it cannot be used in an emergency" (Rombach, 2003). Specifically, the data indicates that processes that follow the preceding admonition do quite well in emergencies and have been credited with saving the day under dire circumstances. In other words, effective processes are ones that have evolved over time to be effective in both ordinary and extraordinary circumstances. This is a common situation in other industries. For example, aircraft manufacturers occasionally get emergency orders from an airline for a critical safety part for one of their aircraft. Their client's plane cannot be flown until this part is installed, but the manufacturer does not have one on hand. The manufacturer has a process that does not skip any of the inspection or quality control steps, meets FAA requirements, and gets the part into shipping in record time. The concept of streamlining a process when an emergency situation occurs without skipping any steps is one most software project managers have yet to embrace.

Myth #10: The marketplace requires that we get to market as quickly as possible. Using some sort of prescribed method or process is just going to slow things down.   There is data to support only the first part of this myth. Depending on whose study one reads, the first to market with a product addressing a specific market segment can expect to lock up between 60 and 80 percent of that segment. By lock up, I mean that it will be very expensive for the competition to displace the first firm without expending more than the amount of revenue that they can expect to see from that market over a three-year period.

The second part of this myth is another matter. One can easily deduce that having a defined process that is well thought out (this does not take months or weeks, only a few days), a plan to execute, milestones to hit, and quality targets supported by checks and balances to reduce the number of bugs generated should take less time to execute than the "Oklahoma Land Rush" mode of development suggested by this myth.

Myth #11: There is so much software out there that either is included with various development environments or can be licensed inexpensively—we can employ it and write very little new code.   Nice try, but it generally does not work that way with commercially successful software. The reason is that commercially off the shelf (COTS) systems have been written with a particular user model, a specific class of application capabilities, and other commercial considerations. People want some form of uniqueness in the software they are paying for. If the software is the same (or nearly so) as other products, they might ask why it was built in the first place. Also, in interactive systems, serious performance and response time issues can be associated with using certain COTS systems commercially. Last, integrating COTS packages from different manufacturers is a major challenge and element of cost.

Myth #12: If we institute processes into this organization, people will either leave the company or become unproductive.   This myth is a long-standing argument against change—any change—usually voiced by managers who really have not got a clue as to what can be achieved and what is going on in other companies. It turns out that instituting processes and procedures into a software organization can dramatically increase morale, with commensurate increases in productivity and quality (McConnell, 2003). That's what the data shows.

Those instances of failures that one hears about often lack the details about what the organization really did. All we hear is that they tried this method or that and had problems. Investigations into such situations that I have conducted have shown that the project manager involved got scared because code did not come rolling out the door immediately, panicked, and directed that the procedural approach be abandoned and coding begin immediately.

Forget About Godzilla—Watch Out for Ducks

Maintaining control over any part of a project is difficult, but controlling the schedule might be the most difficult of all. Why? Because we can get more money, reduce features, and buy faster computers and better software tools, but we can't stop the calendar. Many software projects have failed miserably because of late delivery or even no delivery. Postmortems on such efforts usually reveal that management did not fully comprehend how far behind schedule the project was until it had missed a major milestone or had fallen behind by an atrocious amount that could not be overcome. What we never hear is that the project got behind schedule because it was attacked by Godzilla. What I mean by that is that the schedule slip was not due to a single, catastrophic event. Instead, the project died because it was bitten to death by ducks. If you have ever been nibbled on by a duck, you can imagine that it would take a lot of them to kill you. Furthermore, it would be very difficult to pin someone's death on one duck or another. Similarly, in software project management, each time some-one does not meet his or her commitment or misses delivery by a day or more, that is a duck. If you generate enough ducks, the project is doomed. The moral here is that small slides could occur each day and add up to a very large slide that jeopardizes the entire project. In Chapter 7, "Estimating Project Size, Cost, and Schedule," I will demonstrate how the use of the Earned Value Management (EVM) method can help a software project manager identify the "ducks" early on and take the remedial action needed before the project gets out of control.

Summary

Although it might sound like a daunting task, being successful at managing software projects is relatively simple. All we have to do is successfully navigate software's Bermuda Triangle. Although easier said than done, this involves recognizing that management is not an exact science with right or wrong answers and remembering the following:

- Much of what we learn from the physical world and our everyday lives does not apply to managing software projects.

- Quality affects more than just the product; it also affects the performance of the people producing the product.

- If we aren't careful, small slides in the schedule can build to tsunami proportions that cannot be overcome, with or without death march mode.

I'll extend the preceding list in the remainder of this book to incorporate additional guide-lines worth remembering, including these:

- People are the most valuable resource a project has.

- Trust and mutual respect between the project manager and those directly involved in developing the product improve team morale and our odds of success.

- Within reason, running more tasks in parallel is far more effective in shortening development flow time than adding people or cutting features.

References

(Brooks, 1995)   Brooks, F. P., Jr. *The Mythical Man-Month: Essays on Software Engineering.* Reading, MA: Addison-Wesley, 1995.

(Rittel and Weber, 1972)   Rittel, H. W. J., and M. M. Weber. "Dilemmas in a General Theory of Planning," Institute of Urban and Regional Development, Working Paper No. 194. Berkeley: University of California, November 1972.

(Deming, 1986)   Deming, W. E. *Out of the Crisis*. Cambridge, MA: Massachusetts Institute of Technology, 1986.

(Townsend, 1970)   Townsend, R. *Up the Organization: How to Stop the Corporation from Stifling People and Strangling Profits*. New York: Knopf, 1970.

(Rombach, 2003)   Rombach, D. "Teaching How to Engineer Software," keynote address at the Conference on Software Engineering and Education. Madrid, March 2003.

(McConnell, 2003)   McConnell, S. "10 Myths of Rapid Development," lecture presented at Construx, Inc. Bellevue, WA, January 2003.

Part II
Software Development as a Process

In this part:

Chapter 3
Building the Software Development Team

When you bring a group of people together, it's called a start. When you get a group of people to stay together, it's called progress. When you get a group of people to work together, it's called success.

—Lou Holtz, American football coach

People have been analyzing other people's behavior since the time of the Greek philosopher Hippocrates (400 BC). Understanding people is essential to the first step in managing a software project—putting together an effective software engineering team. So all we have to do to put together such a team is to find the "right" people, in terms of skill, education, and experience and then hire them—right? Unfortunately, it's just a *little* more complicated than that. Picking team members involves predicting the interpersonal relationships that will occur among people as well as their interactions with you, their manager. Basically, you, the project manager, must answer the following questions correctly: "Can these folks work together?" "Can they get the job done?" "Can I work with them?" Granted, there are project situations in which you are forced to work with people you find difficult to communicate with, or even people you dislike intensely or who dislike you. That comes with the job. I've been in those situations, and I've been successful by focusing on the project, working through personality differences, and whenever possible, making those conflicts work for the project rather than against it. It takes a lot of energy, but it can work. One goal of this chapter is to help you avoid these situations when you have the opportunity to build your team from the ground up, or at least to work through these problems in an existing team. At issue here is another question, "If these people work together, will they work well together as a team and perform to the best of their abilities?" Last, a fifth question that you and your team need to evaluate is, "Do they have the needed skills?"

In this chapter, we'll look at the skills and techniques you'll need to select individual team members and build a high-performance team. I've used many of the techniques described here; most are not found in software engineering books because, as stated at the outset of this book, success in software engineering is considered by most to be primarily a technical issue, not a management one. Since you will be building your team in parallel with the development and execution of your project plan, you will probably return to the methods and processes described in this chapter throughout the execution of your project.

Team Building as a Process

There might be as many ways to build a software development team as there are software project managers. All software project managers who have been successful at team building have a personalized formula that they will try to use over and over again, in the belief that history will repeat itself. They frequently discover that it does not. Software project managers are made, not born with some innate skill. Other software project managers who have been less than successful at building teams often reflect on what they should have done differently, what they should have sensed about certain prospective team members, and how they might prevent similar failures in the future. In many cases, this retrospective still does not work. A generic model of the team building process as summarized in this chapter is presented in Figure 3-1. A lot of what your company currently does is probably represented in this figure, but one unusual item might be the activity labeled "Administer personality test." This aspect will be expanded upon in the remainder of this section.

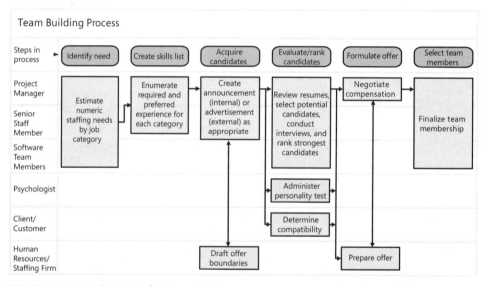

FIGURE 3-1 A generic model of the team building process.

So what does work? To begin with, we need to understand just what it takes to create an effective software development team. In reviewing my successes and challenges in this area and those of some of my colleagues, I must concur with some research that identified five key factors that determine a technology project team's effectiveness (Chen and Lin, 2004):

- **Domain knowledge and experience**   This is the training and experience that the prospective candidate brings to the project. Each company has its own scheme for determining the skill levels needed within a team to conduct a project. This factor is usually given the highest priority by software project managers. The level of expertise is relatively easy to establish through interviews by asking the prospective team member detailed technical questions.

- **Experience as part of a team**   This factor is often overlooked by software project managers. They can often be blinded by the technical skills of a prospective team member and fail to notice that the prospect is really an independent performer or a "cowboy" who does not see himself or herself as part of a mutually supportive group. These types might be exceptionally effective at working alone, but they might have difficulty in a team situation. One way to assess potential candidates' team experiences is to get them to describe the kinds of relationships they have had in current and prior work experiences. Did they act, to some extent, as a technical resource, assisting less-skilled team members, or did they help coordinate the work within the team or in other ways provide and/or utilize a team-based resource? Ask how they resolve technical problems: do they try for a time and then ask a colleague for help, or do they go it alone no matter how long it takes?

- **Communications skills**   For years, the software industry has complained about the lackluster communications skills possessed by software engineers. Perhaps if they were serious enough about it, they would complement coding proficiency tests with communications skills tests to determine whether the candidate can write a coherent sentence or explain something to an audience verbally. This is one of the biggest failings of most software professionals. To assess the candidate's communications skills, you might have them put together a brief (say, 5 to 10 minutes) presentation on a topic related to their current or previous work or what they will be doing in this new assignment. See how they respond to questions. Alternatively, have them write a short essay there at the interview but in a private setting on some topic in a 10-minute to 15-minute period. Can they write coherent sentences? Can they communicate under pressure?

- **Flexibility with respect to job assignments**   This is related to whether prospective team members view themselves as being focused only on the type of software development work they are being hired for or are willing to pitch in when things get difficult and do whatever it takes for the team to be successful. Tasks of this nature include debugging someone else's code, cleaning up the data extract from a database tool that has some bugs that can be fixed only post-extract, doing some statistical breakdowns of the content of a data file, and other tasks that were not included in the job description or mentioned during the job interview.

- **Personality traits**   This is the toughest factor to deal with. Software project managers are rarely trained in psychology to the extent that they are qualified to effectively deal with this issue. Instead, they rely on whether they "like" the individual and whether the other team members have a positive reaction to that person. While that can be an effective combination of criteria, like other schemes, it is not foolproof. This factor is fundamental to successfully building a team. As in sports, if the team members do not get along, your software project is going to suffer. A caution is in order here: Avoid favoring those candidates who think like you do and always agree with you. Your blind spots could become the team's blind spots, which can lead to issues in the future.

Most project managers are fairly comfortable with addressing the first four factors in this list. However, the last factor can be cause for concern. This issue extends beyond whether the software project manager is comfortable with each team member and vice versa and touches on whether team members are mutually comfortable with each other. This gets into the domain of personality traits.

There are several models of personalities and the sets of traits that describe them. One of the most widely accepted and researched in the project team environment is the Myers Briggs model (Myers and Myers, 1995). This model provides a means of not only categorizing an individual's personality but also assessing how compatible that person is with other personalities according to the Myers Briggs Type Indicator (MBTI). This personality model describes each of us as having four dimensions to our personality, with each dimension having two opposing personality preferences, as follows:

Focus of Attention

- **Extrovert (E)**   Someone who is comfortable communicating with others. Extroverts derive their energy from working with groups.

- **Introvert (I)**   Introspective people are comfortable working alone. Their energy is drained by working within a group.

Seeking Information

- **Sensing (S)**   These are fact-oriented and data-oriented people who derive their information from the details and often find small errors in documents that others missed.

- **iNtuitive (N)**   These are speculators who employ intuition and theory to get the "big picture." They will most often focus on how the arguments within a document were laid out rather than on the detailed typographical errors the document contained.

Decision Making

- **Thinking (T)**   These people make decisions by relying on principles, laws, rules, logic, and objective analysis.

- **Feeling (F)**   As the name implies, people in this category will strongly consider the feelings of the people involved and are focused on maintaining harmony within a group.

Relationship to the World

- **Judging (J)**   These people are oriented toward outcome. They make decisions in a rapid manner—they like to get things done and are frustrated by delays.

- **Perceiving (P)**   These people are very process oriented. They tend to be open minded and make decisions slowly, often considering new possibilities.

Reviewing the preceding, we can see that there are a total of 16 possible combinations of personality traits. As you might have guessed, not all 16 possibilities are compatible with one another. Compatibility between types in technology project situations is shown in Table 3-1 (Chen and Lin, 2004). Note that this is a *normalized* representation, meaning that the highest possible value is 1.0. The higher the compatibility value, the greater the compatibility, and vice versa.

Table 3-1 Personality Type Compatibilities

	1 – ESTJ	2 – ESTP	3 – ESFJ	4 – ESFP	5 – ENTJ	6 – ENTP	7 – ENFJ	8 – ENFP	9 – ISTJ	10 – ISTP	11 – ISFJ	12 – ISFP	13 – INTJ	14 – INTP	15 – INFJ	16 – INFP
1 – ESTJ	0.67															
2 – ESTP	0.33	0.67														
3 – ESFJ	0.83	0.50	0.67													
4 – ESFP	0.50	0.83	0.33	0.67												
5 – ENTJ	0.83	0.50	1.00	0.67	0.67											
6 – ENTP	0.50	0.83	0.67	1.00	0.33	0.67										
7 – ENFJ	1.00	0.67	0.83	0.50	0.83	0.50	0.67									
8 – ENFP	0.67	1.00	0.50	0.83	0.50	0.83	0.33	0.67								
9 – ISTJ	0.50	0.17	0.67	0.33	0.67	0.33	0.83	0.50	0.33							
10 – ISTP	0.17	0.50	0.33	0.67	0.33	0.67	0.50	0.83	0.00	0.33						
11 – ISFJ	0.67	0.33	0.50	0.17	0.83	0.50	0.67	0.33	0.50	0.17	0.33					
12 – ISFP	0.33	0.67	0.17	0.50	0.50	0.83	0.33	0.67	0.17	0.50	0.00	0.33				
13 – INTJ	0.67	0.33	0.83	0.50	0.50	0.17	0.67	0.33	0.50	0.17	0.67	0.33	0.33			
14 – INTP	0.33	0.67	0.50	0.83	0.17	0.50	0.33	0.67	0.17	0.50	0.33	0.67	0.00	0.33		
15 – INFJ	0.83	0.50	0.67	0.33	0.67	0.33	0.50	0.17	0.67	0.33	0.50	0.17	0.50	0.17	0.33	
16 – INFP	0.50	0.83	0.33	0.67	0.33	0.67	0.17	0.50	0.33	0.67	0.17	0.50	0.17	0.50	0.00	0.33

What this provides us with is one, but not the only, indicator of who would or would not make a potentially high-performing team member from a compatibility standpoint. To apply this model effectively, each team member would have to complete the MBTI questionnaire, have it evaluated, and agree to let you, the manager, see the results. Many corporations currently administer this or a similar profile as a condition of employment, with the permission of prospective employees for their managers to view the results.

Perhaps an even more important factor to be used in selecting team members is determining how tolerant each team member is of other people's idiosyncrasies. While this is not part of the MBTI, it does relate to the issue of team experience.

You might wonder how you would deal with a situation where key team members are incompatible and cannot be replaced. I have had the experience of managing such teams. What I did in most cases was to first ensure that the incompatible team members did have the project's best interests at heart. Then, with the help of outside psychological consultants, we determined just what it was that each did that inadvertently upset the other party. This worked and also helped me to identify when they backslid into the behaviors that led to problems in the first place. Gentle reminders were enough to get things on an even keel again going forward. If you find yourself in a similar situation, try seeking professional help for you and your team.

Conducting Interviews

Putting a team together is a key to success and will take some well-designed effort. Whether hiring people from outside the firm or selecting people from within the company, you are eventually going to have to conduct some interviews. One thing to remember about interviews is that everybody dislikes them and is usually nervous during them. Prospective employees are nervous because they want to get hired. The project manager is nervous because evaluating someone is always an uncomfortable task and because the manager has a million things to do that are not getting done while he or she is conducting an interview. But you might as well resign yourself to getting through the interview process as quickly and as effectively as possible.

First, let's look at some ground rules set forth by case law and current labor laws at the state and federal level in the United States and many other industrialized countries. Please note that this is not an all-inclusive list but focuses on the most common and potentially costly types of mistakes that you, the manager, might make during an interview. I have directly observed or had related to me by others some interview questions and behaviors on the part of interviewers that can get a company sued. To make sure that you are familiar with today's rules regarding what you can and cannot (legally) ask during an interview, contact your human resources department. If your company is too small to have such a resource, get a current reference text on labor law, contact a labor law attorney, or call your local Department of Labor office and obtain a copy of the appropriate publication on the subject. In the United States, you should also contact your local Equal Employment Opportunity (EEO) office. Under current law, you cannot ask a prospective or a current employee or one transferring into your group about certain topics, including the following:

- The person's religion, political affiliation, country of national origin, or belief system

- The person's marital status, sexual orientation, or current and past relationships

- The person's age

You can ask a number of questions, some of which are required by law, including the following:

- For new hires, you can ask whether they are authorized to work in the United States (or whatever country you are hiring them to work in) and require that they provide evidence to support their answers. The presumption here for current employees is that you or your human resources department has already verified this.

- Focus on their experience with the kinds of system development your group engages in, the development support software they have used, the number of years they have worked in various roles, and so forth. Remember, you're trying to assess whether they can do the job based on past experience.

- Ask whether they are comfortable with the interview format—for example, some people might feel claustrophic in a small office with several interviewers and might prefer a larger room.

- Ask whether they need any kind of special accommodations—for example, a person who is hard of hearing might need an amplifier system.

There are a plethora of articles and textbooks on conducting employment interviews, so I won't try to duplicate them here.

In fact, your company might have a standardized process for conducting interviews that you are required to use. If your company does not have a standard process that is used for all candidates for a specific position, develop one as soon as possible to avoid lawsuits by those who were interviewed but not selected and who might feel that the selection process unfairly discriminated against them. The most effective approach I have used for interviewing and selecting prospective software engineers was based on our need to hire C/C++ programming professionals. At the time, we could not find enough qualified people to fill our open positions, and this was jeopardizing our commitments to customers and some aggressive schedules we had agreed to. It seems our competitors were hiring some of our best people away with what seemed like astronomical offers that we could not match. I found that anyone capable of buying and reading an introduction to a C/C++ programming textbook was calling himself or herself a C/C++ senior software development professional. My senior software engineer and I came up with a scheme to separate technically viable candidates from those who would not work out. This approach has proven effective even in today's labor market:

1. I had a senior software engineer draw up a programming test in the form of code snippets in the programming language that the interviewee would be writing in. Each snippet was preceded by an explanation of what the code was supposed to do and a description of what it did do. The interviewee was asked to explain why the code did not work correctly and provide the changes that would make the code work as advertised.

2. We focused on each job candidate's approach to solving the problems and asked the candidates to describe aloud their observations and the approaches they were using to track down the causes of the software errors.

Such code snippets are readily available at various Web sites that contain coding puzzles and code examples and counter-examples. Remembering that job candidates are nervous during interviews, the senior software engineer and I observed how they went about trying to solve the problems. Given that they were probably not performing at their best under these circumstances, we were more interested in how they went about attempting to solve a problem than in whether they succeeded. In one team development effort, we had two people at different extremes with respect to their performance take the same test. One appeared quite nervous due to discomfort with the English language and solved only three problems in the allotted 30 minutes; the other solved all 10 in a record time of less than 10 minutes. We hired both, and they both were spectacular performers. Again, the key selection criterion focused on the candidates' solution approaches and not on whether they got the right answer.

The rest of the team will have to work with this person and should have some interaction with him or her during the selection process. Have the rest of your team meet with the candidate individually and provide you with feedback regarding their comfort level with working with the candidate. Knowing your current team members is important here, since each will have unique characteristics with respect to evaluating other people's work, their interpersonal skills, and so forth. Having team members interact with the candidate, thereby becoming part of the selection process, also helps ensure that candidate's acceptance by the team if he or she is selected. The selected candidate becomes the team's choice, not just the manager's choice. Here are a few guidelines for the other team members to follow. (Your company might already have a structured interview process that addresses these issues.)

- Prepare your questions in advance, and compare these with what other interviewers are going to ask. It is OK to have the same question(s) asked by more than one interviewer.

- Compare responses with other interviewers.

- Have everyone who will have to work with this person on a daily basis interview the prospect individually for the same amount of time—for example, 20 minutes or 30 minutes.

- If at all possible, have the entire group and the interviewee have lunch together or socialize in some way in order to observe how they interact in social settings.

Keep in mind the questions that we are trying to answer through the use of interviews, including the following:

- Can this individual do the work?

- Is this person compatible with the prospective team?

- Does this person have the requisite interpersonal skills to deal with other groups (for example, the quality assurance team and the test team) and, potentially, with the customer?

- Does this person really have the experience and the employment record stated on his or her resumé and job application? (The human resources department or an outside firm can verify the employment history.)

Some large companies have had their human resources departments draw up an interview process to be used by all managers who are hiring professional staff members. If you are employed by one of these companies, you might not be able to use the preceding procedures. In any case, it is important to keep in mind that if you deny employment to someone and that person feels that you and/or your colleagues discriminated against him or her, you and your team might be required to present documentation of how you arrived at your hiring decisions in a court of law. This support documentation could include any notes, observations, or discussions regarding one or more candidates. Always be consistent in your treatment of job candidates, and document everything clearly, consistently, and concisely.

If you really want to find out what this person might be like to manage and work with, you might try having them fill out a questionnaire like the one shown in Figure 3-2 on the next page. You should tailor the questionnaire to suit your organization and try filling it out yourself before having anybody else complete it. The idea is to explore the issue of compatibility. For example, if you support the notion of conducting walk-throughs at key points in the project and the questionnaire indicates that this person does not think much of the idea, that is a factor in hiring. Also, having a job prospect fill out such a survey at the start of the interview day, before any interviews are conducted, helps everyone to focus their questions on any issues raised in the questionnaire.

Incompatibility with the manager and/or colleagues can be a serious issue. One project that I contracted to be project manager on had a team of fewer than 10 people. Most had little experience, but two were more senior and had the level of experience needed to help hold the project together. Everything went well through the planning, requirements gathering, and definition stages. As we began design, assignments were made or volunteered for. As part of the process for developing the design, each software engineer was required to walk through his or her part of the design. Walk-through guidelines had been developed during the planning stage of the project and included having one person act as a moderator and a second person act as a scribe during the walk-through. The job of the scribe was to record action items. An action item was a deliverable (usually a correction) with a date by which the deliverable was due. The job of the moderator was to ensure that people did not drag out the meeting beyond its nominal 1-hour limit and to prevent people from getting into sidebar discussions and so forth.

One of our two key developers was completely intolerant of anybody critiquing his work. He was defensive, even on points that were obvious errors. To make matters worse, when this person was in the position of being a reviewer, he was overly critical, abrasive in his comments, and occasionally rude. Even though we discussed the fact that these behaviors were jeopardizing the project, the person persisted. He had actually been assigned to this project because he was one of the few people in the organization who had experience and who was available for reassignment. But perhaps this situation demonstrated why he was available, and by mutual agreement, the person was transferred to another group. The point here is that if a preferences inventory such as the one included in the Workplace Preference Profile, shown in Figure 3-2, had been done, the problem could probably been avoided.

The preferences inventory should be considered a generic starting point from which you can develop your own document. This revised inventory would be tailored to the types of systems your organization builds, your preferences, the preferences of the other people in the group, company policies, and so forth.

Workplace Preference Profile

Candidate's Name _____ Today's Date _____

Using the scale shown below, enter a whole number value between 1 and 5 in response to each statement. The purpose of this profile is to assess mutual compatibility between you and this organization.

Strongly disagree	Disagree	Neither disagree nor agree	Agree	Strongly agree
1	2	3	4	5

_____ I prefer to work independently.

_____ In a disagreement with a colleague, when I know I am technically correct, I will usually stand my ground and not concede until I have convinced him or her I am right.

_____ I prefer to work with very little structure or rules but will still do a good job.

_____ I find coding standards, standard processes, reviews, and the like to be inhibiting, thereby preventing me from getting the job done.

_____ I believe in commenting code in such a way that others who are familiar with the programming language but not the application will become effective at maintaining it quickly.

_____ Given a situation where I either have to comply with the organization's process for doing things or just get the job done, I would prefer to just get the work done and fill in the required process items if there is time.

_____ I believe that the best way to achieve a highly efficient development team is to work toward consensus on all major issues.

_____ I prefer to do the hard parts of a software-related problem first.

_____ I often provide assistance to other members of my team, even when time is tight and schedule deadlines are near.

_____ If the budget for an effort is increased with no change in requirements, I put additional effort into the analysis and design phase.

_____ When I am stuck on a programming problem for more than 10 minutes, I frequently will seek the assistance of a colleague to solve it.

_____ I write code that is easily modified after I have left a firm, and I rarely get calls from the person who became responsible for it inquiring about how it works.

_____ I see no reason for extensive comments in code; after all, if someone knows the programming language well, they will figure out what it does.

_____ Given the choice between writing efficient code and code that is simple, I will go for efficiency.

FIGURE 3-2 The Workplace Preference Profile.

Checking References

As an advisory, always have your human resources department or an outside firm verify the candidate's references and employment history. They will do a more consistent job than you will; they will observe the legalities, thereby protecting you and your company from potential liability lawsuits; and they are trained to correctly record and interpret responses. The legalities are nothing to ignore. For example, a number of court cases have resulted from previous employers "bad-mouthing" their previous employee. In those instances, the courts held that the person involved had been harmed by the negative comments from the previous employer and was entitled to monetary damages. If you are called regarding a previous employee, refer the caller to your human resources department. If your firm does not have a human resources department, all you can confirm without putting yourself and your company at risk is the start and end dates of employment, the job title(s), and the job description. Make sure that you get and respond to such requests in writing to ensure that you are really being legitimately contacted by the firm you think you are speaking with and that this is not some other matter (for example, a divorce proceeding, a bill collector, and so forth).

Checking out references is best done by a professional firm. As stated earlier, they are trained in this area and will give consistent, reliable results. References can be a very important issue. Once, during the peak of what appeared to be a shortage of software professionals in the 1990s, I hired a firm to check out the references of an individual whose resumé and interview were exactly what we were looking for. However, the individual indicated that, although she would prefer to work for us, she did have another offer that would expire shortly. This increased the pressure on us to get an answer back to her quickly. I pushed the reference checking firm for an answer, and they indicated that they were unable to confirm two of the references because the people were no longer with the firms indicated and they were having trouble tracking them down. Also, they had contacted the overseas university that the candidate claimed to have graduated from with a technical degree but had not gotten a response. The reference checking firm indicated that this was not unusual. In hindsight, all of this should have set off alarm bells for me. The pressure from upper-level management as well as overworked technical people was intense. I conferred with our senior software engineer, and we agreed that we should go ahead and take a gamble on this person or risk continuing to be woefully understaffed. We soon found out that this was a bad gamble. This individual refused to comply with the coding standard that we had developed jointly with our premier client, frequently submitted code to the build that she claimed was working code only to have the code bring the build down, and refused help from anyone when she got stuck on a coding issue. This was a costly lesson for us all. Even though we dismissed the person within three months, the costs of this episode were high and continued well beyond that time frame. It cost us in terms of the excellent working relationship we had with our client and in terms of the confidence our team had in my judgment and that of our senior software engineer.

The Business School Conundrum

Since most managers have not been trained in management methods and techniques, they are very uncomfortable interviewing anyone for a management position. A case in point happened to me recently. I was being interviewed for a senior program manager position. Before the interview, I was given a "test" and asked to fill it out before the interview began. The test consisted of a set of riddles, and I was to fill in the answers. It turns out that the riddles were literally "outside the box"—they had appeared on boxes of breakfast cereal. It was obvious that the manager was not equipped to ask management-related questions. Examples of management-related questions would include giving the candidate a project management situation that had no right or wrong answer and having the candidate discuss why he or she would take one action or another.

Here is a technique you might use in interviewing that will give you some much-needed information about the candidate. What we're trying to find out with this exercise is how the candidate might behave in a crisis or an uncertain situation—in other words, a situation in which there is no technically correct answer or analysis that will clearly spell out the answer. I have used this technique before, and it is quite revealing. I call it my Business School Conundrum.

Tell the candidate to imagine that he or she is a senior program manager at your firm and is responsible for a new product. This product is going into a heretofore untouched market segment. Therefore, the firm that is first to market will likely capture a dominating market share. The company has sunk so much money into developing the product that if the product is not successful with a large market share, the company might go under. There have been rumors that your number-one competitor is developing a competing product but is having some technical difficulties. Their release date could be soon, but no one is sure. The effort has not gone according to plan, but the product is finally ready to ship. The first wave of thousands of items is currently sitting on the shipping dock awaiting the arrival of the overnight delivery truck. Prerelease products have been shipped to sales and marketing representatives, who plan to take them to reviewers for major magazines, newspapers, and Web sites specializing in evaluating computer-based products of this type. The media have been notified of the ship event and await samples. They plan to write reviews for magazines and Web sites that will coincide with the first release of computers containing your company's product.

Into your office come the director of software engineering, the director of hardware development, and a couple of your top developers and testers. They announce that there is a problem. Twice that day when their people were using the product, it produced a "blue screen of death" scenario—that is, the computer system locked up and could not be powered down without disconnecting the desktop from the wall outlet or, in the case of portables, removing the battery pack. The reproduction scenario (that is, the sequence of actions required to reproduce the problem) could not be nailed down in either case. The symptoms are causing everyone to lean toward a software problem or a BIOS problem. They have not had time to investigate, and reproducing the problem has proven elusive. You turn away to look out the window and collect your thoughts when you see the overnight delivery truck pulling into the security station about two blocks away. You have one minute to make the decision to ship or not to ship. You get no other information.

At this point, you, the interviewer, should make a point of looking at your watch and telling the candidate that he or she has one minute to make a decision and must be able to explain that decision to you.

Even though the candidate might be nervous, the key here is to find out what he or she was thinking about that led to a particular decision, not whether the decision is right or wrong. Strictly speaking, either decision the candidate chooses has both positive and negative consequences. At this point, the candidate is likely to be in a high-pressure, decision-making mode. It is better to find out now rather than later how the candidate goes about making decisions under such conditions.

Let's look at brief descriptions of the two choices:

- **The candidate chooses not to ship.**   A key issue here is whether the candidate believes that only perfect products are going to cut it in the marketplace or is willing to settle for products that are "good enough." You might want to explore what the candidate believes qualifies as good enough. If that means anything that appears to work and is just shot out the door in order to grab market share, this might be a serious issue. Also, this position indicates that the candidate might be willing to put his or her own belief system and self-esteem ahead of the company's survival. In other words, the candidate would not knowingly ship a product with a serious defect because that would reflect badly on the candidate. Conversely, the rumors about the competitor might be just that, and there might be time to delay shipment until this issue is resolved.

- **The candidate chooses to ship.**   The candidate likely sees the survival issue and is not willing to risk the company's future to satisfy pursuing perfection. But we must probe into why and what will be done (if anything) after shipment. After all, it is possible that one or more reviewers will experience the serious fault, and that could have a chilling effect on reviews and the product's market. Did the candidate consider putting together a "red team" (for example, consisting of software, hardware, BIOS, and testing people) to track down and fix the problem as soon as possible? And would the candidate notify people in the field not to release the early products to the press—or if they have done so prematurely and the problem arises, tell them that they have the beta version and that the Release to Manufacturing (RTM) version does not exhibit this behavior? Also, the original equipment manufacturers (OEMs) who will get these early versions are probably not going to install and ship them as soon as they arrive, so we might have some flow time.

There is a lot more that could be said here, but you can see how this scenario opens up a basis for a dialog to find out just how the candidate approaches high-pressure decisions. It turns out that in a pressure situation, people revert to their inherent tendencies. Since you and your team will encounter high-pressure situations, it is better to find out now how the candidate might behave under pressure, rather than later, when it really counts. In this scenario, candidates tend to drop the veneer they put on in order to get a job or impress people and go to their basic instinctive approach to problem solving.

It's DISC Time

In this section, we'll look at a model of human behavior called DISC. This model was introduced in 1928 by William Moulton (Moulton, 1928). Since then, it has matured through the work of many others in the field of human behavior and has become one of the most widely used tools of its kind.

The DISC model consists of four dimensions:

- **Dominance** Measures how well a person addresses problems.

- **Inducement** Relates to the individual's interactions with others.

- **Steadiness** Measures performance in a stable, steady environment.

- **Compliant** Measures the degree to which a person complies with the rules and regulations imposed upon them.

For each of the four DISC dimensions, there are highest and lowest extremes. Remember, there are no better or worse values on such scales; they are used simply to measure what is present in the person's behavior. The extremes for each dimension are described in Table 3-2.

Table 3-2 Bounds of the DISC Dimensions

Trait	High Extreme	Low Extreme
Dominance	Fearlessly addresses problems directly	Addresses problems methodically, with a plan
Inducement	Outgoing, social, very persuasive	Cautious, reserved, focused on facts
Steadiness	Tends toward secure situations; needs to know boundaries, structured environment	Prefers lack of structure, undefined environment; wants complete freedom
Compliant	Abides by the rules set forth by others; aware of the consequences of ignoring the rules	Sets own rules; prefers "doing own thing"

What all this has to do with selecting team members is that if you put together a group of brilliant people who are at the lowest end of the Compliant dimension, your chances of getting standards and policies followed are practically nil. There are many ways to obtain accurate DISC assessments for you, your team, and prospective team members—check the Web and elsewhere. Just in case you plan to do a little research on your own and do some cursory assessments without the aid of a professional, be aware that only 4 percent of people behave primarily in one of the DISC dimensions, about half will behave primarily in two DISC dimensions, and slightly less than half (46 percent) will present three or more dimensions as their primary drivers. However, when tensions are the highest and stress the greatest, people will exhibit one core trait.

The Apollo Syndrome

Some years ago, a researcher discovered some principles about team building that, at first, seemed to be counterintuitive (Belbin, 1996). He was studying teams working in information technology. The common wisdom at the time was that the best information systems teams are made up of the best and the brightest information systems people. The team members were selected on the basis of tests that measured each individual's ability and aptitude. Eight teams were involved in the study. These highly skilled, high-aptitude teams were called "Apollo teams." They were so named after Apollo, the Greek and Roman god of the sun.

The results? Apollo teams often finished at or near the bottom in actual achievement ratings. Actually, this is not unlike some professional sports teams that have been composed of the most expensive and, presumably, most talented players but that have failed to perform as a team.

As is often the case, the results of this study prompted more study. This focused on a more in-depth analysis of the results. Investigators found that several factors sabotaged the operational effectiveness of the Apollo teams, including the following:

- Team members argued with each other over minor points, with each member pointing out the flaws in the other's argument while refusing to admit flaws in his or her own argument.

- The group was ineffective at making decisions, often not arriving at any decision on high-priority issues that had to be decided in a short time frame.

- The team was difficult to manage in the sense that each member took his or her own course of action, without coordinating with the work of other team members. From a management standpoint, the term "herding cats" seemed applicable to the situation.

- Some team members recognized that there were problems and tended to overcompensate by avoiding confrontation at all costs. This actually made matters worse.

A few Apollo teams were successful. These teams exhibited the following characteristics:

- The team did not have any highly dominant individuals.

- Each team had a distinctive style of leader.

The successful leader of an Apollo team had a tendency to be skeptical and suspicious. He or she guided group discussions toward his or her own agenda. The setting of objectives and priorities was a tenet of these leaders' management style. They did not dominate the group or try to engage participation, but they were tough and were able to hold their own in any discussion without dominating it.

Although there is considerably more detail on these points in Belbin's work, the key point to remember here is that the success of Apollo teams, or *any* team, depends on the manager who manages the team. The manager who is successful will not be afraid of innovation, experimentation, or failure but will maintain direction and enough control for the team to succeed.

Ashby's Law and the Ideal Team Member

One issue in this early part of the twenty-first century is the availability of a large number of highly skilled, trained, and experienced software professionals. The economy in this era is such that while some employers are laying off workers, other employers are hiring. This results in having several people to choose from to fill open positions. As a result, the people they do hire have to fulfill a "laundry list" of skills, education, experience, and so forth. Some of the job listings I saw on the Web during the "high-tech implosion" listed as many as 42 skill/experience items as required; most listed somewhere between 10 and 20. Most employers feel that because it is an employers' market, they might as well describe the ideal job candidate, and if that person happens to exist, hire him or her.

To paraphrase Ashby's Law of Requisite Variety, *the better a system is at performing one or a group of tasks, the less able it will be to do anything else* (Ashby, 1956). When a firm advertises for and finds the ideal candidate for a slot—that person who is a perfect fit—they might be putting themselves in jeopardy. Why? Because as the technology and marketplace change, the person who met this multidimensional specification was targeted at today's needs, not tomorrow's. Targeting for tomorrow's needs means hiring someone who does not have the exact set of experiences we think we need. Hiring this close-fit person versus the perfect-fit person means that information, methods, practices, and experiences that were acquired outside the domain we need help in will be brought to bear on it. This results in the team being exposed to new ideas and practices and better enables the organization to cope with the rapid pace of change evident in the software profession. The next time you feel like finding that ideal job prospect, ask yourself whether the team members have complementary skills or simply the same set of skills replicated several times. This latter situation has led to some teams having blind spots or common flaws that will go unnoticed. These can lead to project failure.

Management Styles

Depending on who you talk to in this industry and where they have worked, the styles of software project managers range from highly aggressive to passive. These extremes are indicative of the lack of training and screening of project managers that exists in our industry. Let's face it, at one extreme are people who cannot lead, and at the other are people who are likely to abuse the power that leadership bestows upon them. What's worse, our industry focuses on success in terms of profit and spends too little time or money trying to separate the best managers from the poorest—as long as they perform. This fails to recognize how much more profitable a project could have been if it were led by a project manager who motivated the team to work at its highest level of productivity. What we are referring to here are management or leadership *styles*.

Several distinct styles of management have been analyzed and categorized. Each has its own strengths and weaknesses. The issue that the software project manager has to cope with is which style seems most natural to her or him and whether it will be an effective one for leading a specific group of software professionals.

As stated at the beginning of this book, management is about power—its acquisition and its use. To better understand management styles, we need to understand where power comes from. One management expert has identified four primary sources of power (Kreitner, 1998):

- **Coercive power**   This stems from an employee's fear of the repercussions associated with not complying with a manager's wishes—for example, fear of what might happen if a report is turned in late.

- **Legitimate power**   This derives from the fact that a person is in a superior position (organizationally) to others. It is similar to coercive power but has more of an implicit flavor. This type of power works well in the military, where people are expected to take orders and follow them without question. However, it is rather ineffective in civilian life. Why? Because, eventually, people stop paying attention to a boss who is constantly bombarding them with orders to do this or that without indicating why or getting at least tacit concurrence from those being commanded.

- **Referential power**   This stems from a type of charisma wherein people identify with the manager and support whatever initiatives the manager comes up with. Unfortunately, history and business journals are full of instances of people misusing their charisma to get others to commit or cover up crimes.

■ **Expert power**   This is quite common in the software field. It involves the possession and sharing of information (for example, a shortcut to trapping a bug or estimating project cost) that the power holder has. It too can and has been abused. Expert power often results when the best software engineer on the team is chosen to be its manager. The difficulty here is that such individuals are great at what they do because that is what they love to do. Managing or leading is not usually part of that scenario.

Any manager's power is a combination of more than one source of power. Since none of the sources of power cited here works all that well, a fair question to ask is, "What does work?"

We have known the answer for a long time: *empowerment*. This term relates to the practice of providing each member of the team with the knowledge, training, tools, and environment he or she needs to be successful.

I have often been asked how one achieves management success. I respond by saying that a leader must simultaneously play two roles: the manager setting the direction of the group and the servant whose job it is to remove obstacles that could prevent the group from performing at its highest level.

A model of what might be called the *empowerment cycle* is shown in Figure 3-3; it is adapted from Kreitner (1998).

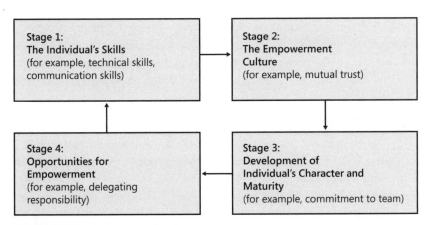

FIGURE 3-3 The empowerment cycle.

Notice that each stage feeds into another, resulting in increases each time through the loop. This cycle is a continuous one in that the team does not pass through it once but over and over throughout the project. Each time through the cycle increases positive attributes for the team member and, as a result, for the team as a whole. Let's look at how it works:

Stage 1   At the start of the team's development, this stage represents perhaps the initial technical skills and communication abilities possessed by each team member and the team as a whole. Over time, with successive passes through the cycle, these will increase.

Stage 2   This is a natural outcome of the software project manager establishing an atmosphere of mutual trust between the software project manager and the team and encouraging the same trust among team members. The manager is essentially demonstrating belief that the team is competent and is willing to shore up any shortcomings in skills by providing training or other assistance. The software project manager has to also maintain the delicate balance among team members between competitiveness and ethical behavior.

Stage 3   As team members become more self-confident as individuals and as members of an organization, it becomes obvious that these people are no longer a bunch of strangers thrown together to complete a project but rather a mutually supportive group.

Stage 4   The success of this stage is the key to the completion and repetition of the cycle. It is more dependent than any other stage on the actions of the software project manager. Retaining decision making and not enabling the team to take responsibility for certain decisions can stop this evolutionary cycle dead in its tracks. But delegating responsibility for certain kinds of decisions to the team members, demonstrating confidence that they will make prudent choices, and accepting these choices can result in expanded skills and judgment, taking the team through to stage 1, albeit at a higher level of technical knowledge and communications. At this point, we start the cycle all over again.

The effect of these stages is to create an environment wherein the software project manager and the development team become partners seeking successful completion of the tasks at hand rather than a superior issuing orders to subordinates who follow them. This both alleviates much of the software project manager's burden of managing the software project and expands the manager's scope of influence and effectiveness.

So what is the best management style? By now, it should be obvious—*empowerment*. As one expert put it, "The more power you give away, the more you have" (Walters, 1992). The success of this approach stems from the fact that by sharing power, you have drawn each team member into being a partner in the success of the project—and we all want to be successful. Perhaps the most common fault of all managers I have ever worked with is their inherent inability to empower their team members. This indicates a lack of trust and self-confidence, resulting in an inability to delegate. These managers also tended not to have anyone reporting to them that they deemed more knowledgeable than themselves. Unfortunately, nearly all of these managers verbally stated that they were team players who were empowering their people when nothing could be further from the truth.

A Maturity Model for Software Project Management

Some years ago, a revision of the Software Engineering Institute's (SEI) Capability Maturity Model (CMM) was published (Paulk et al., 1993). As you might already know, the CMM represents a framework within which organizations can assess their ability to achieve certain levels of quality in software development efforts. While this concept is covered in considerably more detail in Paulk et al., suffice it to say that immature organizations (for example, CMM Level 1) tend to produce unreliable results, while those at the higher maturity levels (for example, CMM Levels 4 and 5) produce high-quality results.

There are five CMM levels, with CMM Level 5 being the highest and most desirable. These levels form a basis for a similar type of assessment from a management standpoint. Table 3-3 depicts a five-level maturity model for project management that parallels that for the software development process. Notice that the management processes and activities evolve from extemporaneous at CMM Level 1 to more like a production line or contracting firm at CMM Level 5. Another way to view this progression is in terms of project outcomes. At Level 1, a successful outcome is, in gambling terms, a "long shot." At Level 5, a positive outcome is highly likely, provided other factors (for example, people with the right skills, adequate understanding of the problem domain) are present—meaning that success is likely and failure highly unlikely. Various degrees of certainty are present in the levels between these two extremes.

TABLE 3-3 Maturity Scale for Software Project Management

Level	Label	Description/Characteristics
1	Informal	Management approach not consistent from one project to the next. Situation best characterized as "chaotic," with management preoccupied with "firefighting" (responding to urgent problems), leaving no time to strategize as to how to prevent fires (potential disasters).
2	Fundamental	Less chaotic than Level 1 and more consistent. At least tacit attention given to requirements analysis and management, existence of a quality assurance function, configuration management, and consistent approach to project planning.
3	Manageable	More consistent results with higher quality than Level 2. Represents the first level where software project management is institutionalized with support from senior and executive levels within the company. Marked by institutionalization of group reviews, walk-throughs, coordination of effort with other groups (such as marketing), training and skill expansion, a defined development, and a proactively maintained management process.
4	Reliable	Marked by focus on high-quality, reliable software at a higher incidence than Level 3. The management of quality processes and their measurement is an adopted discipline.
5	Optimal	Management extends into planned process and technology evolution coordinated with change management and the product suite. Focus is on preventing errors and continual process and product improvement.

Figure 3-4 shows the population of firms that I have had firsthand and secondhand knowledge of over the years. Please note that these were not formal assessments but represent approximate ratios. (The figure is provided strictly as a means of depicting the relative occurrence of project management maturity in my experience and that of my colleagues.)

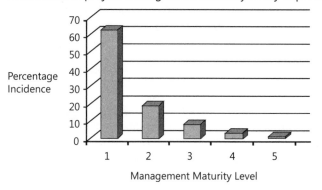

FIGURE 3-4 Experience-based occurrence of manager maturity levels.

Another issue to keep in mind is that even if a group within a company achieves a CMM Level 5 certification, that does not necessarily include all other parts of that company. For example, the Boeing Company announced that a group (and presumably the group's management as well) had achieved CMM Level 5, but other groups are currently considerably lower.

Moving from One CMM Level to Another

A question of great concern to many software project managers is, "How long will it take for my organization to move from one CMM level to the next?" Although the data has not been collected for all level transitions, some data is available for the time it will take for an organization to transition from CMM Level 1 to 2 and from Level 2 to 3, as shown in Table 3-4 (McConnell, 2003). If these times seem too long, keep in mind that the goal is a significant change in the culture of an organization, not just a single project accomplishment.

TABLE 3-4 Transition Times Between Some CMM Levels

Levels From/To	75th Percentile	Median	25th Percentile
CMM Level 1 to 2	40 months	26 months	16 months
CMM Level 2 to 3	24 months	19 months	16 months

Task Maturity Levels

With all due respect to the SEI CMM model just described, there is a very practical matter that needs to be addressed by project managers but often is not. It relates to the way in which people are initially assigned tasks when they join an organization. As Fred Brooks pointed out, adding people to a late project makes the project later (Brooks, 1995). In other words, adding people to a software project, even highly qualified people, might not help matters much. Many people in the software profession have learned the veracity of Brooks' statement the hard way—they added people to a late project, and the situation got much worse. Yet the explanations regarding the forces at work that cause this to happen have been largely absent and quite localized to a specific project effort.

One researcher outside software engineering has succinctly identified these forces (Graham, 2002). His model looks at the maturity of tasks and the performance level of persons assuming duties at each task level; see Table 3-5.

TABLE 3-5 Task Maturity Levels

Task Maturity Level	Appropriate Management Style
Low	"Hands-on," requires management involvement, close supervision, possibly the assistance of a mentor or senior software engineer or manager.
Medium	"Management by objectives," involves setting goals, mutually agreed to by the software engineer or manager and the project manager, and then reviewing these goals on a regular basis to determine what progress has been made to ensure that they are achieved in a timely manner.
High	"Management by exception," involves the individual or manager working independently, essentially without supervision. Interaction with the project manager occurs for either of two reasons: ❑ To set goals or objectives. ❑ An issue exists that requires management intervention.

The most common mistake managers make is that they assume that more senior or experienced software engineers will "hit the ground running"—that is, they can begin work immediately. This means that the expectation is that the new hire or transfer will perform at the Medium or High maturity level right from the start. However, even the most experienced software engineer or project manager must start at the Low maturity level until such time as they have mastered the requirements of that level. Once that has occurred, they move up to the next level.

Now let's get back to Brooks's admonition. You can see that if people are placed at the lowest level first, more management time and senior software engineer time will be required with them. This might well reduce the productivity of the group significantly. If we try to defeat this phenomenon by putting a senior person into a High maturity level position, the objective will not be achieved, and problems will occur. This is because there is no basic understanding of the forces at work, the organizational culture, the processes used to complete project-related tasks (for example, builds, testing), and what the project is really about. This will also greatly reduce progress. Many of us knew that Brooks was right, and now we have a more elaborate explanation as to why.

To summarize, everyone starts out at the lowest task maturity level, no matter what position he or she was hired into. Each person then moves up the task maturity ladder. The time spent at each level is strictly a matter of the combination of the individual's performance and his or her experience level. More-experienced, higher-performing individuals will move faster than those with less experience.

Development Phases and Personalities

It doesn't take long to realize that different people approach life and problem solving in different ways. As mentioned at the start of this chapter, people have been trying to figure out people for a very long time.

One model of personality and behavior that we discussed earlier in this chapter is the Myers Briggs model (Myers and Myers, 1995). That personality model views personalities as being composed of four dimensions. Within each dimension, there are two choices, giving us a total of 16 possible combinations or personality types.

What has this got to do with software project management? Just this: for at least a quarter century, there has been a tendency in the software industry to use one person for many roles throughout the software development life cycle (SDLC). This is intended to save money but might be more costly than most managers realize. A common job classification in firms that do this is programmer/analyst. In other words, this person can be used to gather requirements and analyze them as well as develop the code needed to fulfill those requirements. This seems reasonable, but is it?

If we break the SDLC into four phases and assign to each phase a personal characteristic that would enhance a person's ability to successfully complete that phase, we get the information shown in Table 3-6.

TABLE 3-6 **Relating Desired Behaviors to SDLC Phase**

SDLC Phase	Desired Characteristics and Needed Skills
Requirements	Able to listen, be compassionate, gather facts, be nonjudgmental, ask questions only for clarification and not for assessment of the skill or fitness to job of the person being interviewed, and make decisions with only limited data.
Design	Able to create multiple alternative solutions, withholding selection of one or more as prime candidates for implementation until reviewed by others and evaluation criteria developed.
Code	Works (largely) independently, interfacing primarily with a computer, and works logically, holding ego in check. Able to work within the constraints of the development environment and overcome other constraints, rules, and issues not of his or her own making.
Test	Strict, disciplined application of principles, processes, practices—logical, objective. Strictly focused on being the messenger, not the message—dispassionate regarding results.

Notice how different the behaviors are throughout the SDLC. These are really four different kinds of people. Certainly, people can learn to adapt to situations, but first they have to be aware of the need, as described in this section. If we use the abbreviations for the MBTI personality type factors discussed earlier and align these combinations with the SDLC phases described in the preceding table, we obtain Table 3-7.

TABLE 3-7 **Alignment of Type Factors with SDLC Phase**

SDLC Phase	Type			
	I or E	S or N	T or F	J or P
Requirements	E	S	F	P
Design	E	N	F	P
Code	I	N	T	J
Test	I	S	T	J

The evaluation of type requires the use of a test by a licensed and authorized professional, but by now you should have noticed that there are no duplicate patterns in Table 3-7. While you can guess at your type or that of another person, the point of this discussion is not whether the Myers Briggs model is accurate or even to help you find out what your profile is. Instead, it is to demonstrate that, in assigning people to a project, it is important to think beyond that and to consider the phase for which that person is appropriate (or inappropriate) to enhance your project's chances for success.

The Process of Team Building

Team building can take place in a number of ways. The two primary ones are:

- **Building a team from "scratch"**   Some consider this to be the ideal. After all, you will be putting together a group of your own choosing. However, this does have some drawbacks. One serious one is the fact that, to some extent, we all tend to select people who share our views on software development and have similar values. As a result, there is a danger that the entire team will have the same blind spots that you, the manager, have. For example, if you do not place a high value on code documentation, the code will tend to be largely undocumented. The problem stems from the fact that there is no dissenting opinion regarding downplaying or overemphasizing one practice or another. As an advisory, if you find yourself in a situation where you will be building your own team, have other managers participate in order to improve the mix of candidates.

- **Being assigned an existing team and having to supplement it with new people**   This can also be a mixed bag. For example, the previous manager might have quit or been fired because the team was blatantly unmanageable, would not perform, or was not working for some other reason. This happens, but it is rarer than you might think. If the team was without a manager for more than a few weeks, one of the team members might have become the *de facto* manager and might resent having to step down. This is not uncommon, but it is workable if you provide this person with the opportunity to have some leadership role as a programming lead or similar position. The big advantage in having to work with a team you did not create yourself is the diversity of opinions and approaches present in the team. This ensures a better balance among various viewpoints but might challenge your negotiating skills in trying to reach some form of consensus or at least a decision on your part in a timely manner. Be prepared to listen and treat each viewpoint with respect and value. We will revisit this topic in Chapter 9, "Improving Team Performance," and discuss how it can be used to improve productivity.

The process of team building is illustrated in Figures 3-5 through 3-7.

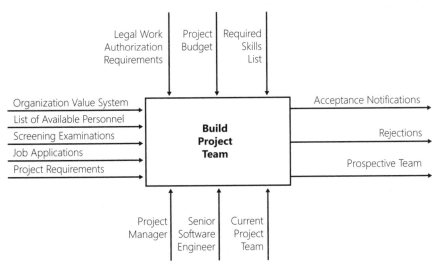

FIGURE 3-5 Top-level view of the Build Project Team process.

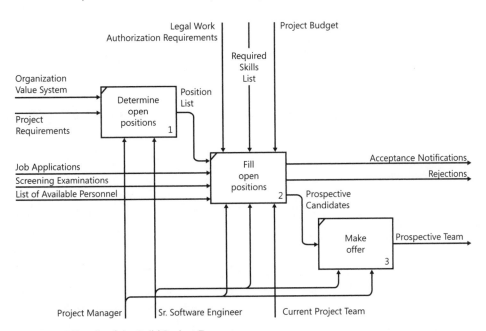

FIGURE 3-6 Details of the Build Project Team process.

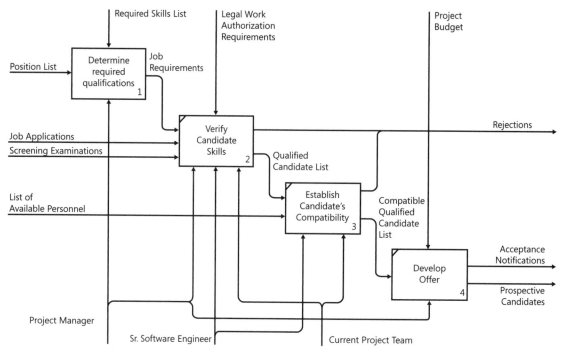

FIGURE 3-7 Details of the Fill Open Positions process.

Descriptions of some of the higher-level activities are presented here. The Build Project Team activity is composed of three subactivities:

- **Determining open positions**   This requires enough understanding of the project to accurately estimate the levels of expertise needed and the number of people needed at each level. Typically, a more senior software engineer might take the role of team leader or lead developer. This person will be the technical resource for the group and will actively participate in the development of the less-proficient. A senior software engineer can effectively direct the activities of two to nine people, depending on the complexity of the project, the skill level of the team members, and other factors.

- **Making an offer**   As project manager, you have some authority within the company. However, this authority must be used with caution. For example, you should not indicate to the candidate that he or she has the job or how much the offer will be. Why? Since you are part of the power structure within the firm, the candidate has a reasonable expectation that you speak for the company. This could put the company at risk. Let the human resources person take care of this, or if your firm is too small to have such a person, do what human resources would have done—notify the candidate in writing indicating the offer amount and the amount of time he or she has to respond before the offer is withdrawn. Remember, money is not everything to the candidate. There is a delicate balance between what it will take to get the person to join and what they are expecting.

Teams: One-Time Throwaways?

Frequently, I have heard software project managers complain bitterly about how difficult it is to figure out this team building business. Invariably, they relate how they had very good success on a project for a client and had an excellent, high-performing team put together. Then along came a similar project, and the same team was assigned to this new effort. But the new effort failed miserably. Sometimes, one or more team members left the organization, and at other times, the team followed the project to the end but encountered internal bickering and poor performance and generally had a very difficult time of it. Managers relating such stories still don't get it. Teams are ethereal. Very much like sports teams, it is rare that a team can have a championship season and follow it with yet another championship season, even with the same team members. People grow and change, learn, and form relationships. Teams are dynamic and cannot be expected to remain essentially frozen over time for as long as we need them. Each new project is a new team building exercise.

Another Reason Why Software People Are Challenging

As you've seen, people who study various disorders and qualities of the human psyche have started to take a keen interest in the software profession. One of these people, Dr. J. J. Ratey, was recently interviewed on the subject of Attention Deficit Disorder (ADD) and its treatment (Ratey, interview, 2001). He had recently coauthored a book that detailed various research results on the subject (Hallowell and Ratey, 1995). He noted that in some of its milder forms, ADD is not an altogether negative characteristic to have. He indicated that the fastest-moving, most-hard-driving software companies have a relatively high proportion of people exhibiting some symptoms of this disorder as compared with the general population. The symptoms they exhibit include not being satisfied with the status quo and always looking to make changes. Even the next, most-advanced, achievement is quickly abandoned in favor of another, somewhat unattainable, one (Lewis, 2000). In the context of a high-technology environment, these traits are valuable assets rather than liabilities.

This list of characteristics might not represent what a software project manager would consider an ideal person to manage. But being aware of these characteristics offers us a challenge. The challenge is to keep people, particularly our most-talented people, focused and engaged in doing what needs to be done to bring the project to a successful conclusion. At issue, though, is whether the software project manager is innovative enough to overcome the high performer's disdain for following a process, repeating a procedure, and staying the course to the end of the project.

Summary

Building a team is not a deterministic task. We don't just build a team and operate it like some type of machine without having to continually review whether things need to be changed. The people on the team change, the needs of the project change throughout its life cycle, the team members' skills usually improve, and sometimes the team members outgrow what they are doing and want to move on. Also, some team members grew up in an era where they were rewarded and cheered at almost every turn. Their expectation is that work will be the same. They are often disappointed at the lack of nearly continual positive feedback. As a software project manager, you will need to identify these folks and find some means of keeping them engaged. Regardless, it is the manager's job to ensure that whatever transpires, the project effort continues as close to plan as possible.

References

(Chen and Lin, 2004)   Chen, S. J., and L. Lin. "Modeling Team Member Characteristics for the Formation of a Multifunctional Team in Concurrent Engineering," *IEEE Transactions on Engineering Management* **15**(2), pp. 111–124, 2004.

(Myers and Myers, 1995)   Myers, I., and P. Myers. *Gifts Differing: Understanding Personality Type*. Palo Alto, CA: Consulting Psychologists Press, 1995.

(Moulton, 1928)   Moulton, W. M. *The Emotions of Normal People*. New York: Harcourt, Brace and Company, 1928.

(Belbin, 1996)   Belbin, R. M. *Management Teams—Why They Succeed or Fail*. London: Butterworth Heinemann, 1996.

(Ashby, 1956)   Ashby, W. Ross. *An Introduction to Cybernetics*. London: Chapman and Hall, 1956.

(Kreitner, 1998)   Kreitner, R. *Management*, 7th ed. Boston: Houghton Mifflin, 1998.

(Walters, 1992)   Walters, L. S. "A Leader Redefines Management," *Christian Science Monitor*, p. 14, 22 September 1992.

(Paulk et al., 1993)   Paulk, M. C., B. Curtis, M. B. Chrissis, and C. V. Weber. "Capability Maturity Model, Version 1.1," *IEEE Software* **10**(4), pp. 18–27, 1993.

(McConnell, 2003)   McConnell, S. "Software Development's Low Hanging Fruit," lecture presented at Construx, Inc., Bellevue, WA, 22 April 2003.

(Brooks, 1995)   Brooks, F. P. Jr. *The Mythical Man-Month: Essays on Software Engineering*. Reading, MA: Addison-Wesley, 1995.

(Graham, 2002)   Graham, V. *Are People Being Managed to Maximize Performance?* Cordova, TN: Kaizen Performance Group, 2002.

(Ratey, interview, 2001)   Interview by Steve Shirer with Dr. J. J. Ratey, KUOW Radio, Seattle, WA, 26 April 2001.

(Hallowell and Ratey, 1995)   Hallowell, E. M., and J. J. Ratey. *Driven to Distraction: Recognizing and Coping with Attention Deficit Disorder from Childhood Through Adulthood.* New York: Simon and Schuster, 1995.

(Lewis, 2000)   Lewis, M. *The New New Thing.* New York: Penguin Books, 2000.

Chapter 4
Developing and Maintaining the Project Plan

Improving quality requires a culture change, not just a new diet.

—Philip Crosby, *Let's Talk Quality*, 1989

Whatever form they take, software project plans are imperfect because no one can accurately foretell the future. From the time of the Romans, who planned battles and city layouts, people have developed plans but have often needed to change them. So why bother planning? In the software world, a plan preprograms the software project team for success. It is an abstraction—a model of what we think we need to do over the life of the project to be successful. In Chapter 3, "Building the Software Development Team," we detailed how to put together a software development team. Now it is time for the team to get together to lay out the project. The team tries to imagine what must be done first, second, third; who will do what; how long each task might take; and what can be done in parallel and so forth. This is like acting on a bumper sticker that reads, "Visualize Success."

However, for more than two decades, the effectiveness of software project plans has been questioned. At the heart of this discourse is the lifecycle model or process used to structure the execution of these plans. We discuss how to select an appropriate lifecycle model in Chapter 5, "Selecting a Software Development Lifecycle Model: Management Implications." Suffice it for now that we view the project plan as "what" must be done, while the software development lifecycle we select is viewed as "how" we will get it done. The fact is, whichever lifecycle model you use to structure your plan, you need to start with a plan and understand that changes to it are inevitable.

Of the projects I have worked on, the ones that had intractable difficulties were the ones where the project plan was developed without the participation of the people who would be driven by it—the project team. Granted, at the start of the project we might not have very many people involved, but we are acquiring talent as fast as we can. Ensuring that all those affected by the plan buy in to the plan helps to ensure that we do not overlook significant issues, that multiple viewpoints and backgrounds are brought to bear on the problem, and that those who develop the plan have a vested interest in the success of the plan. There are plenty of opportunities for latecomers to the project to contribute to the plan, which affords these team members some degree of buy-in going forward. Imperfect or not, project plans are necessary—if only to provide a means to assess how far we have come and how far we have to go during the project. It is important to remember that plans are not carved in stone: plans must change throughout the course of a project to accommodate unforeseen events.

There exists a school of thought that proposes that software development is different from other industries because in software we cannot predict all future activities the way that, for example, project planners in the construction industry can; therefore, for software development, planning does not present a value proposition. It is worth recounting here a recent experience I had on the construction of a 1,200-student kindergarten through 12th grade school. I was asked to assist the project manager who visited the site every week for two days to review the status of tasks, costs, and so forth. Every week, multiple facets of the schedule had to be revised, sometimes because of weather, supply disruptions, labor disputes at other firms, items missed on the blueprints—just about everything was in play. The project's flow time was reduced by employing a "design build approach." Under that scheme, the design of the facility evolves just ahead of or somewhat in parallel with the construction effort. Such a scheme can lead to "just-in-time" discoveries. For example, as the prefabricated walls were being placed, we discovered that the main IT/communications room for the entire facility was only 3 feet wide. A seemingly simple correction involved moving one wall by 7 feet and into an adjacent room, but this necessitated changes in plumbing, exterior window placement, and the fire suppression system. As a result, the project plan had to be changed to meet the opening date despite these construction delays.

From a planning standpoint, software development is similar to building construction in that discoveries, unforeseen technical problems, and market forces come together to drive the development team to overcome difficulties to hit release dates providing (at least) critical content. The software industry is just more challenging than other industries because the repeatability of often critical tasks just is not there.

In this chapter, I present classic methods of developing and monitoring a project through the project plan (referred to herein as the software development plan) together with some not-so-classic methods of planning. I discuss the use of a few classic project management tools, including Gantt charts, PERT networks, and the Work Breakdown Structure. To appreciate the problems that planning addresses, try to shift your focus away from the actual generation of the code toward the higher, more global view of issues surrounding code generation, testing, configuration management, the infrastructure needed for success, interactions with the customer, acceptance testing, the logistics of delivery, and project funding—in other words, the entire project domain.

The Project Charter

The purpose of the project charter is to justify and legitimize the project. This is accomplished in the project charter documentation by focusing on a few key issue sets that must be resolved to the satisfaction of senior management before the project can start.

In its most common form (Project Management Institute, 2004), the project charter overlaps some with the software development plan. However, it is up to each individual organization to decide whether it wishes to employ one or the other or both.

The subject areas that the project charter addresses include the following:

- **Business issues**   These include the risks, assumptions, costs, return on investment (ROI), and related matters.

- **Expected results**   A description of the product, feature, or service the project is expected to deliver.

- **Scope**   A discussion of the boundaries of the project—partly to prevent scope creep and partly to ensure that there is agreement on what will and won't be part of the project.

Another way to organize the content of the project charter is more specific (Project Management Institute, 2004):

- Business case

- Product description

- Project manager and/or key personnel identified and a commitment to assign (provided the project goes forward)

- Constraints

- Assumptions

It is obvious that there is some overlap between the concept of a software development plan and the project charter. If your organization chooses to employ both vehicles, the time order is as follows:

1. Develop project charter.

2. Obtain approval to proceed.

3. Develop software development plan (SDP).

4. Obtain approval for the SDP.

5. Proceed with project.

Regardless of which approach you choose, the key is to create something that will work for your organization rather than using something because it appeared in an institute's study or a textbook.

The Software Development Plan

Developing a plan before spending a significant amount of money on it seems to make the most sense. Yet every year thousands of projects proceed without a plan. This is a lot like going on a backpacking trip into the High Sierras without a topographical map or any idea where the various trails go from the 8,000-foot trailhead. You might know where you want to go but have not considered just how you are going to get there. This is similar to starting a software project without a plan or with a plan that is inadequate. In this context, *inadequate* means that the plan does not consider significant issues that will be encountered or strategize how to deal with them.

A software development plan (SDP) is a means of improving the project's chances of success. It accomplishes this by explicitly stating what will be done, what risks are foreseen, how risks will be mitigated, how long it will take, how much it will cost, what methods will be used in the various phases and why, and other factors. Including all that information sounds like a rather formidable task, but it can take as little as a day if you simply adapt a previously developed SDP.

Even with an example to work from, your first SDP will take longer to develop than subsequent ones will because, even though companies rarely change the methods they use, many sections of the SDP must be created from scratch the first time. Other sections will remain very nearly the same from one project to the next.

One aspect of the SDP that is often overlooked is the potential of its spread throughout the organization. For example, if one project develops a plan and the project is successful, its plan is likely to form the basis for other SDPs developed afterward. What this does is build a culture that uses successful practices and refines them over time—teams might outgrow some practices, experiment with others, and adopt the most useful ones. This encourages experimentation with new methods that appear superior to previous ones because experience using previous methods makes it possible for teams to analyze and identify just where improvements in the process could be made.

The major headings of an SDP are presented in Table 4-1 together with a brief description of the content of each. Note that this is only a suggested starting point. Your company or project team might find it necessary to reorganize or revise this. However, the issues (for example, deployment strategy) must all be addressed.

TABLE 4-1 **High-Level Topic Outline of a Generic SDP**

Main section title	Description
1. Introduction	Tell the reader just what this is. The language changes if this is an internal effort. For example:
	This software management plan was developed specifically for the ABC Project under Work Order 123, Contract XYZ. It is directed at maximizing the benefit to Company X by setting forth processes, procedures, and standards consistent with commonly accepted software engineering practice and the corporate policies of the developing company, SW Software Corporation.
2. Purpose	State why you are going through the time and effort to create this SDP. For example:
	The purpose of this document is to set forth the processes, standards, and guidelines to be used on Project ABC. The benefits of this project are expected to include:
	❑ Reduction in errors and, hence, development and maintenance costs on future projects
	❑ Faster ramp-up time for project personnel on future projects
	❑ Creation of a common set of terms and concepts used across the project
	❑ Definition of a process that can be evaluated by using metrics and that can be used on other software development efforts
3. Scope	State what this applies to. This document could be used on a single project, but it could have been written to cover all projects (in other words, a company standard). For example:
	This document sets forth the management processes to be used on Project X. It also applies to any and all software purchased, constructed by contractor(s), or maintained in relation to Project X (herein referred to as, "The Project").
	As used herein, the term *software* shall include source code, documentation of all aspects of the development, testing, and maintenance of the executable (for example, test cases, error reports) and all other relevant materials related to The Project.

Main section title	Description
4. Organization	This is an enumeration of the sections that make up the document. For example:
	This software maintenance plan is organized into four sections:
	❑ The Methods that will be employed
	❑ The Processes to be used
	❑ The Inspections and Reviews Schedule and related materials
	❑ Costs, flow time, and risk factors
	Each of these is elaborated upon in its respective section.
5. Methods	This section states and gives a brief explanation of the methods to be used on this project. Appropriate references should be provided to direct the reader to the basis for the use of each method. As much as possible, the issue of why a particular method is being used should be justified by explaining why one or more alternative methods were considered but rejected. Tell readers why these methods were rejected. One way to organize this section is as follows:
	❑ Analysis methods
	❑ Design methods
	❑ Programming language selection
	❑ Test methods
	❑ Configuration control methods
	If specific software or computer-aided software engineering (CASE) tools are to be used, discuss them under the appropriate methods category.
6. Processes	Again, using the breakdown from earlier, document and explain the processes to be employed. The most compact way to do this is by using Integration Definition Language 0 (IDEF0) diagrams. Be sure to include a table indicating what sort of reports or artifacts will be forthcoming over the course of this project.
7. Inspections and Reviews	Throughout the course of the project, there will be reviews of what has been done, the overall viability of the project, and what is to be done, all directed at deciding the state of health of the project.
	An easier way to deal with this is to reuse the process diagrams from earlier and identify the point at which reviews and inspections will occur.

Main section title	Description
8. Cost, Flow Time Analysis, and Risk Factors	This section can go earlier in the document. The cost and flow time issues are presented using methods presented earlier in this book. However, risk issues need to be stated, followed by how you plan to address or mitigate each one. Following are some problem statements but without the benefit of mitigating strategies:
	❑ This project pushes the state of the art. No one has actually done anything like this before, but it appears feasible. However, after we begin implementing this, we might discover that it will not work. The probability of this happening cannot be calculated at this time.
	❑ We are relying on the expertise of a small cadre of individuals to carry this project off. If one of them dies or leaves the company, the viability of the project will be in serious doubt.
	❑ External market factors might be an issue. Are there already other products out there occupying a significant market share? Is there really room for another product in that space? Is there really a demand for this thing? (Marketing people will have to be involved in this one.)
	❑ Internal market (software made for internal use by the developing firm) factors might be an issue. (The project sponsor will be needed here.) Of what potential benefit is this software to this company? What are the cost/benefit tradeoffs with respect to making this software internally versus buying commercial off-the-shelf (COTS) products that have the equivalent functionality?
9. Summary	As you can see from the preceding, if only half of the issues raised by the creation of such a document were addressed, a lot of dot com firms might never have even been launched. The goal here is not to prevent software from being built but to ensure that the project being embarked upon will have a high likelihood of success because you, the project manager, have considered all of the relevant issues and have strategic and tactical approaches to deal with them.

Allocating Flow Time

Allocating flow time to the various phases of your project can predestine it to failure *or* give it a chance to be successful. Too little flow time, and the software engineers will not believe they can get the work done. Too much flow time (as though that has ever happened), and the requirements might evolve beyond what can be done with the funds available. The goal is to come up with a flow time and task list that fall somewhere in between these two extremes. The following guidelines have worked and continue to work regardless of which lifecycle model is employed on a software project:

- Allocate at least 60 percent of flow time to requirements definition and analysis, and design in some form (for example, preliminary design and detailed design). You designate such a high percentage of time because lack of understanding in these areas results in "discoveries" late in the project, which cause setbacks, cost overruns, and schedule slides. Late discoveries have a secondary effect of encouraging the team to abandon planning, thereby setting into motion a process that will inevitably result in project failure.

- Allocate 40 percent or less to coding and testing.

- The more work done early in the lifecycle (particularly prior to coding), the less work that must be done later.

- Changes made early in the lifecycle are cheap compared with those that occur after the start of coding.

- Your project plan will contain more detail for the period of 2 weeks to 2 months beyond the planning period. After that, there are too many unknowns to support high detail.

- The better the processes and policies of your software development organization, the faster and less expensive software development will be.

Keep in mind that the preceding are guidelines, not hard-and-fast rules. The key to success is to find a project planning approach that is well suited to your team, your project, and your client.

Using the Work Breakdown Structure

If you have ever done repair work on your car or home or built something (such as a book-case), you probably wished you had done a better job of planning. For example, if you ever changed the oil on an old air-cooled Volkswagen, at least once you had the old drain cover off and discovered that you did not have a new fiber gasket and copper washer kit in hand. Because the old one is usually so brittle from heat that it cracks upon removal, reusing it to get to the parts store is a leaky mess at best. The next time you attempted this chore, you probably mentally checked off whether or not you had the gasket and washer kit, the new oil, the right-size wrench, and so forth as well as reviewed the order in which to perform each task in the process. This process of identifying tasks, needed resources, the point at which each resource will be needed, the order in which each task must be executed, and so forth is an important part of what we refer to as planning.

As the name implies, the Work Breakdown Structure (WBS) is a depiction of a larger task (the "work") broken down into smaller, less complicated tasks organized into a structure (for example, tasks, subtasks, sub-sub-tasks). It depicts this as a time-ordered sequence of events. Each event represents the start or end of a task. The presumption is that when the last task is completed, the project is finished. This might be truer for the development portion of the project than it is for maintenance, and ongoing support is another matter. An additional benefit of the WBS is that it enables us to track progress against our plan and to take corrective action early enough to make a difference. Figure 4-1 depicts a portion of a generic WBS in the format described in the Project Management Institute's Body of Knowledge, 2004 (Project Management Institute, 2004). Although this is an accepted format, the most common format used is that supported by Microsoft Office Project, as shown in Figure 4-2.

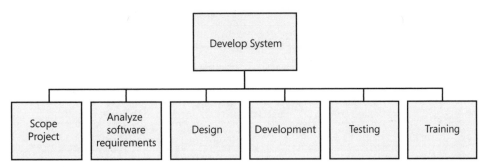

FIGURE 4-1 A generic WBS in a common format.

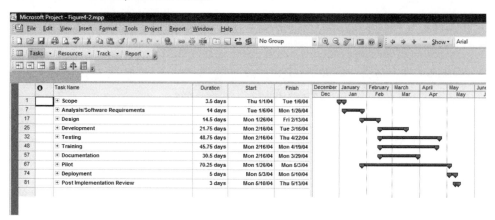

FIGURE 4-2 A high-level WBS using Office Project.

Regardless of the format, the first item with respect to flow time should be the creation and distribution of the methodology set to be used for the project. The product of this activity is used to initiate future team members and to synchronize the team as to how they will do business on the project.

The Gantt chart format (shown in Figure 4-2 and discussed in more detail later in this chapter) depicts a high-level view of a software development project. It can easily be broken down into a more detailed view, as shown in Figure 4-3. In the figures, note the column marked WBS. In Figure 4-2, items are whole numbers; whereas in Figure 4-3, item 3 has been expanded to reveal its underlying structure or task decomposition.

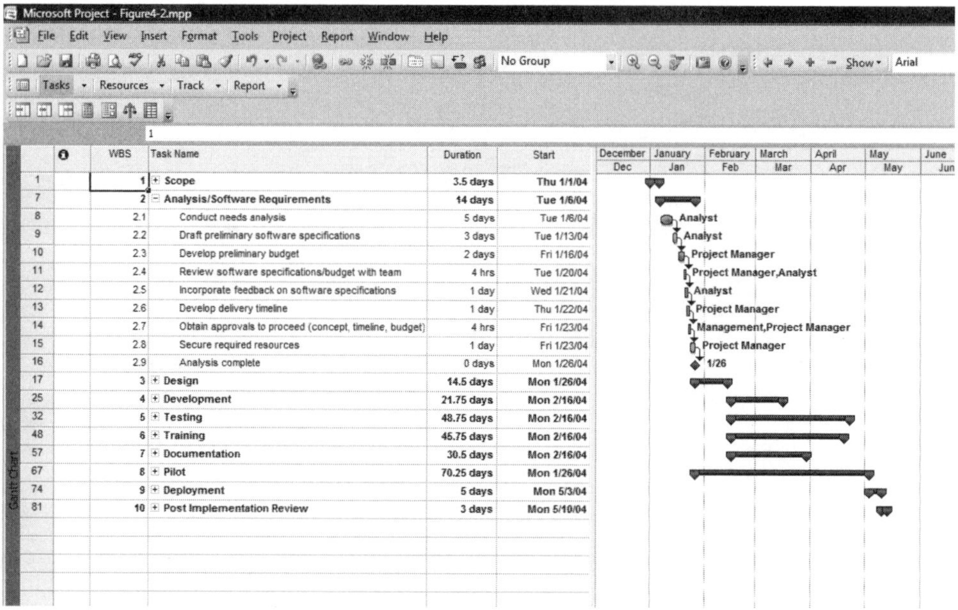

FIGURE 4-3 A more detailed view of the WBS.

There is no formula for developing a WBS, and neither is there a formula that tells you when to stop breaking down tasks. Basically, developing a WBS involves a process of multidimensional decomposition. What you are doing is trying to imagine what must be done first based on the various precedence relationships you know of. In other words, later tasks depend on the successful completion of certain earlier tasks, and so on. In Figure 4-3, note how some tasks must occur right where they have been placed, some could have occurred earlier or later without negatively affecting the project, and others occur in parallel. For example, reviews are events that must occur at particular points because what is being reviewed must exist before a review can occur. Also, reviews are usually called for in the contract and required to occur at specific points in the software development effort.

Developing the WBS

In overly simple terms, a WBS is just a list of tasks that have to be done that are presented in the approximate order in which they must be completed (some are done in parallel), including each task's start and finish dates. For example, the high-level WBS presented in Figure 4-2 is a simple view of a project. To understand what is really required to execute the project plan successfully, we need more detail about how each of the five major tasks in Figure 4-2 will be accomplished, as shown in Figure 4-3.

Let's examine the Analysis/Software Requirements phase (one of the major tasks) in more detail. We can mentally step through what has to be done to complete this phase. It can be easiest to identify these steps (also known as tasks) in the order in which we think they should occur; the key is to make sure we do not miss any steps. Once we are confident that all steps are listed, we can reexamine the sequence to ensure that steps occur in the correct order.

A preliminary list of tasks required to complete the Analysis/Software Requirements phase might look something like this:

- Meet with customer.

- Obtain a narrative description of what the system will do, and with the customer assign relative priorities to each function.

- As well as possible, confirm that functionality and performance requirements will be met.

- Establish a date and an agenda for the next meeting.

- Identify what new hardware must be purchased and order it so that it will be delivered in sufficient time to support tasks that need it.

- Conduct sufficiency review pursuant to the start of the design phase to ensure that the personnel, software support, hardware, and other support personnel and systems are in place.

What we are doing is decomposing each major task into its components. The goal is to get to components that are small enough that we can accurately estimate the associated flow time, personnel hours, and other costs with some degree of confidence.

One difficulty related to cost estimation using this technique is that you do not have a design. This is like estimating the cost of building a house with only a verbal description of the structure and no blueprints (Project Management Institute, 2004).

Using Flowcharts, Gantt Charts, PERT Networks, and Rummler-Brache Diagrams

The flowchart, Gantt chart, and PERT network are the three most popular ways of depicting a project plan. Each takes a very different approach to depicting the project, as described in the following subsections.

Flowcharts

The flowchart in its present form was created by John von Neumann, who regarded flowcharts as a "means of documenting a computer program after it has been written" (Peters, 1978). The flowchart is a handy charting technique for describing a project or nearly any process. It consists of only a few graphic elements.

- **Decision symbol**   A diamond with a statement of a question or condition (for example, Budget Approved?). It most frequently has two outcomes, Yes (True) and No (False), but also supports a multioutcome form.

- **Process symbol**   A rectangle with a statement of an activity (for example, Build Test Suite).

- **End points**   An ellipse representing a starting or an ending point in the process. The text contained in the graphic symbol indicates whether it is the starting point of the process (Begin) or the termination point (End).

- **Directed line segments**   Lines with arrows connect the various portions of the process and assist the reader in understanding the direction of the logic flow.

An application of the flowchart to the problem of planning a project is shown in Figure 4-4. The main problem with the flowchart is that it is strong on logic flow and weak on data flow. Also, the relationships in time among various project elements are either difficult to interpret or not addressed at all. Still, some users of flowcharts find them to be useful tools in creating and executing a project plan.

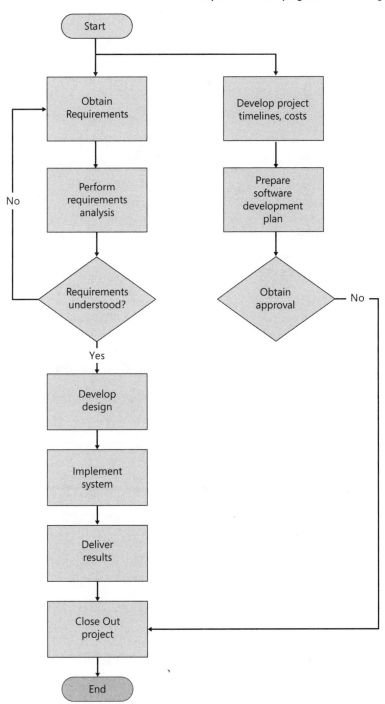

FIGURE 4-4 A flowchart.

Gantt Charts

An American engineer named Henry Laurence Gantt (1861–1919) was the first to publish this graphic format, so it was named after him. The Gantt chart is the oldest of the project planning methods I discuss. It has been used largely in production operations. In recent years, it has been used to describe and coordinate software and other nonmanufacturing activities. The Gantt chart has several advantages over other project plan charting methods, including the following:

- It provides the ability for the manager to specify the start date, the time duration, and the end date for each activity.

- It is more compact and displays less of the logic controlling decision making. Logic is a major issue in project planning because usually the relationships, information flow, and task dependencies are the source of problems, not the logic of the plan. Overemphasis on logic flow in a charting method increases risk because other important factors (such as information flow) can be overlooked.

More complex software projects often result in extensive use of Gantt charts, which themselves can be bulky and unwieldy. Figure 4-5 displays the information in the flowchart shown in Figure 4-4 in Gantt format. This chart was developed using Office Project.

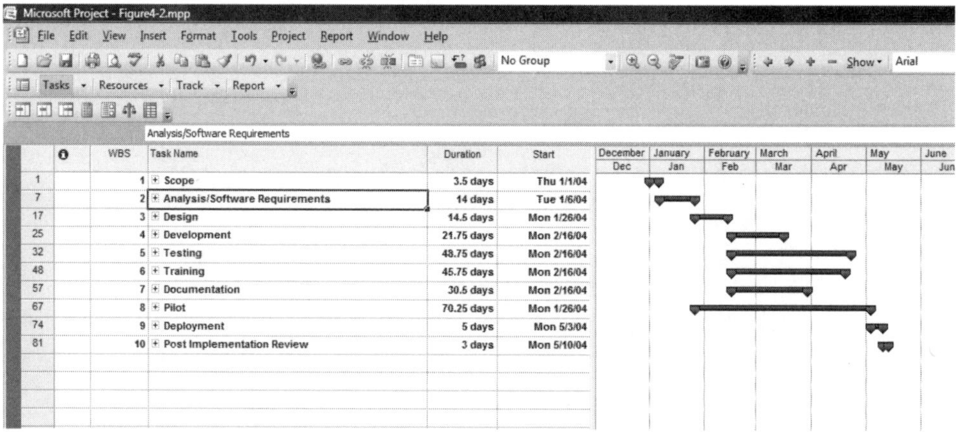

FIGURE 4-5 A Gantt chart.

PERT Networks

As Gantt charts were used on more and more complex processes, the need for an improved graphical method for planning and controlling projects became apparent. The Program Evaluation and Review Technique (PERT) network was developed in conjunction with the U.S. Navy's Polaris submarine-launched missile development effort. The fact that the project resulted in combat readiness nearly two years ahead of schedule led some to believe that PERT was some sort of panacea for success (Anots, 1962), but it was anything but. One PERT user observed, "No management technique has ever caused so much enthusiasm, controversy and disappointment as PERT" (Anots, 1962).

PERT networks are composed of several familiar elements plus a new concept:

- **Event 0** This is a milestone such as the start or end of a task.
- **Activity** This is a resource- and time-consuming process that begins and ends with an event.
- **Time** This is composed of three estimates of how long an activity will take—the shortest (most optimistic), represented by T_o; the longest (the most pessimistic), represented by T_p; and the most likely (the time you think it will actually take), represented by T_m. The time estimate represented by T_e is computed using the following formula:

  $T_e = (T_o + (4 * T_m) + T_p) / 6$
- **Critical path** This represents the most time-consuming path through the network. The term *critical* is applied because a delay in any of the activities on the critical path results in a delay, overall, in the project.

A PERT network dataset consistent with the project model presented in Figures 4-2 and 4-3 is presented in Figure 4-6.

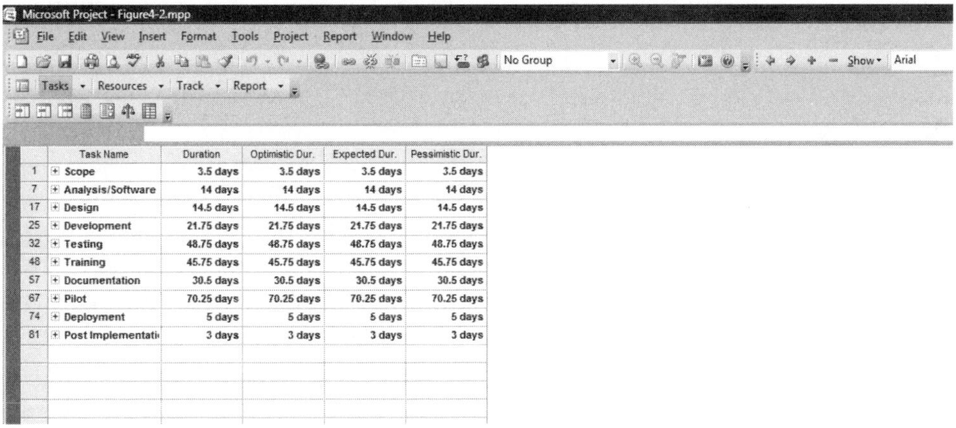

	Task Name	Duration	Optimistic Dur.	Expected Dur.	Pessimistic Dur.
1	Scope	3.5 days	3.5 days	3.5 days	3.5 days
7	Analysis/Software	14 days	14 days	14 days	14 days
17	Design	14.5 days	14.5 days	14.5 days	14.5 days
25	Development	21.75 days	21.75 days	21.75 days	21.75 days
32	Testing	48.75 days	48.75 days	48.75 days	48.75 days
48	Training	45.75 days	45.75 days	45.75 days	45.75 days
57	Documentation	30.5 days	30.5 days	30.5 days	30.5 days
67	Pilot	70.25 days	70.25 days	70.25 days	70.25 days
74	Deployment	5 days	5 days	5 days	5 days
81	Post Implementati	3 days	3 days	3 days	3 days

FIGURE 4-6 A PERT network dataset.

Rummler-Brache Diagrams

This type of chart was developed in response to the need for a multidimensional view of business processes (Rummler and Brache, 1995). The dimensions depict multiple processes proceeding in time from left to right, all in parallel. Perhaps this is why they are often referred to as "swim lane charts." In Figure 4-7, note how the phases or stages of the process proceed from left to right, the roles of various contributors to the successful completion of the process are listed vertically on the left, and the actual activity in the process at any particular stage is delineated vertically. Also note how the vertical span of an activity clearly spells out which participants are involved. This multidimensional scheme provides the software project manager with a compact alternative to the Gantt chart, which can be cumbersome for multiyear projects.

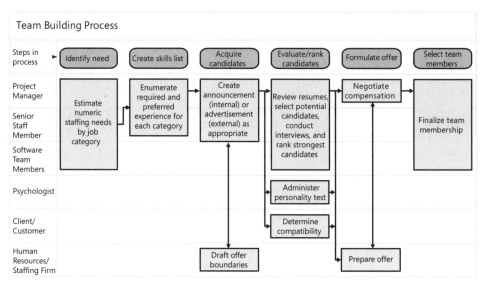

FIGURE 4-7 Example of a Rummler-Brache diagram.

Person Loading

One key to survival as a software project manager is to get the tasks and the money right. An aspect of software project management that is often overlooked is person loading (in person-months, or PMs). That is, calculating the number of people working on the project at any one point in the development effort. A common tool used to estimate person loading is the Work Breakdown Structure (WBS), discussed earlier. The WBS usually is embellished with a list of assigned people and the project expense projections and timelines. At issue in regard to person loading is whether you really need to have the entire team assigned to the effort right from the start. Usually not. Often, you can start with a smaller team that is responsible for the initial steps in the process, including a feasibility study. If the project does not make it past the initial steps, you never need to do development, regardless of whether you are using Agile development or not, so no more human resources are needed.

Today, most organizations are organized using a blend of functional and project responsibilities. This organizational strategy is referred to as a *matrix organization*. In a matrix organization it is often difficult to guarantee the availability of a specific person, which creates somewhat of a dilemma. The solution most project managers use is the ramp-up and ramp-down approach, using as early a lead time as possible to get commitment on one person or another. What usually occurs is that projects start small, ramp up to a critical mass of people, and stay that size with some tapering off toward the end. This approach also helps to stabilize the *burn rate*, the rate at which money is being spent. It also helps provide a reasonable estimate of the cost of an effort as a function of time.

A more popular technique for monitoring and controlling projects is the use of the Gantt chart, discussed earlier. But that graphical view can also be represented as a simple table. Notice how the information shown in Table 4-2 captures the sense of a flow time and includes details of personnel assignment and costs. In Table 4-2, 1.0 means 100 percent committed to the effort, 0.25 is 25 percent committed, and so forth. The Xs indicate the start and finish of the commitment. Right from the start, the amount of budget remaining is depicted. This is actually a more important figure than is the number of hours remaining because in some instances you might use more expensive labor (for example, a senior software engineer rather than a software engineer) than originally planned for. Also, note the line marked "management reserve." This can range from 2 percent to 5 percent of the total budget. It represents the amount of money set aside by the software project manager to accommodate changes in the overhead and general and administrative expenses that can occur during the project or after it at the end of the fiscal year. Depending on the amount, these funds can also be used to overcome unforeseen circumstances such as risk prevention. Depending on how much change occurs when computing the final values for these figures, a team could end a project showing a small profit but realize a loss at the end of the fiscal year. Unused management reserve is reclassified as profit.

TABLE 4-2 A Simple Cost and Person Loading Chart

WBS phase/month	Jan	Feb	Mar	Apr	May	Jun
1.0 Requirements	X	X				
2.0 Design		X		X		
3.0 Code			X		X	
4.0 Test				X	X	
5.0 Deliver						X
Resource Loading						
Project Manager (T. Jones)	1.0	1.0	1.0	0.5	0.5	0.25
Analyst (A. Smith)	1.0	1.0				
Developer (F. Thomas)		1.0	1.0	1.0	0.25	
Tester (J. Valdez)				1.0	1.0	
Installer (R. Wright)					1.0	0.25
Totals [PMs]	2.0	3.0	2.0	2.5	2.75	0.5
Aggregate Labor	2.0	5.0	7.0	9.5	12.25	13.0

WBS phase/month	Jan	Feb	Mar	Apr	May	Jun
Labor Variance						
Cost [budgeted K$]	14.0	21.0	15.0	17.0	16.75	3.25
Aggregate Cost (K$)	14.0	35.0	50.0	67.0	83.75	87.0
Actual Cost (K$)						
Cost Variance (K$)						
Aggregate Actual K$						

Another practical tip for using this tracking scheme successfully is to break out the labor categories into the individual people who will be doing the work. This has two risk mitigation factors:

- It enables you to account for rising labor costs. For example, if a person is due for a raise, include that cost difference in your estimates at the point at which the person will get the raise.

- It prevents overcommitment of a person by preventing other managers from scheduling that key person for their project at the same time you plan to use him or her. Overcommitting people is a common problem. For example, at one firm an installation team was required to travel to the customer's site and spend 1 to 3 weeks installing the product. Only a small number of people could do this. However, the marketing staff made commitments that would have required the installation team either to be in three places at once or to clone themselves. Needless to say, the customers were perplexed, delivery was late, and the installation team was overworked. The problem came under control after specific individuals were listed for specific tasks on a chart similar to the one shown in Table 4-2.

Optimizing the Project Plan Using the Design Structure Matrix

The WBS represents a significant portion of the overall project plan. It lays out what will be done, when each task is expected to start and finish, who will do which task(s), and so forth. A nagging concern I always have had about such plans is not so much whether they are "right" but whether they could be improved. As it turns out, a concept discussed earlier in this text that is the basis for the Requirements Self-Interaction matrix approach has been adapted for analyzing processes (Browning, 1998).

The Design Structure Matrix (DSM) is a method that was developed to address issues in systems development where the following conditions are present:

- Product development is slowed by *cycling* or recycling through a sequence of activities. The process of testing code, identifying bugs, correcting bugs, and retesting is an example of cycling.

- Product requirements are unstable, causing some indecision, revision of work already completed, schedule delays, and so forth.

DSM is most appropriate in product development where many of the following conditions exist:

- There is a lack of and/or failure to use applicable planning methods.

- Product requirements are unstable and can change late in the software development lifecycle.

- Multiple activities completing at different times cause some downstream activities to become idle or overloaded.

- There is a lack of integration and coordination of activities in the organization.

- There are strongly coupled development activities that often result in considerable rework late in the project.

- Product development schedules are optimistic, unrealistic, or poorly formed.

- Attempts at speeding the development cycle lack a systematic approach, often resulting in further exacerbated delays and rework.

I turn to the use of DSM because PERT networks and Gantt charts simply do not address the kinds of highly coupled relationships, interdependencies, and cycling issues that are prevalent in software engineering. The DSM is a square matrix. In it, one row and one column are allocated for each activity. Activities are listed vertically in their expected chronological order. Hence, the earliest activities appear in the upper rows and the later ones appear in successively lower rows. The diagonals in a DSM are placeholders with off-diagonal cells representing interfaces between activities. The DSMs in Figure 4-8 show the basic configurations for relationships (Smith and Eppinger, 1997; Osborne, 1993).

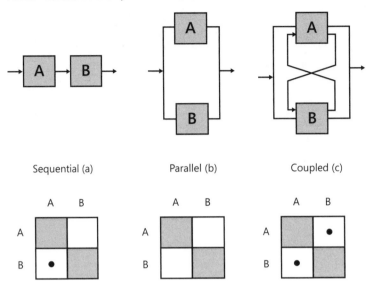

FIGURE 4-8 Graphical and DSM models of logic types.

DSMs are read counterclockwise. Cells below the diagonal indicate feed-forward. For example, in Figure 4-8(a), the DSM is read as, "Activity A must precede activity B." The reason for this interpretation is that the result produced by activity A is needed by activity B to do its job. Cells above the diagonal are used to document feedback, which translates into rework and iteration of the process being described. If activities in rows and corresponding columns i and j, respectively, of the DSM have no direct interface, the cells ij and ji in the DSM will be empty. If both ij and ji are marked, this indicates a two-way dependency (for example, Figure 4-8(c)). This type of interdependency is often referred to as a "chicken and egg" problem, not addressed by Gantt or PERT.

A simple example can demonstrate the use of the DSM before we delve into its application to software project plan evaluation. Most mornings most of us accomplish the simple process I use in this example: the process of putting on our shoes and socks. Although there may be differences in how some of us accomplish this task, let's assume the following sequence of events: Get Socks, Get Shoes, Put on Socks, Put on Shoes, Inspect Shoes.

By putting this sequence of activities into the DSM format, we get the DSM shown in Figure 4-9. To save space, the headings at the top of each column (such as "Get socks" at the top of the first column) were eliminated.

Task						
Get socks	▨					
Get shoes		▨				●
Put on socks	●		▨			
Put on shoes			●	●	▨	
Inspect shoes			●			▨

Figure 4-9 Example of DSM activity sequence before optimization.

A key to interpreting DSMs is to understand the dependencies inherent in the method. For example, in the shoe example, earlier steps in the process provide what is needed by later steps. Conversely, the later steps depend upon the earlier ones. Figure 4-10 demonstrates this facet of DSMs by superimposing the roles played by rows and columns in the matrix.

	P	R	O	V	I	D	E
A	A	B	C	D	E	F	G
B		▨			●	E	
C	●		▨			P	
D		●	●	▨		E	
E		●			▨	N	
F						D	
G							▨

Figure 4-10 The depend/provide relationship in DSMs.

Just to make sure you understand what is going on in the DSM notation, I can state the relationship roles another way. We have added the letters A through E for ease of reference. As noted earlier, the off-diagonal markings denote a dependency of one element (for example, "Put on shoes") on another. Reading across a row reveals to which other elements the element in that row provides support. Scanning down a column reveals which other elements the element in that column depends on. Stated another way, reading across a row reveal outputs while reading down a column reveals inputs. Thus, in Figure 4-9, element "Put on socks" provides something to or supports element "Put on shoes."

Even this simple problem shows how you can unwittingly incur rework or unnecessary cycling. Note the existence of a marked cell above the matrix diagonal. It indicates at least the potential for rework. By inspecting the shoes as the last step, we might discover they are not presentable. This would force us to cycle back by getting a different pair of shoes and replacing the current ones with this second pair. By moving the "Inspect shoes" activity to a point earlier in the overall process, we avoid having to rework by changing shoes. Making that change results in the DSM shown in Figure 4-11.

Task					
Get socks	▓				
Get shoes		▓	●		
Inspect shoes		●	▓		
Put on socks	●			▓	
Put on shoes		●		●	▓

FIGURE 4-11 Example of a revised DSM activity sequence.

This is, essentially, what concurrent engineering is about. We have shortened the feedback loop in the process with the assumption that we will reduce the variance in total process lead time.

Note that Figure 4-11 also has a marking above the diagonal. This indicates some cycling might occur. That is, we might wish to "Get shoes" and "Inspect shoes" at the same time to avoid cycling. The key point here is that moving the inspect activity earlier in the process represents saving valuable resources. In a software project, rework later is much more expensive than changing the process by design and having what rework does occur happen early in the process. The advantage of using the DSM approach is that on more complex problems, it points out these resource-saving opportunities more clearly than casual inspection can.

In a real software project, the preceding analysis can be the equivalent of moving the testing or inspection activity to a point earlier in the software lifecycle. This reduces the amount of resources that have to be invested prior to determining whether we will get any benefit from them. While we are on the subject of resources, when analyzing processes using the DSM approach we need to be sure that they are sufficient to support whatever arrangement we contrive. Figure 4-11 indicates that "Get socks," "Get shoes," and "Inspect shoes" could all occur in parallel, resources permitting. The question the project manager has to answer is, "Does this project have the resources to achieve this parallelism?"

A few additional, more advanced features of DSMs include the following:

- Off-diagonal cells can have a value (for example, 0 through 9) other than simply being marked or unmarked. A common use of the nonbinary form is the documentation of the probability of occurrence of an activity, percentage of rework, amount of data, data transfer rate, and other indicators, as appropriate.

- Activities can be overlapped in time.

- Critical-path calculations can be approximated by inserting the duration of activities along the diagonal.

- Activities that can be executed in parallel might still be prevented from executing because of resource constraints. These constraints must be accounted for in more complete models.

Now let's examine a software engineering–related model. Let's take a look at a "typical" software lifecycle, as shown in Table 4-3.

TABLE 4-3 Software Development Phases in Sequential Order

Order	Phase name
1	Requirements Definition
2	Requirements Analysis
3	Preliminary Design
4	Detailed Design
5	Coding
6	Testing
7	Distribution
8	Installation

This is pretty standard stuff and represents nothing new. Now let's put it into the DSM form, as shown in Figure 4-12.

	1	2	3	4	5	6	7	8
Requirements Definition	▓							
Requirements Analysis	●	▓						
Preliminary Design	●	●	▓					
Detailed Design	●		●	▓				
Coding				●	▓	●		
Testing	●	●		●		▓		
Distribution					●	●	▓	
Installation							●	▓

FIGURE 4-12 DSM form of a generic software project plan.

The issue might be how to shorten the total flow time for this project. Inspection of Figure 4-12 shows the Testing phase to be somewhat unusual because, strictly speaking, tests should not be based on the code but on the requirements and, to some extent, the system design. This means that all or some part of testing could be moved to a point in the lifecycle ahead of coding. Obviously, we can't test what has not been coded.

Testing takes a lot of forms with major differences from author to author and company to company, but typically it might follow this series of steps:

- Generate unit test cases
- Generate system test cases
- Generate user interface test cases
- Conduct unit tests
- Conduct system tests
- Conduct user interface tests

I have put this into the first form of a DSM in Figure 4-13 using this two-stage testing activity. All that is needed to generate unit tests are the data format and some knowledge of the call or initiation sequence. Parts of other tests fall into the same category. Hence, we could split Testing into two distinct but related activities:

- Generate test cases of various types
- Conduct (execute) tests

	1	2	3	4	5	6	7	8	9
Requirements Definition	▨								
Requirements Analysis	●	▨							
Preliminary Design	●	●	▨						
Detailed Design	●		●	▨					
Coding				●	▨	●			
Generate Test Cases	●	●		●		▨			
Conduct Tests				●		●	▨		
Distribution					●		●	▨	
Installation								●	▨

FIGURE 4-13 Revised DSM reflecting two stages of test activity.

Now we can make some further observations. Note that the activity "Conduct Tests" depends only on the existence of code to test and on test cases to test with, but the activity "Generate Test Cases" does not depend on the existence of code. This last item is because, as we noted earlier, test cases should be generated from what the code was *intended* to do (that is, requirements). This lack of dependency of the "Generate Test Cases" on its immediate predecessor means we can move it ahead of the coding activity in the sequence of events, as shown in Figure 4-14.

	1	2	3	4	5	6	7	8	9
Requirements Definition	▨								
Requirements Analysis	●	▨							
Preliminary Design	●	●	▨						
Detailed Design	●		●	▨					
Generate Test Cases	●	●		●	▨				
Coding					●	▨	●		
Conduct Tests				●		●	▨		
Distribution					●		●	▨	
Installation								●	▨

FIGURE 4-14 Revised DSM reflecting resequencing of test case generation.

At this point, we have Detailed Design and a major part of the test phase occurring concurrently. I have used this strategy on several projects, and although there were a small number of data format changes causing minor rework, the team was able to reduce total project flow time significantly. What happens is that software engineers have unit test cases ready and waiting as soon as they have coded a module. The policy was that the software engineer had to pass all unit tests before the code would be incorporated into the daily or current build. An added benefit of basing at least the unit tests on the requirements is that we found out very early in the coding process just how well we understood the requirements.

Risk Management

In Chapter 2, "Why Is Software So Difficult?" I quote Mike Deutsch, who states that nearly every aspect of software project management involves some form of risk management. That said, I have found that the most effective means of managing risk is by using a combination of strategic (that is, planning to avoid risk) and tactical (that is, preparing to take remedial action if adverse events occur) methods. Strategic planning addresses what we can foresee, whereas tactical planning enables us to address what we can't foresee.

The Software Engineering Institute defines risk as "the possibility of suffering loss." A considerable amount of information on risk has been published in recent years, with more resources likely in the future. If we look at the risks involved in a software project, we can see that they are closely related to the software development lifecycle. The farther out we plan in time, the lower our confidence level is and conversely the higher the risk and likelihood of change(s) to the plan. But simply considering the existence of risks is not enough. We need to assess how likely a risk is to occur, what impact it might have on the project, what we can do to mitigate its effects or prevent it, and whether or not the mitigation represents good value, and then we must share this process and knowledge with the software development team.

Figure 4-15 presents a model of the process for addressing risk as part of a software project manager's usual activities; Figure 4-16 provides more detail. Although the processes presented in these figures imply that risk management is something we do once and then move on, such is not the case. Risk management is a proactive, continuous activity in which the software project manager and anyone else involved in project decision making engages throughout the life of the project.

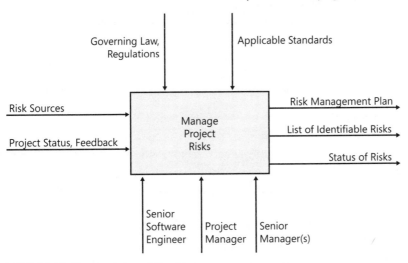

FIGURE 4-15 High-level view of the risk management process.

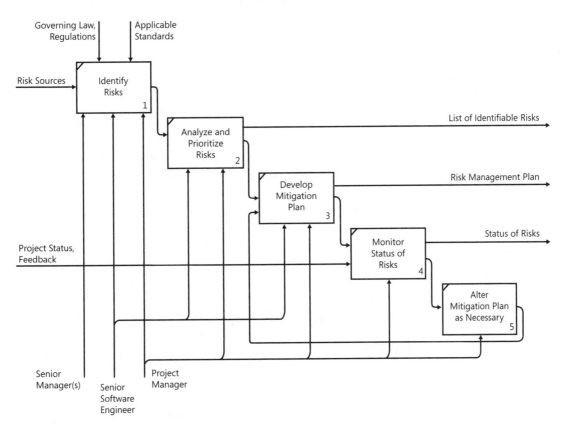

FIGURE 4-16 A more detailed view of the risk management process.

Risk management is a way of looking at the project plan and asking the following two questions:

- What could go wrong?
- How is the plan constructed to minimize the loss associated with each event?

Trying to imagine events that can cause the team to fail is disquieting. For most managers, this is a particularly difficult process because most software project managers used to be programmers, and programmers are probably (when creating estimates) the most optimistic people in the world. But imagine failure we must. Just as we can learn from our real mistakes and failures, we can definitely learn by imagining mistakes and failures and contriving a plan to prevent them or at least minimize their impact on the project. Considering the severity and likelihood of risk occurrence provides a sanity check for the project. The key is to ensure that the *entire* software development team recognizes where the plan is at risk and is proactively involved in reducing that risk. One situation to avoid occurs when only certain members of the team are aware of risk issues that are not addressed at status meetings. This can reduce motivation to execute the project plan because these team members perceive that the plan will fail anyway because of one risk or another.

Sometimes You Just Can't Win

It can be frustrating to imagine how things can go wrong and then to take preventive action, only to have them go wrong anyway. Here is a cautionary tale: The head of Information Systems for a major airline once noticed that the main road into Los Angeles International Airport, Century Boulevard, was frequently under construction. He began to wonder just what would happen if the construction company inadvertently cut power to the building that housed the airline's central data processing systems that run the passenger airline reservation system. The potential for monetary loss was in the millions. So he decided to install an onsite power generation system that ran on natural gas. This reduced his anxiety until he realized that construction crews could just as easily break a gas line. This prompted him to install a large natural gas storage tank containing enough fuel to run the facility for 24 to 30 hours. This tank would supply fuel to the power generation system if the pressure from the city-supplied gas line dropped below a certain threshold. The manufacturer of the device that detected pressure changes certified that the device had a reliability rating of 0.999999, or a probability of failing of about a one in a million. Well, you probably have already guessed what happened. During the peak of the Christmas season reservation period, a backhoe went through the main electrical line supplying a four-block area, another went through the gas line, and the automatic pressure sensing/switching device failed. This cost the airline millions of dollars in lost revenue and left the manager asking what more he could have done. The moral of this story is that although we greatly increase our chances of mitigating the impact of adverse events, there are no guarantees that we will avoid them altogether.

Three aspects of risk management that are most important are the following:

1. Continuously monitoring and evaluating the variables or factors that can set us on the path to failure.

2. Sorting through what can go wrong and identifying which events must be dealt with strategically (for example, the automatic switchover system described in the sidebar) and which can be handled tactically (for example, manually switching over the gas supply at the tank) when they happen.

3. Developing and implementing strategies to deal with those high-priority risks identified in step 1 (for example, avoiding single-point failures by having key personnel cross-train with colleagues to avoid possible loss of operability if key individuals are absent or leave the company).

Table 4-4 lists the principles of effective risk management.

TABLE 4-4 Principles of Effective Risk Management

Item	Description
Systems viewpoint	Consider all aspects of the project, the product, the processes—literally everything involved in the project when viewed as a system.
Projection in time	Imagine, going forward, just how the project or specific aspects of it will play out, what vulnerabilities are present, and how to mitigate them.
Open communications	Make sure that everyone is aware that sharing concerns, observations, and suggestions carries no penalty.
Continuous management	Realize that risk management is not a deterministic process but one in which the team is engaged every day.
Unified vision	Members of the team share the same basic elements of what the product is, what the problems are, and so forth, even though they might disagree on some details.
Working as a team	Vital to reducing cost, improving or maintaining quality, and achieving project success (on time, on budget, satisfying client requirements).

The best way to demonstrate what we have discussed about risk management is to apply this knowledge to an actual software development effort. In an example, we will list each area of risk and its likelihood of occurrence and then describe a mitigation approach for each issue. Table 4-5 contains some of the factors that I considered during the development of a commercial software product using a Petri net simulation system for business process reengineering. The numbering scheme ranks the highest severity or probability at 1. The underlying principle that makes the analysis in Table 4-5 effective is the consideration of not just how serious a risk area might be but also the likelihood that it will occur.

TABLE 4-5 **Example of Risk Mitigation Factors Analysis**

Relative severity	Relative probability	Category/Description/Mitigation
5	7	Requirements—Least likely. Contract requires renegotiation of delivery price if changes occur and client has fixed budget. Early requirements well done and clear. Mitigation—Not an issue, but will monitor for conformance.
3	6	Design—Not as serious as might have been. Proof of concept design was more complete than required and found to be excellent. Mitigation—Ensure that the as-built design conforms to delivered system by configuration management and peer review audit.
2	2	Coding—Nobody had ever tried coding this type of system in this time frame and budget. Mitigation—Acquire highly skilled individual who could do the job here proved out in the proof of concept.
1	1	Testing—This is a stochastic system (Petri net simulation); it would not be possible to come close to a high percentage of possible cases. Mitigation—Use analytic methods to assess the approximate number of tests needed, analytic tools needed to ensure test coverage. Obtain multiple certified and refereed models in the literature to check results.
6	3	Installation—Damage during shipment en route is a major concern. Mitigation—Hard drive would be carried on aircraft and rest of system shipped by land carrier.
4	4	User training—Level of knowledge of subject of users is not known. Only a few have been interviewed. Mitigation—Survey user community early, build class in modules so that advanced students can attend only advanced sessions.
7	5	Support—Cost of support during warranty period is not predictable. Mitigation—Keep error content to a minimum to reduce support.

Summary

The concept of planning has been around a long time. For some people, actually creating a plan is a major headache. The source of the pain appears to be the number of variables that must be considered and the haunting knowledge that, along the way, they are making assumptions that can prove to be incorrect. But plan we must. The crucial thing about planning is to be a skeptical optimist. That is, expect the best and plan for the worst. In reality, what happens is usually somewhere in between. After you have developed an overall plan, it is ready for refinement through the selection of an appropriate software development lifecycle, as described in the next chapter.

References

(Project Management Institute, 2004)   Project Management Institute. *A Guide to the Project Management Body of Knowledge*. Newtown Square, PA: Project Management Institute, 2004.

(Peters, 1978)   Peters, L. *Software Design: Methods and Techniques*. New York: Yourdon Press, 1978.

(Anots, 1962)   Anots, I. "The Management Side of PERT," *California Management Review* **4**, pp. 16–27, Winter 1962.

(Rummler and Brache, 1995)   Rummler, G. A., and A.P. Brache. *Improving Performance: Managing the White Space on the Organization Chart*. San Francisco, CA: Jossey-Bass, 1995.

(Browning, 1998)   Browning, T. R. "Use of Dependency Structure Matrix for Product Development Cycle Time Reduction." *Proceedings of the Fifth International Conference on Concurrent Engineering Research and Applications*, Tokyo, Japan, July 1998.

(Smith and Eppinger, 1997)   Smith, R. P., and S. D. Eppinger. "A Predictive Model of Sequential Iteration in Engineering Design Structure Matrix," *Management Science* **43**, pp. 1104–1120, 1997.

(Osborne, 1993)   Osborne, S. M. "Product Development Cycle Time Characterization Through a Model of Process Iteration." Master's thesis (Management/Engineering), M.I.T., Cambridge, MA, 1993.

Part III
Management Methods and Technology

In this part:

Chapter 5
Selecting a Software Development Lifecycle Model: Management Implications

Success in software engineering is the result of a system—not a secret.

—*L. Peters*

Whether you are new to or experienced in the business of software engineering, you will encounter many versions of the *software development lifecycle*. The software industry treats a common engineering model of a project (that is, the lifecycle) as something special and unique to software with the view that there must exist a "right," magic-bullet-type, lifecycle (Brooks, 1987) and a bunch of wrong ones. This perspective might stem from the scientific and engineering backgrounds of some software project managers, but anyone who has worked on a few projects recognizes that each project has its own unique issues resulting in a lifecycle tailored to that specific project.

In this chapter, I examine the most common software development lifecycles from a process modeling view, beginning with the basics and comparing and contrasting the various versions currently in use. The origins of the general software development lifecycle lie in other engineering disciplines more than 2,000 years old. Presented in this chapter are descriptions of software lifecycles that various authors have idealized and documented. Each should be viewed as a generic starting point for specific projects that requires some customization by you and your team to make it most effective for your project. Near the end of this chapter, I present a tabular comparison of lifecycle model features followed by a section titled, "Selecting a Software Development Lifecycle," which provides guidance on how to select the software lifecycle model that is best for your group and project.

The Software Quality Lifecycle

Over the years, some of the most significant advances in the area of software quality and reliability have occurred in high-availability software, including military systems, banking systems, flight control software, and health-related software. In the military arena, Willis and Deutsch developed the software quality lifecycle (Deutsch and Willis, 1998). The idea was to depict how a software system becomes imbued with quality. This approach spans the entire development lifecycle and is mutually supportive of both development and quality assurance. I present this lifecycle model first to set the tone for the lifecycle selection process.

A lifecycle is more than simply a map that guides a project from beginning to end. It sets into motion processes that are intended not only to get the work done but to do so in a manner that ensures that quality results. These processes improve productivity, reduce cost, and increase your chances of continued success with your stakeholders and customers.

A distinction is made in the software quality lifecycle between *defects* (conceptual errors that can be detected and corrected through the review process) and *errors* (mistakes in the implementation discovered through execution in a test environment). The beauty of this approach is that it captures in one complete view the concepts involved in creating software quality, as shown in Figure 5-1. Its contribution to the quality of the software system results from providing a holistic view of what is required to instill quality from the start and to formalize the process (such as by using reviews). The software quality lifecycle can be adapted for use in conjunction with a software development lifecycle. For example, it could be used with most of the software development lifecycle models presented in this chapter in the testing and installation phases; moreover, it could be applied to any stage from requirements through delivery.

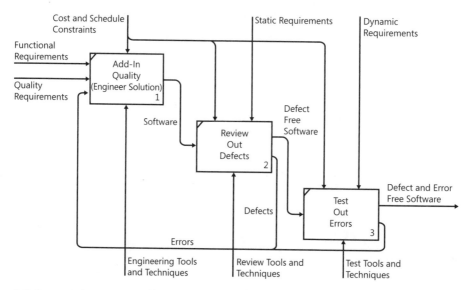

FIGURE 5-1 A detailed view of the software quality lifecycle.

Viewing Software Development as a Process

In some ways, software development is similar to other engineering-oriented industry processes. It begins with requirements, develops a design, executes (implements) the design into a deliverable, tests and corrects the deliverable, and delivers the results to the client. Regardless of the specific product, all engineering disciplines start with a problem or concept and take it to fruition—a product or process. A more detailed list of software-related activities occurring in this process is presented in Table 5-1, as adapted from an IEEE standard (Boehm, 1988).

TABLE 5-1 List of Activities in Software Development

Software development phase	Similar engineering phase
Process implementation	Adoption of industry standards
System requirements analysis	Specification
System architecture design	Conceptual design
Software requirements analysis	
Software architecture design	
Software detailed design	Blueprint
Software coding and testing	Implementation
Software integration	
Software qualification testing	Inspection cycle
System integration	
System qualification testing	
System installation	System delivery
System acceptance and support	Punch list completion/final delivery

A few observations about the list in Table 5-1 are in order:

- The concept of planning the project appears to be a given or is just plain absent.

- In actual fact, a considerable amount of cycling (repeated work to correct errors) occurs in real projects from design to code and test to integration and back again.

- A more complete view of the process would include management-related issues such as acquiring and assigning personnel.

- Planning preprograms the team to think about how to be successful. The first time a team uses planning, an act of faith is required—believing that planning and process development/refinement will have positive effects on the project.

In describing an overview of software engineering management, we will be using the IDEF0 modeling method described in Chapter 3, "Building the Software Development Team." Our high-level model of software project management is presented in Figure 5-2. Note that Figure 5-2 is an example of only one model of software engineering project management. There are many other ways to portray it. Specific companies and projects in a company can differ from this model in terms of the labels used for different resources, the various applicable controls, and other details. For example, I have used a broad term, "Domain Rules, Legal Considerations," for a complex data stream. In the health services industry, these might include privacy rights, governmental regulations, and so forth. This generalized term was used to ensure that these key controlling factors are not ignored. Figure 5-2 should be considered a starting point from which to develop a customized model of software engineering project management as practiced by you and tailored to your team and project.

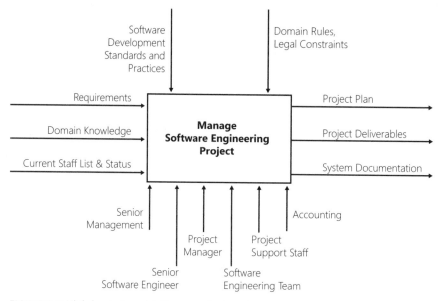

FIGURE 5-2 High-level view of software project management.

Figure 5-3 expands the process shown in Figure 5-2 into four activities that are, in general, done in the order they appear from left to right:

- **Develop Project Plan**   I discuss this activity further in the next section.

- **Revise Development Plan**   This involves updating and refining the plan.

- **Develop Project Deliverables**   In this activity, the creation of the code, testing, debugging, and so forth occurs. This is the portion of the process that most companies focus on, while ignoring the rest. This involves preparing whatever has to be provided to the client as part of the contract or work agreement. It involves packaging what was developed into a presentable deliverable and making sure that all deliverables have or will be accounted for so that the contract can be declared to be complete.

- **Deliver Product—Close Out Project**   This activity can be simplified if there is no delivery activity. Examples of delivery activities include installation of the product at the client site, on-site instruction in the use of the product, and conducting a briefing at the client's site when the final deliverable has been put under the client's control. What really is essential in this activity is the closeout portion, which consists of a *postpartum* meeting (some people call these *postmortem* meetings, but that is a Latin term for *after death* and, hopefully, the project did not die) after the product has shipped. The objective is for the project team to compare notes on what went well so that success-oriented practices can be repeated in the next project. Also noted are practices that were not effective so that the team can ensure that these practices are not used on similar projects in the future. This is also the point at which the senior programmer or lead programmer presents some of the statistics that (hopefully) were gathered over the course of the project. Often, these reveal nuances that might have gone unnoticed were they not presented to the team at once. These might include the amount of time it took to correct bugs by category, the number of bugs overall, productivity figures, build issues and solutions, and related matters. The statistics might also include the relative effectiveness of software tools or of the development environment used. Usually, a social event follows this meeting so that the team can celebrate (or commiserate).

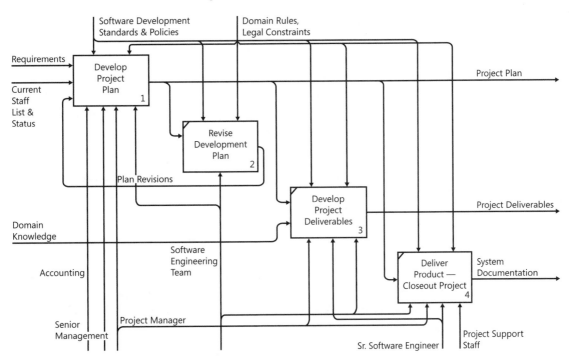

FIGURE 5-3 The four activities of software project management.

Islands of Knowledge

Some companies use a project model in which key people with specialized knowledge collaborate to produce results. Project planning, process development and improvement, and other practices seem to them to be too textbook oriented and out of step with the real world. Surprisingly, this "islands of knowledge" approach can occasionally be successful—but success comes at a high price. These key players tend to burn out, leave the company, or otherwise become unavailable, which puts the project in jeopardy.

What usually seals the fate of such organizations occurs when they take on a project that includes technological challenges far beyond anything they have ever attempted. This is where process development and refinement could pay off, if only they were used. When things get really difficult, someone always suggests that some planning and process development might help get the project back on track. But the usual response to this suggestion is, "We don't have time to do that—maybe later when things let up a bit, we will do it, but not now." Like a self-fulfilling prophecy, they never do get around to process development and instead get eaten up by the entropy (wasted effort), cost overruns, and schedule delays. On those rare occasions when teams are successful using the islands of knowledge approach, management's conclusion is that this is just the way things are and chaos is always the order of the day. Besides, why abandon a successful approach? Because periodic reinforcement of a behavior tends to increase that behavior, this project model becomes a tough habit to break.

The Develop Project Plan activity is detailed in Figure 5-4. It consists of five related activities that carry out the task of developing a project plan. A brief description of each activity follows:

- **Conduct RSM Analysis**   This activity involves performing a requirements self-interaction matrix (RSM) analysis of the current requirements. This is discussed in detail in Chapter 7, "Estimating Project Size, Cost, and Schedule." It reveals where linkages and potential problems exist in the requirements statements as well as the level of independence certain requirements have from others.

- **Develop Preliminary Design**   One key factor in developing a cost estimate is the existence of a system design. The system design should contain enough detail so that an approach like function point analysis can be applied. This activity uses the requirements and some project personnel to generate the preliminary design.

- **Estimate Cost, Schedule, and Variations**   This activity results in a statement of what the project is likely to cost, what it could potentially cost (the variations), and an estimate of how long it will take to complete. It should also include a discussion of the foreseeable risks likely to be encountered and a plan for how these risks will be mitigated. The cost estimate should include a contingency budget as well, as discussed in Chapter 7.

- **Assign Personnel**   This is where the positions and required skill sets identified in the Estimate Cost, Schedule, and Variations activity are filled.

- **Conduct Internal Review**   The purpose of this activity is to ensure that everyone involved in the project and those potentially affected by it have a chance to comment on the project's organization and (eventual) conduct. Basically, this amounts to obtaining an approval to proceed. It amounts to a sanity check regarding the proposed system. A lot of projects I have consulted on would never have launched if such a review had been conducted because their flow time, business case, and associated risks were more than the project team could handle.

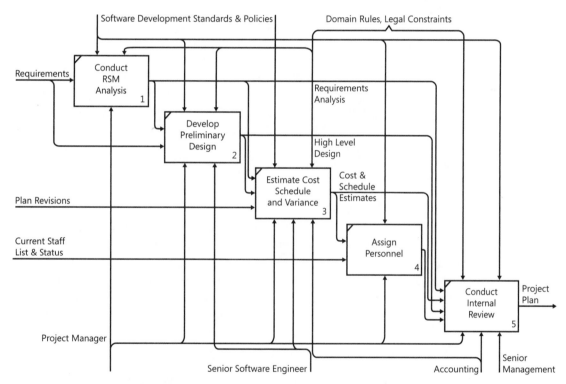

FIGURE 5-4 Details of the Develop Project Plan activity.

Modeling Processes

Processes are a time-ordered set of activities directed at a goal or outcome. Management and engineering processes are not exactly recipes for success. Recipes in the culinary arts provide step-by-step instructions that, if followed, guarantee the same outcome every time.

Their repeatability makes them static, and there are few unforeseeable problems. This differs greatly from software development in that processes are dynamic in the sense that we lay out a set of activities and a plan for accomplishing them only to find that changes must be made as time passes to accommodate one unforeseen circumstance after another. I have often wondered where the concept of a lifecycle-related process came from. It turns out it dates back to the early part of the twentieth century.

Discovering How to Model Processes

Based on his observations at a meat-packing plant, Henry Ford envisioned the first true auto-mobile production line. The idea of reversing the process of breaking an animal carcass down from a single object into various cuts of meat and waste products might seem trivial to some, but nobody else prior to that time seemed to have captured the concept of an assembly line production process. At that time, automobiles and other goods were created by work crews working in a mode we would refer to today as self-directed teams.

The idea of the production line brought with it some new challenges. The solution to one challenge marked the beginning of a new discipline that came to be known as industrial engineering. The problem this new discipline addressed had not arisen before: how do you graphically depict a production line? By graphically depicting the process, the engineering team would be able to analyze and refine the production process. For sure, blueprinting was around, but blueprints provide a static view of a project; they do not convey the idea of the dynamic, the flow of parts and labor from one workstation to another.

Between 1915 and 1925, a notation we refer to today as the *block diagram* began to be used as a means of describing the flow of raw materials and subassemblies into what became the Model T and later automobile models. These were actually dataflow diagrams that used rectangular shapes instead of circles to represent processes. The process models of these early production lines revealed the potential for many improvements and refinements in the production process. For example, one study resulted in Ford specifying to some suppliers that they ship their products to Ford in wooden boxes made up of certain types of wood cut to specific dimensions. Anyone fortunate enough to still own an intact Model T should know that the floor boards in their antique car used to be boards in these shipping crates.

Effective process models are capable of revealing several classes of process problems:

- Inefficiencies in the process such as loopbacks and rework
- Choke points that could cause downstream efforts to slow or stop
- Opportunities for consolidation of steps to streamline the process
- Oversights, such as leaving out a required activity (or activities)

One aspect of process modeling that is often overlooked is that a process model is an abstract representation. As such, it presents the process from a different perspective that can reveal facets of the process not readily seen in the live process.

In software, modeling processes graphically helps to normalize the team's viewpoints by presenting a common set of information for evaluation and communication. Graphical modeling is analogous to using a different part of the electromagnetic spectrum to observe a scene. For example, the human eye uses the visible portion of the electromagnetic spectrum to see and obtain visual information about our surroundings. However, accessing other portions of the electromagnetic spectrum can provide useful information; for example, using an instrument that detects infrared energy is useful for finding where a house might be losing heat on a cold night. In software project management, benefits can be realized similarly by viewing the software development process from different viewpoints. Other perspectives can reveal sources of problems and suggest solutions. This strategy can work well when it is used on a continuous basis. Solving today's project management issues does not mean we have solved those of tomorrow. Keep the process model accurate, and continually adjust what is happening in the project to address current issues.

Lifecycle Model Basics

In reviewing the lifecycle models presented here and those you might find elsewhere, you'll find some common properties worth noting. One is that they are all intended to avoid or prevent many of the classic problems that have been cited in the literature, including cost overruns, lack of features, lack of customer acceptance, poor maintainability, poor reliability, and late delivery. Each author of these models has taken a different and sometimes radical approach to lifecycle model creation. Most have reported their approach in conjunction with one or more project team successes using it. Rarely has an author of a lifecycle model advised teams to avoid using the model under a defined set of circumstances. So each is offered by its originator as something of a panacea—a lifecycle that will work for everyone. As you shall see later in this book, success in software engineering is neither a secret nor a set of formulated practices but a system whose focus should be people. The people part of the equation can, at times, make just about anything work as long as the people side of the equation is adequate. Making sure that the team is up to the task is the manager's primary job—not coding, not testing, but team creation and management.

There are three basic types of software lifecycle models:

- **Classic phased**   Lifecycles of this type follow the traditional approach of defining requirements, creating a design, implementing the design, testing and refining the results, and delivering the finished product. A complaint about this approach is that neither the customer nor the developing organization really "see" a working product until very late in the project. For many, this translates into higher risk because we do not know if the client will accept what is being built until a serious commitment of funds and flow time has already been made. Some authors and managers have varied this model to include user interface development early on to ensure better customer acceptance by gaining feedback early in the lifecycle. These approaches are also referred to as being analogous to the Big Bang theory in that little or nothing is available and working until very late in the project.

- **Evolutionary**   This style of lifecycle model and the management methods to support it are based on acceptance of the fact that the requirements will evolve during the development effort. This is because software is so pervasive in the enterprise that its impact cannot be fully comprehended early in the project. Instead, its impact becomes more obvious over time and results in new ideas being put forward and accepted. The evolutionary lifecycles require close scrutiny by the project manager because they can and have resulted in runaway development—that is, the system is developed at a rapid pace without observing the usual protocols related to testing, documentation, and correlation of the results with requirements and customer feedback. In this model, the idea is to get something up and running early, let the customer use it with limited functionality, obtain feedback from the customer about its acceptability, build in more functionality based on the feedback and other considerations (such as legal reporting requirements in the banking industry), and continue the process until the system is "complete." This approach raises a serious issue: how do we stop this process? After all, the customer's appetite for features is often insatiable. One response from proponents of this approach is to stop when the scheduled project flow time, money, and/or the development team are exhausted.

- **Amorphous**   Amorphous lifecycles are even less structured than evolutionary approach models are. Of all the lifecycle approaches, amorphous models rely most heavily on the efforts of individual software engineers rather than on a process being carried out by software engineers. Control of this type of lifecycle is limited and difficult, but possible. Because it involves simply letting the development team do their own thing for a period, one approach to maintaining some semblance of control is to give the team fixed due dates for funtionality and let them get there any way they see fit.

In the sections that follow, I present examples of these approaches; often it might be difficult to distinguish one model from another. At the end of this chapter, I summarize each model's characteristics and provide a classification of these software lifecycle models.

The Lifecycle Models

Engineers in the times of the Romans and earlier went through the same general process that today's software engineering managers do—that is, a multistep process in which the project moves from defining what needs to be done to project completion. Although there are significant differences between the kinds of projects software development teams work on and the projects of the Romans, the differences lie mostly in the details and not in the general progression of the development process, from gaining agreement from the client to project completion and handoff for continuing maintenance. The process is shown in a visual style based on IDEF0 in Figure 5-5. A more detailed look at the process is presented in Figure 5-6. Integration Definition Language 0 (IDEF0) diagrams are composed of Activity cells. The graphic convention is that input data enters the Activity cell only from the left, output data leaves from the right side, resources (such as people and equipment) enter from the bottom, and controls (such as flags, approvals, and rules) enter from the top.

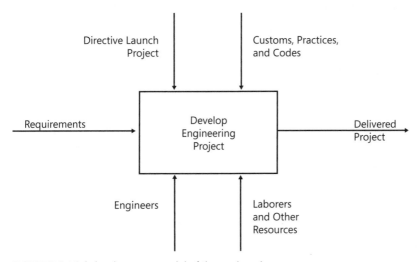

FIGURE 5-5 High-level process model of the engineering process.

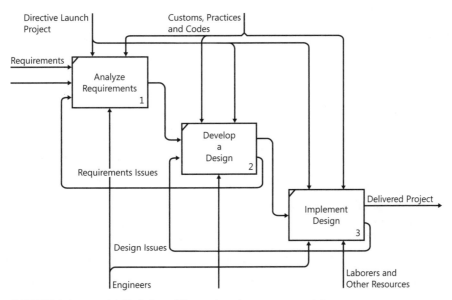

FIGURE 5-6 A more detailed view of the engineering process model.

This is the general form of all of lifecycle models: progression from the *problem* to the *solution* through the use of some scheme based on incremental progression.

Another way to look at the software lifecycle model concept is that the lifecycle is the process that governs the flow of activities, artifacts, and results from start to finish in chronological order. It is used as the basis for the task and subtask lists employed in project management tools (such as Microsoft Office Project).

Although the popularity of a few of the lifecycle models mentioned in this chapter makes them de facto standards in the software industry, a "standard" software development lifecycle currently does not exist.

Waterfall Model

The name of the waterfall lifecycle model comes from its physical appearance, shown in Figure 5-7, and the process by which the results from one phase flow into the next. An alternative name for this model is the "Big Bang" lifecycle because working results first appear near the end of the process, something like how scientists describe the Big Bang theory of how the universe was created. The waterfall model is simple, easy to learn, and easy to use. I and others have used it successfully in its standard and modified forms. The format of this model makes it easy to document, update, and refine using software such as Office Project and other Gantt chart–based project management systems.

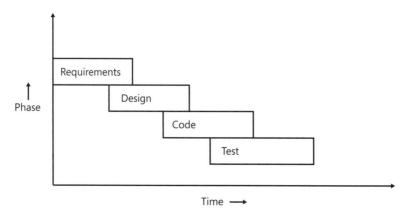

FIGURE 5-7 A representation of the waterfall lifecycle model.

Many people complain about the waterfall lifecycle model. Some experts imply that this lifecycle is not appropriate for software development or is in part responsible for problems in software projects (Boehm, 1988; Davis, 1988). One source of problems in the waterfall approach is that there is little or no functionality that works, and then, at some point well into the project, a system appears. Criticisms of this sort come from software development communities that do not develop the early deliverables called for in the waterfall model (for example, a system design document). The focus of these groups is on producing the executable code while ignoring the long-term value of the other artifacts (such as design documentation) that are a vital part of a sustainable product.

Also, much of the criticism of the waterfall approach comes from those who have managed unsuccessful software projects and who have concluded that the problem was the software lifecycle model used and not the management of the project. These and others propose their own variations. However, variations on the waterfall model still take the project from the stage of not knowing what is going to be built to building it. These variations change some details of how this occurs or innovate by developing the system incrementally using early prototypes and mini-waterfall lifecycles. In the mini-waterfall lifecycle strategy, the complete system is broken down into separate subsystems, each with its own development and build schedule or schedules. In this way, short-term, incremental deliveries reduce the risk and anxiety inherent in a Big Bang development effort.

A more serious criticism of the waterfall model is that it is not a good fit for the iterative manner in which humans solve complex problems. This problem can be solved by frequently updating or iterating the Gantt chart (which looks like the waterfall model) as the project proceeds to reflect both the positive and negative changes that must be made to the project plan.

Slam Dunk Model

The slam dunk lifecycle model predates just about all lifecycle models and is quite simple. The name for this model is derived from the expression in basketball used to describe the act of slamming the ball through the hoop. Customers, managers, and software developers all have a fair idea of what needs to be built. No real process, design, or plan is developed. The approach is trial and error. It does not usually lead to a viable product. Code is generated, debugged, perhaps even demonstrated, and then further enhanced, and so forth. Often, no overall system architecture is developed. In general, this approach has not consistently produced results. It is mentioned here because it is seen by some as viable.

An alternative view of this approach is runaway development. Some years ago, I was involved in a couple of these efforts. Without planning and management controls, the fate of the project was sealed early on. Neither effort resulted in a viable product, but we all learned a lot. One lesson I learned was that slam dunk projects are wasteful and unsuccessful. Although they show a lot of promise early on, no real plan exists to provide the team with a goal and to measure progress toward that goal.

Spiral Model

The spiral lifecycle model was originally developed by Barry Boehm (Boehm, 1988). In part as a result of his employment at the time, this model is oriented toward very large projects. The key to success with this approach is identifying risk early and controlling it throughout the life of the project—a practice engaged in by all successful project managers. Each cycle around the lifecycle spiral represents another phase, as shown in Figure 5-8.

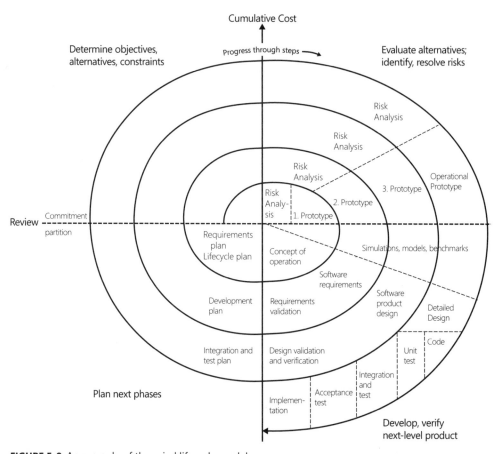

FIGURE 5-8 An example of the spiral lifecycle model.

Cost is represented in the model by the distance from center: the farther from the center the project is, the greater the cost because to get from the center to an outer ring the project must go through several stages over again. A key feature of this approach is the risk gate that is invoked between phases during which risk is assessed, mitigated, or otherwise dealt with, including curtailing or greatly modifying the project. At each stage, cost is incurred, and the costs continue to add up.

The advantage of this approach is that it focuses clearly on the objectives of the effort from several different viewpoints. These same viewpoints are employed in different contexts, and the context changes each time around the spiral. It encourages the reuse of code and exploration of alternatives. Notice that as we proceed from the center of the spiral toward the outer rim, we pass through a series of phases having a common title, *prototype*. This lifecycle engages the concept of prototyping that starts simply with a conceptual view of operation and some risk analysis (that is, "1. Prototype") and ends with an "Operational Prototype" that lies on the outermost rim and, although unnumbered, is actually stage 4 in this cyclic model. Compared with the slam dunk model discussed earlier, the spiral lifecycle model skips the internal cycles during which the team refines their model through design and analysis and jumps right into coding. This is one of the ways that this model is something of a composite of all software lifecycle models.

Let's go through the process to see how it could be used by your team. We start by noting that we will be using several rounds of development, starting with Round 0. Also, assume that the project involves the development of a business process reengineering software system. At Round 0, we might have a set of spiral model–related viewpoints such as those described in Table 5-2.

TABLE 5-2 **Example of Round 0 in the Spiral Model**

Objectives	Develop a business process reengineering (BPR) software product
Constraints	Cost: Come in below cost point of current systems Flow time: Release while market still active Uniqueness: Incorporate unique feature(s)
Alternatives	None considered at this time
Risks	Marketing: Name recognition of new product Market: Limited, with better-known products out Profits: Market might limit volume, cost recovery
Risk resolution	Marketing: License to Big 5 firm, others Market: Research current status Profits: Reduce costs through reuse from other projects
Risk resolution results	Market is limited, but price points are very high Not a clear leader in the marketplace
Plan for next phase	Partner with Big 5 or similar for requirements Comparative analysis with three leading products
Commitment	Funding commitment for next phase in place Tentative interest from two firms

In most instances, the feasibility phase (Round 0) won't be as specific as the contents of Table 5-2 but would look at the possibility of creating the new product, researching which product areas would be appropriate, and so forth. If the prospective product survives the feasibility phase, it proceeds to a requirements definition phase (Round 1) and so on through the spiral. Each round goes through the cyclic pattern established in Figure 5-8.

Notice that at each stage, the objectives to be achieved are stated. It is implicit that not achieving the stated objectives from a previous round can cause the project to be reevaluated or canceled. In this regard, the spiral lifecycle model bears some resemblance to the stage gate approach discussed later in this chapter. The spiral model is purported simply to represent what "really" happens in a software development project. It formalizes and documents the process. However, tracking status and communicating with stakeholders are made very complex in the spiral model, which might be why there are no significant testimonials as to the model's effectiveness.

Evolutionary Model

The idea behind the evolutionary lifecycle model is, just as the name implies, the evolution of the system from an idea to successively refined, feature-enriched, and (presumably) less error laden versions of the system (Cearns, 2002). This model is built upon the concept of "build a little, test a little, repeat," which is illustrated in Figure 5-9. This concept has been refined more recently and published as the Agile programming lifecycle, discussed later in this chapter. The build-test cycle is similar to the way building construction is done: at key points in the construction process, inspections occur (similar to software testing) to ensure that the work done to that point is of sufficient quality to warrant proceeding to the next phase of construction.

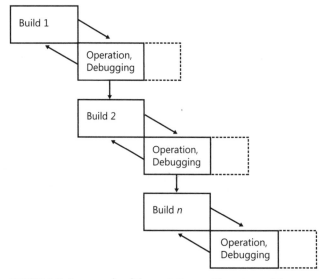

FIGURE 5-9 An example of the evolutionary lifecycle model.

My experience with this approach is on a project for which we combined the evolutionary model with the waterfall lifecycle model. The software development team for the project was very inexperienced. We addressed the architectural issue and through the successive refinement technique were able to overcome the inexperience of the team members. With some discipline, teams can use this approach quite effectively when the team needs to work together to build confidence in themselves and in the team as a whole. This can be an expensive proposition because changes late in the lifecycle become inordinately more expensive. For the project I worked on, we reduced this risk by creating an overall system architecture at the start, stubbing everything in, and replacing the stubs in conjunction with an implementation plan that strategically employed parallelism.

Not surprisingly, some proponents of this concept consider it the best way to develop software. Those who oppose it point out that it deemphasizes the importance of establishing the overall architecture for the system from the start, which subsequently results in a considerable amount of rework late in the lifecycle. Also, the benefits of stabilizing the system and releasing changes in batches (Brooks, 1975) could be lost if the cycle time between one set of changes and the next is too short.

Stage Gate Model

Figure 5-10 depicts the stage gate model. It looks like projects using this model might be doomed to failure because of the sequential nature of the stages depicted here; complaints from several authors about this model concern the sequential lifecycle processes. However, a lot of work is done in parallel to foreshorten development time and ensure timely completion. Also, what happens in each stage is prescribed by the process descriptions adopted by the development team. For example, pair programming, walkthroughs, and continuous testing could all be used as well as other methods and techniques.

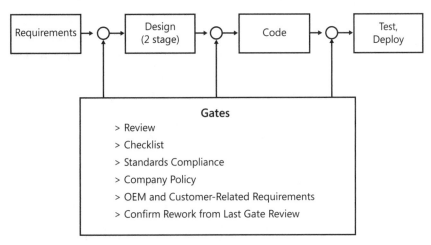

FIGURE 5-10 Phases and gates in the stage gate lifecycle.

The stage gate lifecycle model comes in various flavors, some of which have been trade-marked under the title "Stage Gate." This model has its origins in the manufacturing sector. The idea is relatively simple: Parts and subassemblies are staged. When all of the required parts, subassemblies, inspector signoffs, and any required tests have been completed, they pass through a virtual gate and are assembled into the next largest subsystem or perhaps the final system. In the software arena, this approach addresses the following requirements:

- Reduce risk to the project resulting from out-of-control development

- Improve the quality of deliverables

- Ensure that the processes put in place are followed

- Reduce the flow time through the development process

- Focus on all aspects of the software being produced

- Have a clearly stated set of goals and specific tasks that are achievable in the short term

At first glance, this approach might seem rather Draconian, and it is. But think back for a moment. How many times has the daily or weekly build been brought down by the fact that someone turned in code that should have been unit tested and regression tested prior to acceptance, but the author was in too much of a hurry or forgot or thought that the change was insignificant enough not to make any difference? This lifecycle model enforces the organization's policies, prevents problems, and reduces rework and errors.

The idea of the gate might be a new concept to some managers. Gates are positioned at critical points in the lifecycle. They have a vital role in that before a project can proceed to the next stage, a review committee examines artifacts (such as presentations, documents, test cases) appropriate to that stage and evaluates them against standards established for that project and for the company overall. The committee makes one of four decisions:

- **Go**   Everything is in order, and the project can proceed to the next stage.

- **Cancel**   The project is in serious enough trouble that it should be disbanded here and now. Yes, some projects would have been better off if they had been canceled!

- **Hold**   At this point it would be best to suspend the project for the time being (for example, the market for the product is deteriorating, the customer is considering canceling, and so on).

- **Recycle**   Direct the project to correct/enhance the current results and try for approval again.

Draconian or not, this approach works. A number of dot com companies might never have buried so much money in a weak idea if an approach similar to this had been used when they began operations.

My experience with the stage gate lifecycle involved the development of a portion of an operating system. The difficulties we were having gaining stability in previous efforts could be traced back directly to some programmers not following the configuration management and other content control practices adopted in our firm—people were turning in code that had not been walked through with their peers, that was untested, and so forth. Although instituting this lifecycle approach as an experiment caused a lot of complaining from the members of our team, it resulted in the fastest-to-market, lowest bug count we had experienced. This occurred even though this was a new product.

We did have certain advantages that newly formed firms might not: We knew exactly what needed to be done to prevent the occurrence of a long list of issues that had plagued us in the past. The whole process was set up to address those issues. Unfortunately, after such an initial success, an executive abandoned the practice because he felt it caused too many complaints from developers, which inhibited their creativity. Later in this book, I demonstrate that even though team members might complain about being required to do something as part of a company practice, they are much more productive in such a structured environment than in a laissez-faire one.

The challenge for software project managers using this approach is to "stay the course" and not to succumb to complaints from the development team regarding having to move through such strict processes. This aspect of the stage gate method is the source of most complaints about it from managers and developers alike.

Rapid Prototyping Model

The rapid prototyping approach uses the prototype as a means of developing a specification. For those not familiar with the term *prototype*, it means a mockup or stand-in. Prototypes have been used for many years in industries where the final product is too expensive to build and abandon in favor of a more robust or feature-laden version. In software, prototypes often take the form of a series of user actions and corresponding screens enabling the user to evaluate the process of navigating through the interface to achieve some objective. These screens have only the functionality behind them needed to support the navigational activity.

The assumption here is that improving communication with the client through the client's ability to actually see and use the system as envisioned by the developers will ensure that what is delivered is what the client really wants. The danger here has been that prototypes have often become production systems. Clients see the prototype, it has a fair number of important features that work, and the client's reaction is often to believe that the system is complete and only needs some minor cleanup. This approach requires a mature, disciplined development team to prevent runaway coding and to ensure that the client is educated enough to realize that what they are viewing is only a prototype and not a viable commercial product.

Often, once the specification portion is finished, it is difficult to get the development team to quit coding and get back to the problem of designing the solution. This approach treats robustness characteristics such as availability, safety, and security as afterthoughts in the rush to produce a working artifact. An additional problem is the fact that often it is not the customer or the developers who want to accept the prototype as a deliverable but the marketing people—they see something that can be sold and start selling it prematurely.

Agile Programming Model

The Agile programming approach is actually a compendium of best practices gleaned from other lifecycle methods and programming practices that have been successful plus some added nuances. It employs continual interaction with the client by including a client representative on the development team. Although this might sound like a new practice, it was employed on more than one project more than 30 years ago.

Figure 5-11 depicts the Agile lifecycle model (IBM Rational Group, 2003). Many of the ideas this lifecycle model promotes work well on their own. In Figure 5-12, the vertical bars represent 2-week intervals; longer intervals can be used, but it is not recommended. This is the "nominal" time delta. Analogous to a miniature lifecycle, within each of these 2-week periods, a certain volume of work is completed, and working code results. This volume of work is referred to as a set of *story points*. A use case or Stimulus-Response scenario (SRS) technique is used to collect *stories*. The ratio is one use case or SRS per story. Each story is written on an index card or some other recording mechanism that is easily accessible to the entire project group. Each story is assigned an index score (story point) relative to its degree of difficulty. An optional guide is to have story points for a single story range from 1 to 10, but the upper level can be adjusted as more experience is gained using the technique.

Analysis										
Design										
Implementation										
Time Period	1	2	3	4	5	6	..	..	..	N

FIGURE 5-11 A generic view of the Agile lifecycle model.

In Agile programming, software engineers work in pairs. Pairs work at the same development workstation and share a keyboard. A pair is usually composed of a more senior, experienced developer and a less experienced one. Some people argue this lowers the productivity of the senior person. Although this might be true, over the course of a reasonably long project (such as 6 months) productivity for the group as a whole actually increases.

One concern expressed about this almost continual change approach is stability. Each batch of nuances or changes occurs on a short-term cycle, resulting in a lack of maturity in the resulting system. Even though there is continual testing, there is also continual change, which goes against recommendations by Brooks (Brooks, 1975) and others regarding how to ensure that projects are successful. Their recommendation is that changes should occur in a burst, and then no changes should occur while testing takes place (a stable period), followed by another controlled burst of changes, and so forth. In Agile development, this stability issue is addressed by requiring daily builds that run, continual testing, and the application of coding standards that evolve over time. Also, the earlier admonitions regarding changes were based on a Big Bang style of development. That is, work went on for months with no running code, and then, at some point, a build happened.

> **Note** I devote the most text space to the Agile approach because it incorporates so many techniques from other models as well as techniques considered good management and programming practice. In fact, nearly everything about Agile programming has been around for some time. What is unique is the combination of practices and techniques it pulls together into a coherent constellation of policies and procedures.

The development team estimates how many stories it can achieve during the first 2-week period. They do this by simply selecting, in conjunction with the customer, several of the stories and adding up their story points. For example, they might select 50 points' worth of stories for the first 2-week period. A schedule is estimated by taking the total number of points contained in the total set of SRS or use cases and dividing by the number of story points the team believes they will average per 2-week period. For example,

Total Number of Story Points for Project = 2,000

Estimated Average Number of Points/period = 50

Estimated Project Duration (2,000 / 50) = 40 periods

At the end of the first period, the team counts up how many points they actually completed, and they adjust the schedule estimate accordingly, up or down. This early result is used as an assumed work rate. This process is repeated at the end of each subsequent period, and the average number of story points (estimated) per remaining period is recomputed based on the preceding weeks.

If the schedule starts to slide, the customer has the choice of living with the slide, hoping things will get better later, or deferring some features to a later release to maintain the original schedule. Usually, the customer selects lower-priority features or stories and defers them to the next release. Enough of these are selected so that the original date or an acceptable date for first release is achieved. This encourages, even requires, that the customer make some difficult decisions regarding what must absolutely be included in the system and what is optional.

What is really powerful about this technique is that it employs something similar to an engineering principle called *design to cost*. That is, given that we have only this much time and money, this is what we can deliver. Moreover, the customer is in control of which features the system will contain and can determine priorities based on business objectives, the marketplace, and their corporate strategy. This control on the part of the customer is extremely important in gaining acceptance of the results, no matter what they are. A sample of this recalibrating scheme is presented in Figure 5-12.

Analysis										
Design										
Implementation										
Time Period	1	2	3	4	5	6	..	..	..	N
Number of Stories Done	50	40	40	60	70	45	65	50		
Average Number Done Per Period	50	45	43	48	52	51	54			
Number of Stories Remaining										
End Date in Periods										

FIGURE 5-12 Example of an Agile schedule chart.

Another concept employed by the Agile approach is that testing occurs continuously. This is possible because, right from the end of the first period, there is a running system. Granted, it will not have much functionality at first, but over time it will. The customer can use it and give feedback to the development team. All of this takes place very early in the project.

Agile programming employs three bases: customer business practices, developer practices, and quality assurance practices. The degree to which each set of practices affects a project is dependent on the quality assurance practices and their effect on the resulting system. Terms used to describe the practices in each category are presented in Table 5-3 through Table 5-5, by category.

TABLE 5-3 Characteristics of Agile Development

Source	Description
Whole team	Developers, stakeholders, business analysts, quality assurance people all working together as a team.
Planning game	Involves the use of cards or other schemes to identify each feature/requirement that is part of the project; one feature or requirement per card.
Small releases	Releases occur (typically) on a 2-week cycle. Supported features at each of these internal release points are available for the customer to experience and critique.
Customer tests	Tests are developed by the quality assurance group, one per card. Tests are automated as much as possible except for user interface–related testing, which occurs throughout the project with the biweekly releases.

TABLE 5-4 Developer Practices Used in Agile Development

Term/Attribute	Description
Coding standard(s)	Developed (minimally) at the outset. Evolve over time with participation of entire team.
Sustainable pace	Goal is to develop in small increments, avoiding the death march phenomenon.
Metaphor	The basic concept.
Continuous integration	One of the main tenets of this approach—a working system is built daily.
Collective ownership	All stakeholders are responsible, avoiding scapegoats.

TABLE 5-5 Quality-Related Practices Used in Agile Development

Term/Attribute	Description
Test-driven development	Testing is continuous.
Refactoring	Continual revision of structure, refinement of code, improved quality.
Simple design	Applies the Keep It Simple, Stupid (KISS) principle.
Pair programming	People work in pairs, often one more senior than the other, using one development computer and one keyboard. The advantage is the increase in skill and knowledge of the junior or less-skilled person. The senior person circulates among pairs, expanding the impact of this knowledge sharing.

The Agile approach has a considerable amount of merit, a growing number of devotees, and some positive reports regarding its effectiveness in small to medium-size projects. This model gathers early and frequent feedback, thus aligning the approach with iterative human problem solving. However, there are some cautionary notes to acknowledge. One is that this approach, perhaps more than any other that is popular today, could result in runaway programming. This can be overcome only if the project has a cadre of disciplined senior software engineers and a mature software project manager. If it is a small project, perhaps only one or two senior people are required, but someone has to ensure that the project maintains the discipline and practices inherent in this method.

There is a tendency in the software industry to be successful on one project using certain methods and techniques and to infer from that single data point that the next and subsequent projects could all be successful using the same methods, techniques, tools, and people. In fact, nothing could be further from the truth. In the Agile method, more than the others, the pair programming technique practically guarantees that the people who finish the current effort will have more skill and knowledge than when they started it. This can result in some disintegration of the teams as people grow into leadership roles. This is a natural consequence of project experience. But this possible negative aspect is neutralized by the application of the pairing process and other processes in the next project.

Synchronization and Stabilization Model

The synchronization and stabilization approach is employed at Microsoft and, perhaps, other firms. It is similar to the incremental approach. Starting with requirements, the team generates a specification, sets priorities, and divides the effort into four major builds. These major builds are called Release Candidate (RC) 1 through RC 3 and Release to Manufacturing (RTM). RC 1 is the first major build and represents the point in the development cycle, with the widest range of possible changes in code and content, as shown in Figure 5-13.

As time passes and subsequent RCs are established as baselines, the threshold for approving changes to the code rises, the number of newly introduced features decreases, and bug content drops significantly. The most serious and even minor bugs are absent by the time RC3 is established. Note that in the time frame between releases, Agile or any other development lifecycle model can be used. The key here is achieving the goal of stability and maturity in the released product.

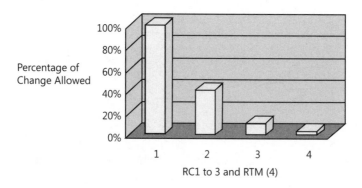

FIGURE 5-13 Change over time in the synchronization and stabilization model.

Comparison of Lifecycle Model Features

Table 5-6 depicts the various features of the lifecycle models to help you compare and select a model to use on future projects. In selecting a lifecycle approach or when creating your own, you will need to do the following:

- Characterize your project, and see how well it matches one or more of the lifecycles discussed.

- For the lifecycle models that are most appropriate, focus on the shortcomings of the lifecycle and determine whether those are serious enough to rule out use of that model.

- As much as possible (it is not possible to get everyone to agree in all cases), gain the concurrence of your development team on which model to use.

- Get commitment from the leadership team—if problems occur, the surest way for the project to fail is to have the leadership of the company panic and abandon the process.

- Gain concurrence or at least tacit approval from your stakeholders.

- Identify what, if anything, must be altered in the best candidate lifecycle for it to work on your new project.

- Be innovative.

- Be flexible during the project and ready to alter the lifecycle depending on the circumstances.

- Take into account the level of experience and maturity of your software development team.

TABLE 5-6 Comparison of Common Lifecycle Models

Lifecycle Model	Pros	Cons	Most Applicable To
Waterfall	Controllable results; consistent with engineering practice	Forestalls delivering results until late in the development cycle	All project sizes
Slam dunk	Gets something going right away	Not truly a lifecycle; results generally unsatisfactory	Not recommended
Spiral	Reflects reality of software development in the large; reports of use quite positive	Complex and intricate; requires extensive management infrastructure	Major multimillion-dollar efforts; ill suited to small efforts
Evolutionary	Begin controlled, working software early on; longer testing period than otherwise possible	Nothing stable for long; high change level without much maturity occurring in software	Small to medium projects

Lifecycle Model	Pros	Cons	Most Applicable To
Stage gate	Practically guarantees adherence to some discipline	Requires an infrastructure, maturity, and process some firms might not have	Medium to large
Rapid prototyping	Get something going early on; lots of review time	Often results in runaway coding	Small to large
Agile-programming	Puts discipline into the prototyping approach	Requires a mature, disciplined team; strict adherence to process	Small to medium
Synchronization and stabilization	Controls changes; long testing cycle to improve quality	Based on premise that quality can be tested into a system	Small to very large

Selecting a Software Development Lifecycle

Deciding which of the various lifecycle models is best for your project can seem like a daunting task, but it needn't be. First, my experience and that of many of my colleagues indicates that as long as you have taken care to select a lifecycle model that you and your team believe to be appropriate to your project, your team can be successful with it—provided you are willing to be flexible in its use, adapt it to your team's needs in a disciplined manner, and monitor its effectiveness throughout the project.

Let's look at a couple of examples. A while back, I was engaged as a project manager and consultant on a software project whose goal was to replace the software and hardware being used to test real-time embedded systems using simulation. The requirements were well known and documented. However, the software was about two decades old and was totally undocumented except for some of the errors that had been discovered and corrected. Without considering which lifecycle to adopt, I began the process of project planning by noting that we were (essentially) starting at the design stage. I proceeded to work with the on-site development team to estimate how much work needed to be done to replace each routine in the system, categorizing these tasks from complex to simple. Using the staffing levels that had been allocated, the number of contractors that could be used, and the rough order in which things could be done, I arrived at the total flow time for the replacement software to be designed, implemented, tested/validated, and put into place. Did I mention that the effort had a hard-and-fast fixed completion date? The flow time estimate came out well beyond the project end date. Given the nature of the system (defense), reducing functionality was not an option, budgets were not going to give, and the situation seemed intractable. Fortunately, I observed that the testing phase could be run in parallel with the design phase because the test data was well known. All that was needed was an overall test plan that could be coordinated with the implementation plan. What resulted was the necessary foreshortening of the overall project length, a process in which various levels of tests were available as soon as each routine was implemented and what amounted to a seriously modified form of a waterfall lifecycle.

Another instance in which the lifecycle evolved during the process was for another project with a hard-and-fast delivery date and budget. In this case, the requirements were very high level and needed embellishment and detailing. The schedule looked impossible until I observed that the company with which I had contracted owned the intellectual property rights on a considerable amount of the software that needed to be reworked. The term *commercial off-the-shelf software (COTS)* had not yet been invented, but we used the concept just the same. In this case, we focused on detailing the requirements phase, had a very short—almost nonexistent—design phase, and then went right to linking up the pieces with a minimum amount of bridging software to be implemented. In this and the previous project, the keys to success included the following:

- Letting the project's character dictate just what kind of a project plan was used
- Not panicking into a slam dunk mode, but taking the time to analyze what needed to be done
- Getting concurrence from the rest of the development team
- Monitoring how well we were executing the plan
- Being flexible enough to replan almost continuously to accommodate unforeseen circumstances

The message here is that success in managing projects results from many factors. The lifecycle is only one of them, but a necessary one. If you have had success with one lifecycle more than with another, before adopting it on your next project, ask yourself whether those previous experiences with this lifecycle were similar enough to the new project to make this choice a good one. If you are new to software project management and have not had the experience of employing one lifecycle model or another, try going with what you understand and what you and your team feel comfortable with, bearing in mind some that alterations might be necessary.

It is tempting to think that because any chosen lifecycle will have to be altered anyway, it is a waste of time to adopt such a model in the first place. The problem with such a position is that both the customer and the development team need to know what lies ahead, commit to achieving the milestones laid out before them, and apply a sanity check to what is being proposed. Without a lifecycle plan, you are asking for a greater leap of faith than either of these groups can tolerate.

Summary

A key point about software development lifecycles is that each one, as published, represents an idealization. As a result, it is highly unlikely that any of them can be used on a real project exactly as published. As you have seen, there is no single lifecycle model that is the best or that works for every project. What we have in these and countless other lifecycle models is a spectrum of approaches from which to choose, knowing that any lifecycle model we pick should be altered to suit the needs of a given project.

In my 40 years of experience in this field, I have seen successful projects that used the "wrong" lifecycle model, and failed projects that seemed to do everything "right." What distinguished them was the flexibility of project managers to sense when things were going well and when they were not. This sensing was achieved through the use of metrics—not simple ones such as lines of code produced, but more in-depth ones such as number of errors detected as a function of time and the number of builds its takes to do an upgrade of functionality, for example. These measures together with close contact with the development team can give a project manager who is paying attention a sense of how things are really going. It should be noted that the lowest bandwidth of communication is e-mail, while the highest is in-person, face-to-face contact.

After establishing some metrics and communications comes the challenge of being willing to try various lifecycle schemes to improve matters. The most successful project managers are those who are not bound by one approach or another but who innovate with a likely model or who modify or even abandon a model if it is not working. Especially challenging to most software project managers is the acceptance of approaches they themselves had not thought of. Face it, when your team members propose a practice they believe will make things go more smoothly, they have a vested interest in seeing to it that it works. After all, they are closest to the problems and might be best suited to resolve or prevent problems going forward.

So the question of which lifecycle model to use is somewhat of a minor one when compared with the importance of adaptability to a challenging and changing technical and business environment while maintaining discipline and a commitment to quality during the execution of the project. Meeting that challenge often spells the difference between project success and failure.

References

(Brooks, 1987)   Brooks, F. P., Jr. "No Silver Bullet—Essence and Accident in Software Engineering," *Computer* **20**(4), pp. 10-19, April 1987.

(Deutsch and Willis, 1998)   Deutsch, M., and R. Willis. *Software Quality Engineering: A Total Technical and Management Approach.* Englewood Cliffs, NJ: Prentice Hall, 1998.

(Boehm, 1988)   Boehm, B. "A Spiral Model of Software Development," *IEEE Computer*, p. 61, May 1988.

(Davis, 1988)   Davis, A. M., et al. "A Strategy for Comparing Alternative Software Development Lifecycle Models." *IEEE Transactions on Software Engineering*, October 1988.

(Cearns, 2002)   Cearns, A. "Design of an Autonomous Anti-DDOS Network (A2D2)." Master's thesis, University of Colorado at Colorado Springs, Colorado, pp. 105-111, 2002.

(Brooks, 1975)   Brooks, F. P., Jr. *The Mythical Man-Month*. New York: Addison-Wesley, 1975.

(IBM Rational Group, 2003)   IBM Rational Group. "Agility and RUP—How They Apply to Your Project." Professional Development Seminar, Seattle, Washington, May 2003.

Chapter 6
Modeling the Target System

If you can't describe what you are doing as a process, you don't know what you are doing.

—W. Edwards Deming

One way to envision software development is as a process or system that consists of the creation, analysis, and use of a series of models that can overlap in time. In Chapter 5, "Selecting a Software Development Lifecycle Model: Management Implications," we examined several methods for organizing a project, referred to as *lifecycles*. Those were methods for modeling our project. They provided a framework within which to plan, schedule, and control our project. But that framework alone is not sufficient to actually create a software system. It is simply a set of rules, goals, constraints, and completion dates. A second type of model is needed—one within which we can lay out the overall architecture, relationships, and operation of the target system. This is known as a *system model*. Although there are similarities between the concepts of a system model and a lifecycle model, the two are fundamentally different. One difference is that the lifecycle model describes how the team is going to build the deliverable system. The system model, on the other hand, describes what the team is going to build. It enables us to depict the activities being managed within the lifecycle whose execution will lead to the creation of a new system that we will refer to as the *target system*. Some activities in the development lifecycle occur sequentially, while others occur in parallel. As we proceed through the lifecycle, these models of the system build upon one another. Each subsequent model is based on results from one or more previous models and often some new information as well. For example, what was learned during requirements definition is employed in design, the results of the design phase are employed in coding, and so on. In addition, many of these models are composed of multiple viewpoints, each having its own distinct advantages and shortcomings. This "evolving models" scheme even describes some of the more recent programming methods (for example, Agile programming).

In this chapter, I present several different methods and techniques for modeling software systems. Each method emphasizes what its author or authors saw as important and ignores what wasn't considered important. Many of these models tend to complement one another in that they provide information that might not be addressed in another modeling technique. Contrary to the advertisements from various vendors in our industry, no single approach or methodology is necessary and sufficient for doing the whole job. Instead, we find that combinations of compatible methods work and that the mix of methods from one project to the next might change, even though the projects might appear to be quite similar. In general, each of these system-modeling methods can be used in conjunction with any lifecycle model, and each is complementary or at least compatible with the other system-modeling methods presented here.

Why Model Software Systems?

Over the last couple of millennia, engineers have found that it is eminently less expensive to build models of systems, analyze the models, and find the problems the theorized system will have than to make such discoveries after the system has been built. Since we can't see software and most of us have not been trained as engineers, there is a tendency to skip analysis and design and simply build and test. This has resulted in costly overruns. With that in mind, various researchers analyzed data in the software field in an attempt to model and quantify the cost of letting an error get through to the final product. This data was correlated to the phase in the lifecycle where the error was detected and corrected. While the numbers vary from author to author, the trend is clear, as shown in Table 6-1 (extrapolated from McConnell, 1996): errors that are discovered later cost more to correct.

TABLE 6-1 **Relative Cost to Repair a Software Defect by Phase**

Lifecycle Phase	Minimum Relative Cost to Correct Defect	"Typical" Relative Cost to Correct Defect	Maximum Relative Cost to Correct Defect
Requirements definition and design	1	1	1
Code and test	5	10	20
Installation and use in field	25	100	Variable—extremely costly if loss of life occurs

This data should prove sufficient justification for doing a better job in the requirements definition and design phases. But often the pressure is on from the most senior management to get into coding as early as possible. Does the following sound familiar to you?

- **Month 1**   A project schedule is set forth based mostly on marketing and corporate issues, with some input from the development team. The development team indicates that this is an 18-month project, but management insists that it be done in 12 months. Requirements are agreed upon, but with some items in need of clarification. Rather than losing flow time clarifying them, the decision is made by management to move forward on the project and resolve these "fuzzy" issues.

- **Month 2+**   A design of sorts (high level, not verifiably linked to the requirements) is created. Management expresses concern that no code has been generated although the project is almost 3 months along. Also, some of the requirements need to be changed.

- **Months 3 through 6**   A lot of code has been generated. Several important functions are working, and a user interface has been developed. In order to save money and flow time, the decision was made early on to employ as much functionality from purchased development libraries as possible. That way, the project reduces the amount of new code to be developed. This should reduce the number of errors encountered during the testing phase. Management is still concerned but quite gratified that 80 to 90 percent of needed functionality is up and running. They are now preparing to announce that the system will be released ahead of schedule.

- **Months 7 and 8**   A number of interface problems among various modules have surfaced. Also, some performance issues (for example, response time and execution time) and computer resource issues (for example, memory and disk storage space) have developed. These have been traced to the extensive use of off-the-shelf code libraries and prepackaged software. It has been concluded that major portions of the system will have to be rewritten from scratch to reduce the response time problems and make better use of computing resources. It is now estimated that 4 to 6 months will be required to replace the problem code. Management presses the schedule issue and proposes that to maintain schedule, some functionality be cut. Some of the developers who authored the functions being cut leave the project or the company.

- **Months 8 through 10**   Testing is revealing some unstable behaviors in the newly developed system, ranging from the "blue screen of death" phenomenon to system lockups. Many of the most serious crashes are difficult to reproduce and occur only randomly. Often, when these crashes occur, they take out the debugger, making the developer's job of correcting the problem extremely difficult and time consuming.

- **Months 10 though 12**   The development team announces at least another 4 months will be needed to complete the effort, especially tracking down and correcting the anomalous system crashes and some additional reworks of purchased software. Management further reduces functionality in order to maintain schedule and demands that the project be done at the end of the 12-month schedule, as originally planned. They emphasize that the company's future might be riding on getting this product out as soon as possible.

- **Months 12 to 13**   The system is released. A "red team" has been formed to develop a service pack to correct known errors as quickly as possible. User reports and reviews are not favorable. The company engages an expensive public relations firm to launch a campaign to save the product by reducing negative press reports.

- **Months 14 to 17**   The developers clear up system crashes, add back previously canceled functionality, and correct the most-serious errors reported by initial users. The competition releases a stable product with more functionality 4 months earlier, capturing an estimated 65 percent of market share.

- **Months 17 and 18**   Management does a "postpartum" review of the project. It concludes that delays in getting the product out were most likely due to starting coding too late in the project.

Now let's compare the preceding scenario with the development of the Columbia Tower Building (since renamed the Bank of America Building) in Seattle. At the time it was built in the 1980s, it was the tallest building on the West Coast of the United States and the tallest west of the Mississippi River. It took seven years to build. Nothing quite like it had ever been built, and there were concerns regarding aerodynamics, earthquake resistance, and other issues. The first five years of the seven-year development time were spent planning, designing, and refining the design and ensuring that the building requirements and economic viability were met, that fire and safety codes were met, and that the logistics of acquiring, shipping, storing, and installing all the various pieces that make up such a building during construction were addressed. Really only the last two of the seven years were spent actually constructing the building.

Another example in the software arena of a much smaller project for which I was responsible was done as an SBIR Phase II effort. SBIR stands for the Small Business Innovative Research program, which is sponsored by the U.S. Government. Phase I involves receiving a small grant to develop a concept. If it appears that the concept is a viable one with respect to developing it into a commercial product, Phase II funding is awarded. We conducted that project "strictly by the book"—that is, the project plan called for a total development time of 18 months, with 12 months devoted to requirements definition and analysis, preliminary design, and last, detailed design. By the time month 13 came around, we had a highly refined system architecture, the system was completely pseudocoded, a user interface had been defined and refined via user feedback via screen mockups, a user's manual had been created, and all test cases were defined. This included the creation of test processes, datasets, and related materials. Coding involved adopting the pseudocode as the comments for the executable source code and inserting lines of source code between comments. Thus, we avoided the prospect of having to cajole the developers into commenting their code. The comments not only already existed, but like everything else at month 13, they also had been walked through and reviewed by the development team and the client more than once. Since the test cases were based on the pseudocode and requirements, the code was tested to see whether it did what it was *intended* to do. Test cases based on actual code tend to test code just to see what it does. Hopefully, this not-so-subtle difference is obvious.

The result was completion of the effort six weeks early. Since the project was a fixed-price effort and I had managed our costs well, we did not lose money on it. No errors were reported by the client in the six-month warranty period. The product was later repackaged and licensed to the largest Big 5–type firm in Canada and marketed worldwide. That project and others like it that I have managed or consulted on have convinced me of the importance of establishing a viable architecture early in the lifecycle, implementing it, and delaying most of the coding until the last third of the estimated schedule. It has also convinced me that schedules must be agreed to by the developers, establishing in them a vested interest in ensuring that the schedule is made. This is even true when fixed dates are imposed if and only if the developers can remake the product into something they think they can actually build in the time allocated.

What has always interested me is scenarios like this: A manager is told in a 10 AM meeting by a contractor that the new parking area will take three months to build and accepts the contractor's estimate. Then, at the 11 AM meeting, the software people tell her that the latest set of new features will take three months to incorporate and perform regression tests on, and she balks at this prospect. The problem, of course, is that the project manager can understand the first meeting because foundations and footings take time to cure, framing and other work take time, and inspections must be done by the local authorities. But it is not only the physical issues that make the three months of flow time seem reasonable. Acceptance of that estimate is aided by the fact that the contractor has a detailed plan of what has to be done, how long it will take, when it will be done, and who will do it. But one cannot see software, so one's physical experience does not come into play. This is further aggravated by the practice of many software people of not creating a detailed plan similar to what the contractor had—that is, a Work Breakdown Structure (WBS) showing estimates, resource allocation, flow times, and the overall process. This raises anxiety levels, because the software people seem to be making up the plan as they go along (and many of them do). The anxiety is often most present in the project manager. This gives rise to the mistaken belief that through threats and cajoling, the manager can somehow dictate that a system be built using whatever flow time he or she desires and get tacit agreement from the development team. The mistake here lies in the view of the development team that the schedule is not theirs. They did not have enough information with which to make an estimate, were not asked for concurrence on the estimate that was made, and want nothing to do with the whole process. All of this confirms their suspicion that management is incompetent. In this scenario, the schedule belongs to management. Since the development team did not agree to the schedule in the first place, they have no vested interest in seeing that the schedule is met.

The common wisdom among most managers is that to get done reasonably close to the schedule, we better start coding as early as possible. This philosophy perpetuates itself. That is, by following it, we practically guarantee that there will be cost and schedule overruns, and those are often seen as being caused by not coding right from the start. Looking at the numbers another way, we can see that premature coding is costly. We occasionally read about people dying due to a programming error. When that happens, the courts have held that unless the company that produced the software had done everything that the profession held to be appropriate for high reliability and safe software, they are liable for the full amount of the jury award. On the other hand, if you follow recommended industry practices but still have loss of life resulting from your software, the amount of any jury award will likely be greatly reduced. To summarize, following a defined and accepted process is both an act of faith and, in some cases, a matter of corporate financial survival.

Requirements Modeling Methods

The statement of requirements represents a contract between the provider of the software and the entity paying for its development. Often, these requirements are expressed in a legalistic style with terms using constructs like this: "The system shall accommodate up to 10 users subject to the response time maximums specified in Paragraph III-A-1.4.1." Can you imagine having the requirements for the home you're building stated in a similar way? Consider this example: "Eight-room, single-story building with attached garage. Rooms consist of one master bedroom, two smaller bedrooms, one master bathroom, one standard bathroom, a living room, a family room, and a dining room." Would you sign up to purchase a home with only this type of information available? Probably not. In the physical world, we want to see blueprints, examples of what we are buying, mockups, quality specifications, and other descriptive tools that will help us to better appreciate exactly what we will be getting. The virtual world of software is altogether another matter.

Using Dataflow Diagrams

DeMarco introduced the concept of using *dataflow diagrams* (DFDs) as a statement of requirements (DeMarco, 1987). This has the added benefit that DFDs are relatively easy to translate into some form of design. This satisfied the needs of the software arena in a simpler form than its predecessor, the SADT/IDEF0 diagrams developed by Ross (Ross and Brackett, 1976). The idea in both instances is to graphically state requirements. This approach provides us with a means of engaging the client and the software team to the extent that both can critique and "debug" the graphic showing the existing system (if there was one) and the graphic showing the "to be," or future, system. This communication of needs by the customer and of concerns and questions by the development team greatly reduces the chance that we will "miss the mark" in the delivered system.

An example of a DFD is shown in Figure 6-1.

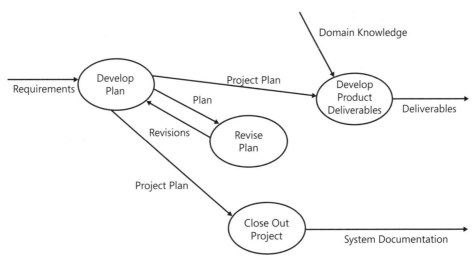

FIGURE 6-1 An example of a DFD.

A DFD is composed of the following elements:

- **Process elements**   These represent transformations of information. Process elements are represented as labeled circles. The label text consists of an action verb and object noun combination (for example, *Revise Plan*).

- **Dataflow elements**   These document the flow of information. Dataflow elements are represented by directed, labeled arrows. The labels consist of descriptive nouns (for example, *Project Plan*).

- **Datastore elements**   These represent repositories of information. They are represented as labeled pairs of parallel lines (not shown in Figure 6-1). The label text describes what is stored (for example, *Current Users*).

- **Source elements and sink elements**   These document where information begins and where it ends or goes from the viewpoint of the system. They are represented by labeled rectangles. Label text takes a form similar to that for datastores. (For example, *Deliverables* effectively exits Figure 6-1 as a sink.)

- **Data dictionary elements**   These are used to define terms and to document (via pseudocode) how each process transforms incoming data into output. Data dictionary elements are not explicitly cited in the DFD but are used to define the content and meaning of the terms the DFD is comprised of.

I usually create hierarchical or multilevel DFDs using the following process: Starting with a single process, the DFD is decomposed, or broken into its constituent parts, comprising a lower level in the hierarchy but with a higher level of detail. In other words, the upper portions of the DFD hierarchy contain less detail than the lower ones. For example, at the highest level in the hierarchy, we might have the term *Automobile*, and at the next level down in the hierarchy, we might have terms like *Propulsion System, Transmission, Drive Train, Chassis, Body,* and so forth. Some of the lower-level processes might still be complex enough to break down further at the next-lower level of decomposition. *Balancing* (that is, ensuring that data represented at a higher level is accurately represented at lower levels, with no data suddenly appearing or disappearing through the decomposition process) is achieved through the data dictionary. In other words, at the higher levels in the DFD structure, we might have a dataflow with a label like *Customer Record* but not find that label used at the next level of decomposition. At that next level of decomposition, we might find dataflows with labels like *Customer ID, Customer Address,* and so forth. The data dictionary would tell us that *Customer ID, Customer Address,* and other elements make up a *Customer Record,* so no data items have been lost or surreptitiously created between one level of decomposition and the next.

Using IDEF0 to State Requirements

The diagram shown in Figure 6-2 is an example of the IDEF0 notation. It represents the same system as the DFD shown earlier in Figure 6-1, but certain items provided in Figure 6-2 were left out of Figure 6-1 because the DFD does not address them (for example, resources in the form of software engineers). The completeness and discipline of IDEF0—its focus on important details, such as the *mechanism* (who or what will accomplish the transformation) and the *controls* (rules or guidelines the system must comply with)—have made it popular with many software engineering managers.

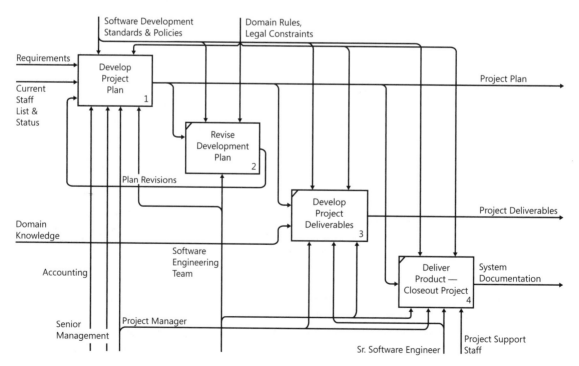

FIGURE 6-2 An IDEF0 diagram that is equivalent to Figure 6-1.

IDEF0 diagrams consist of *activity cells*, as shown in Figure 6-3. An activity cell processes information, performs some form of transaction, or otherwise performs a useful activity. To do this, it requires input, produces output, utilizes resources, and performs its task within the bounds of some rules. As you can see in Figure 6-3, there is a consistent discipline regarding what goes into and out of each cell. For example, inputs always enter from the left, outputs exit on the right, and so forth. Like DFDs, IDEF0 diagrams use levels to describe complex systems. Unlike DFDs, they also include controls (coming in from the top) such as company rules, flags, laws governing the process, and as mentioned earlier, the resources used and feedback referred to as *mechanisms* (for example, money, equipment, and specific labor categories). Further explanation of IDEF0 notation and its applications to business processes can be found in Marca and McGowan (1993).

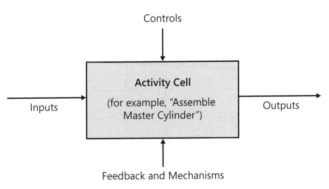

FIGURE 6-3 Details of the activity cell.

Requirements Analysis Using Self-Interaction Matrixes

At some point, a textual, legal version of the requirements list will be produced. This is the handiest way for all stakeholders to determine, via a checklist, that the software does what it was contracted for or intended to do. However, few managers recognize the value of performing an analysis of the requirements. They would much prefer to simply check off requirements as they are fulfilled by developed code. This lack of requirements analysis can be disquieting to the development team. They have probably experienced situations where not having a firm grip on the interplay between one requirement and another caused delays and rework. Putting this analysis task behind us will improve the development team's productivity by getting everybody in sync. The term *analysis* is used here in the engineering sense of the word, meaning "to examine, refine, and/or reorganize." A relational analysis among the requirements, documenting how they affect each other, is rarely done. What is the value of such an analysis? The value comes from documenting which requirements are affected, positively or negatively, by changes in one or more other requirements. One of the primary sources of problems for software projects has been that the requirements always change and that the impact of these changes is rarely understood, often with disastrous results. When requirements are changed, unexpected side effects can occur that hurt the development effort. The concept on which requirements analysis is based, as presented here, dates back about two decades (Warfield, 1976). The process, described here, involves the use of an $n \times n$ matrix, where n represents the number of requirements:

Step 1   Create an $n \times n$ matrix.

Label each row and column with the appropriate requirements element, as shown in Figure 6-4. I've used reference letters (i, j, and so on) to denote the respective requirements.

	i	j	k	l	m	n
Requirement i						
Requirement j						
Requirement k						
Requirement l						
Requirement m						
Requirement n						

FIGURE 6-4 A generic n x n requirements matrix

Step 2   Identify the diagonal along which each requirement meets itself. This diagonal is redundant and will be ignored.

As shown in Figure 6-5, this is the diagonal that slopes downward from upper left to lower right in the matrix.

	i	j	k	l	m	n
Requirement i	�©					
Requirement j		▢				
Requirement k			▢			
Requirement l				▢		
Requirement m					▢	
Requirement n						▢

FIGURE 6-5 An $n \times n$ requirements matrix with its redundancy diagonal identified

Step 3   Ignoring all elements below the diagonal in step 2, mark the matrix appropriately.

At each row-column intersection, note and mark the nature of the relationship between the requirement on the left (the row) and that along the top (the column). The relationship is denoted using a minus sign (-) to represent no relationship and a plus sign (+) to indicate a relationship, as shown in Figure 6-6. Additional types of relationships can also be indicated, such as *I* for "inhibits," *E* for "enhances," and *NI* for "no impact."

	i	j	k	l	m	n
Requirement i		-	-	+	+	-
Requirement j			-	-	-	+
Requirement k				-	+	-
Requirement l					+	-
Requirement m						-
Requirement n						

FIGURE 6-6 Matrix example showing relationships

As an example of the application of a self-interaction matrix, consider a hypothetical drug administration and monitoring system. Suppose that some 11 requirements were extracted from that description. These are listed in Figure 6-7, using the notation presented in Figure 6-6. To see how this method works for this problem, look at item 4, "Update AMA Tables within 30 days." In the opinion of the analyst, this requirement is affected by the -transfer of records (item 7) but not by the switchover of the system in the event of a power outage (item 11).

This concept has been around for more than 20 years, but it is rarely used in software (Warfield, 1976). I managed more than one project in which we used this technique. In one of these, there were requirements changes that might have caused delays in milestone deliveries. We got negative feedback to these reestimates until we started using this technique. With it, we were able to better inform the client regarding the ramifications of changes they were considering. This gave the client an added dimension of understanding of the system in that they could control their own destiny. Once they recognized the value of this approach, they began to seriously consider the pros and cons of each change and actually approved schedule and cost increases to accommodate those changes most critical to achieving their mission statement.

Requirement	1	2	3	4	5	6	7	8	9	10	11
1. Administer and monitor drugs.		+	+	−	+	+	+	+	−	+	+
2. Check level and alert.			+	+	−	+	+	+	−	−	+
3. Store medication limits.				+	−	+	+	+	−	−	+
4. Update AMA tables every 30 days.					−	+	+	−	−	−	−
5. Maintain personnel roster.						+	+	−	+	+	+
6. Change dosage level.							+	+	−	+	+
7. Record transaction data.								+	+	+	+
8. Run self-diagnostics.									+	−	+
9. Alert if security is breached.										−	+
10. Secure Web linkage.											−
11. Switch to battery backup.											

FIGURE 6-7 Matrix layout for our example

The requirements self-interaction matrix method has been rediscovered more recently and incorporated into a suite of tools by IBM-Rational Corporation (Software Consultants International, 1998). Perhaps part of the reason for its current acceptance is the issue of *leveling*. This is the practice of presenting requirements in a contract format with paragraphs and subparagraphs down to several levels. This decomposition might be quite vexing to some due to the large number of subparagraphs that themselves have subparagraphs, and so forth. But databases can certainly handle the issue. It is more likely that acceptance will come about with the realization that requirements changes are inevitable.

Referring again to our analysis in Figure 6-5, we can see that some requirements (for example, requirement 9, "Alert if security is breached") are relatively independent. If the customer wants to change the way that requirement works, there is little impact on the rest of the system. However, other requirements (for example, requirement 1, "Administer and monitor drugs") are more pervasive. Anything that is changed regarding those requirements will have a much broader impact on the system. My experience with this approach has been both positive and surprising. It has been positive in the sense that the client appears pleased that we understood their problem as well as we did, and they often point out interactions that we might have ignored. It has also been surprising in that there have been occasions when a client has been made aware of the broad ramifications of a change but wants to go forward with the change anyway. In such cases, the cost-benefit tradeoff to the client was worth it, even though the change required extensive rework on the part of the project team.

The benefits of this level of openness and complete detail cannot be overemphasized. This method has the effect of taking the practice of software engineering out of a somewhat haphazard change estimation practice and putting it squarely in the camp of the rest of the engineering community.

System Response Table (SRT) Specification Method and Real-Time Systems

A more compact and more precise means of establishing software requirements developed for real-time embedded systems but applicable to a broad range of systems is Deutsch's Stimulus Response Table (SRT) method (Deutsch, 1988). In this method, the client specifies requirements by stating what the new system is expected to do (the *Response*) when a certain input or inputs or event (*Stimulus*) occurs. This method has at least one advantage: it gives software testers early guidance on what tests need to be created to ensure that the system does what it is expected to do. The problem with putting the creation of test cases off until coding is under way is that those test cases establish that the code does what it does, not necessarily what it was intended to do. This problem is further exacerbated if the developers create the test cases (as in Extreme Programming).

Regardless of how they are arrived at, the requirements can be stated as a series of one-line or reasonably brief statements of what is expected from the system. In the case of real-time systems, we need to make some characteristics clear. The term *real-time system* has been defined in many ways. Over the years, key elements of the available definitions have become common:

- Rapid response
- Concurrency
- Complex environment
- Time critical (for example, hard real-time systems)

The key problem with real-time systems has always been how best to represent them graphically, textually, or in tabular form to the client. This is to ensure that the client's vision of the behavior and content of the system coincides with that of the development team. An examination of this problem is presented in Table 6-2 based, in part, on Deutsch's work.

TABLE 6-2 Real-Time Specification Representation Issues

Real-Time System Characteristic	Modeling Notation Needed
Response to external stimuli	❏ Stimulus-Response scenarios
Multiplicity of operational modes (states)	❏ Event flow ❏ Control flow ❏ State transformations
Included sensors	❏ Stimulus-Response scenarios ❏ External dataflows ❏ External event flows
Concurrency	❏ Dataflow/data transformations ❏ Physical design elements and interconnections
Fast response time (with respect to human timeframe)	Specification by ❏ Stimulus-Response scenarios ❏ Dataflows/data transformations
Complex external environment	❏ External definitions ❏ External event flows ❏ Stimulus-Response scenarios
Complex logic flow	❏ Stimulus-Response scenarios ❏ Discrete event simulation

In Table 6-2, you probably noticed a couple of notational methods that we have not yet discussed. For now, we will focus on the Stimulus-Response scenario (SRS). The SRS was developed and used by Hughes Aircraft Company as a means of representing the requirements for a broad range of systems, but mostly for defense systems. They found that its use enabled them to detect and correct errors in requirements that had gone undetected through the various reviews, inspections, walk-throughs, and audits. The SRS enables the client to convey what their expectation is regarding system behavior and to convey it in a very disciplined way. Basically, the system is viewed as a black box. Through a series of interviews and discussions, the client lays out what responses are expected from that black box when a certain stimulus is applied to it. The technique involves the use of a simple form in which a scenario is given a title and the scenario's stimulus and related response are described. Subcategories of information for the stimulus and its response are C = Condition, S = State, and D = Data. For example, consider what happens when you turn on your computer. The SRS information for this scenario might look like that shown in Table 6-3.

TABLE 6-3 **Example of the Use of SRS Notation**

Stimulus	Step in Sequence	Response
C—User turns on system.	1. Power on.	D—Display Power On light.
S—System power off.		C—Initiate boot sequence.
D—User enters ID and password		S—Power on.
S—System access disabled.	2. Logon.	C—Valid logon.
		D—Confirm to user.
		S—System access enabled.

Of course, some intermediate states have been left out for simplicity, but the concept is a powerful one (as I've personally experienced). Deutsch extends this concept further in what he refers to as the "operations concept model," which facilitates validating software and hardware requirements from an operational viewpoint. This concept is a simple one and might seem pedestrian to some, but it works. As always in engineering, "simple and works" trumps "elegant but does not work or works only intermittently" every time.

Use Cases

Use cases are a more recently popularized means of capturing requirements by communicating with the customer and the developer at the same time (Coleman, 1998). Use cases are described by diagrams and some accompanying text. The objective is to enable the client to better visualize what the system will do and to enable the development team to better understand the sequential and/or parallel nature of system tasks. The DFD helped do this, but it was not nearly as oriented to the kinds of systems in play today—interactive systems. Just as the name implies, interactive systems are ones in which a customer (also known as an "Actor" in use case jargon) interacts in some way with the system being developed. Examples of this include cash machines, boarding pass generators at the airport, online book purchases, and so forth. The basic scenario is as follows:

1. Customer inserts ATM card into device.

2. System prompts customer for identifying Personal Identification Number (PIN).

3. Customer enters PIN.

4. If PIN is invalid, system prompts retry and loops back to step 3.

5. On third unsuccessful retry, system ejects card and shuts down for 30 seconds.

6. System validates PIN successfully.

7. Customer enters transaction code for cash withdrawal.

8. System queries customer for amount in $20 increments.

9. Customer enters amount.

10. If amount is appropriate, system checks balance.

11. If amount is not appropriate, system prompts customer.

12. After three unsuccessful prompts, system ejects card and shuts down for 30 seconds.

13. If balance permits, system annotates account.

14. System issues cash.

15. If balance is too small, system notifies customer and ejects card.

The preceding list leaves out a lot of detail. For example, the ATM could have run out of cash. But we get the general idea of this interplay that occurs between customer and system—something like a well-organized and choreographed dance with specific rules in play and security features at work to protect both parties.

A simpler example, as described in the following list, is that of a customer making a purchase at a convenience store using a self-service checkout system:

1. Customer presses Start button.

2. System displays instructions.

3. Customer scans each item, touches it to the yellow pad to the right of the scanner, and then places the item in the bag provided.

4. System displays item description, price, and current total.

5. Customer presses Pay Now button.

6. System display Methods Of Payment options screen.

7. Customer selects method of payment.

8. Customer pays, takes receipt, and leaves.

Here are some possible error cases:

- Item bar code cannot be scanned—system emits error tone summoning clerk for assistance.

- Item (for example, fruit) has no bar code to scan—customer is prompted to manually enter code from chart provided.

- Customer enters invalid item code—system emits error tone to summon clerk for assistance.

Anyone who has used one of these systems is aware that there are many more ways in which failure can occur, but for our example, we will leave the error list as is and proceed to draw up what we have. Figure 6-8 is a depiction of the scenario we just described.

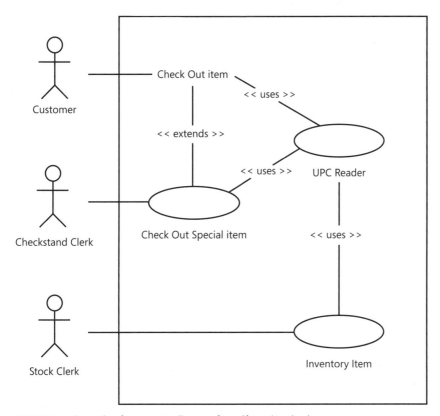

FIGURE 6-8 Example of a use case diagram for self-service checkout at a store.

Note that everything inside the large rectangle is part of the system being described. This rectangle is referred to as the *system boundary*. Everything outside the system boundary (for example, the Customer) is external to the system. The Customer, Checkstand Clerk, and Stock Clerk are referred to as "Actors," in that they have specific roles to play.

Some points about use cases that need to be emphasized:

- There is no standardized way of drawing use case diagrams. There are several firms that have developed a specific style of use case diagrams, and all believe that theirs is the best. I suggest you survey them or develop your own style.

- Use cases, in whatever form, identify relationships, document them, and enable software engineers to describe them in disciplined ways. Ideally, if done well, changes in requirements will result in far fewer changes to the documentation using use cases than other methods.

- There is no relationship between the structure of the use case set and the design of the system.

- As always, use cases are a tool, not a panacea or a substitute for rational thought.

- Use case diagrams require the presence of a textual description since the diagrams lack procedural detail. Again, this underlines the need for development team members to be able to communicate in writing.

In my experience, use cases have proven to be powerful tools for extracting user-system interaction concepts and reducing the existence of redundant information. They are not design tools and do not convey objects or classes for the design of the system. They are, in the truest sense of the word, functional descriptions. But they increase communication among all stakeholders, which can only improve the results from our development team.

Design Methods Overview

When software engineering first emerged, the notion of a software design method was far from anybody's mind. For many years, Von Neuman's flowchart was used to document a design, but the flowchart was intended to document a computer program after it was written (Chapin, 1970). As the profession evolved, the systems got more complex and the demand grew for more and better design methods. Individuals and companies responded by developing their own means of developing and documenting designs. By the early 1980s, there were more than three dozen in all (Peters, 1981; Warnier, 1976), with many more to come.

To understand what the advantages are of designing before building, we can simply envision what any building or device would be like without being preceded by a blueprint—that is, a design. In one respect, a software design method is intended to aid software engineers in expressing their concept regarding the eventual software system in the equivalent of a blueprint. Specifically, the software design must communicate:

- **The architecture**   What the pieces of the system are and how they go together.
- **The relationships**   What goes on between various elements.
- **The human interface**   How the system interacts with users.

What software engineers found in the early 1980s was that there were major differences among practitioners regarding design style that greatly influenced the results of design activity. For example, if one was very functionally oriented, the design might best be represented by a flowchart or some other functional, sequential type of modeling approach. On the other hand, if data structure and data relationships were of the highest importance, these would be emphasized using Jackson's method (Jackson, 1975) or something similar.

Real-time systems presented the software field with an altogether different type of problem and represented the type of software system that had the lowest productivity by development teams. Some authors tried to add flags or other signaling-related objects into their design schemes, but that did not fill the need. What was needed was to take a step back and come up with an approach that would support the concurrency, interrupt-driven, synchronized nature of real-time systems.

Today most systems are predominantly real time (that is, system response is fast enough to affect future user interactions). Use of the PC and its clones has driven us in the real-time direction.

There are several schemes for classifying software design methods. One that is particularly useful employs a four-category system, as shown in Table 6-4. I have not included computer-aided software engineering (CASE) tools, because they have not yet proven themselves as cost-effective aids, and their vendors are often not very financially stable.

TABLE 6-4 Summary of Design Methods

Method Category	System Appropriateness
Data-oriented	Systems that interface with large volumes of data, such as banking, insurance, and government applications.
Function-oriented	Process-intensive systems that are heavily oriented toward classical engineering applications (civil engineering, aerodynamics, and so on).
Object-oriented	Most appropriate for systems that will be implemented in C++, SmallTalk, or a similar language, especially in large system development efforts.
Formal	Well suited (although limited in the size of system to be considered) to efforts involving critical software that must be provably correct.

Due in part to the fact that there is a very thin line separating the requirements definition from the design, many requirements definition tools (for example, DFDs and IDEF0 diagrams) play a significant role in the design process.

Selecting Appropriate System-Modeling Techniques

Regardless of the phase of the project involved, the first thing to remember about modeling systems is that these methods are tools in a toolbox. Each has been consciously created to accomplish a specific set of goals and emphasize a certain domain of information. The other important point is that rarely were any of these methods created because someone set out to create the ideal modeling method. In general, these methods were created to fill a void. They came into existence to solve the problem at hand rather than to solve a more universal set of issues.

An important role for the project manager in this area is one of leadership and decision making. Each member of the development team will tend to want to employ his or her favorite method and perhaps promote that method within the team. Also, the company that developed the technique might have adopted a set of standards that direct projects to use this method or that. It is the project manager's job to ensure that the modeling methods used on the project are

- **Appropriate**   They have been used on similar projects elsewhere, or at least they address the issues that will be important on this project.

- **Documented**   There exists enough instructional material in the form of books and, possibly, on-site courses to enable the team to quickly become proficient with their use.

- **Committed to by the development team**   This amounts to engaging the team in the analysis required to select appropriate methods and then getting them to accept these methods.

The project manager's role in this instance is not to force one method or another on the team but to encourage them to keep an open mind regarding the selection of modeling methods and to drive the team toward selecting what is most likely to work.

A process for selecting appropriate system-modeling methods for your project is documented in Figure 6-9 and Figure 6-10. Be forewarned that regardless of the methods selected, people will want to use what they are familiar with, even if those methods are ineffective. It is the project manager's job to gain consensus on trying something new and to provide the support (for example, training, books, and consulting) needed to ensure success.

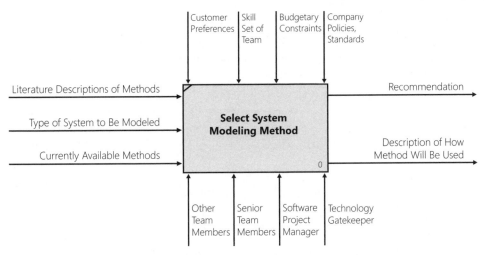

FIGURE 6-9 Overview of the system-modeling method selection process.

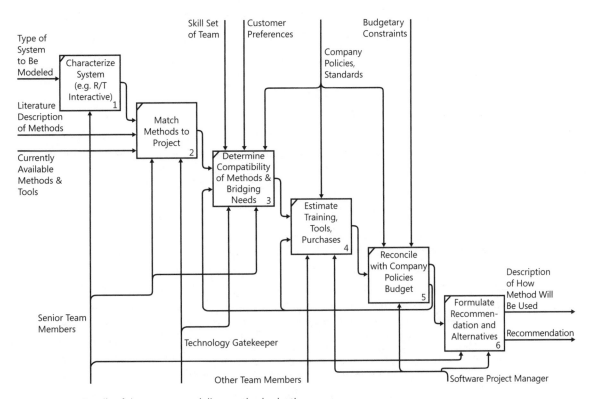

FIGURE 6-10 Details of the system-modeling method selection process.

And Now, a Word from Our Sponsor

The goal of the software project manager is not just to meet requirements but also to ensure customer acceptance/satisfaction. This goes beyond meeting the various constraints and gets into other areas incorporated into the term *Customer Relationship Management* (CRM). One of the best books written on this subject (McKenzie, 2001) looks at this subject exhaustively, but to put our discussion into perspective, I will relate an experience I had early in my career that taught me a lesson that has served me well for more than 30 years.

Our customer was a telephone company that was automating its long-distance (toll) offices. I was assigned the task of designing and developing the measurements packages that operating companies would use. These measurements fell into two categories:

- **Plant measurements** These tallied the number of times that circuits opened and closed and that switches turned on and off, the status of various devices that the Electronic Switching Systems (ESS) interfaced with at the phone office, and other equipment-related data. This data was used to better balance the workload on the equipment to prevent premature failure due to overload and/or overuse.

- **Operational measurements** These numbers were used by the network management people and now software systems to ensure that the telephone switch (ESS) did not get overloaded.

Although the company was devoted to customer service, they knew that they could not achieve their revenue goals if people tried to make long-distance calls and got a fast busy signal. This sound meant that the switch was overloaded. Studies had shown that in such cases, people would retry but eventually give up, which would result in lost revenue.

The company provided people on site to answer the development team's questions regarding what information needed to be gathered, counted properly, and transmitted to the network control centers at appropriate intervals. Problems occurred because the development group management had decided that these measurements were just a nuisance and gave the collection of measurement data the lowest priority for the operating system. As we would find out, this meant that the times when the switch was busiest and the data most vital were the very times when the operating system could not get to low-priority tasks. The attitude among the developers that measurements were a nuisance stemmed from the management's focus on high technology, code elegance, and related issues. As far as the developers were concerned, measurements just interfered with throughput. The problem was eventually resolved, but not until heated discussions occurred in which the client related that they did not care about code sophistication. The client's position was that if they could not get reliable, timely data, the system would be potentially worthless because they would not be able to proactively monitor its health and effectively manage excess traffic.

The moral of this sorry tale is that to maintain a working relationship with a client, we must clearly understand what is and is not important to them. High technology might mean everything to us, but to the client, there is a business objective that must be achieved, and they don't care about the specifics of the technology that gets them there. This is a case of conflicting value systems.

Summary

Each system-modeling technique reflects the specific and sometimes unique viewpoint of its author. Although we did not discuss the flowchart in this chapter, it reflects its author's view that the flow of logic is vital to describing a system or a computer program. For example, in Chapter 4, a flowchart was used to describe the logic flow in managing a project, but it lacked many of the features that managers need, such as flow time, costs, and responsibilities. Other methods focus on functional flow and take into account everything that their authors deem important to adequately describing function flow. Use cases and other methods focus squarely on the interactions occurring between one or more users and the system and include interactions that occur between systems as well. More often than not, members of the development team will tend to insist on using methods with which they are comfortable rather than submitting the modeling method selection decision to close, analytical scrutiny. Unfortunately, many of these methods are used primarily because they are effectively promoted and demonstrated via technical conferences and publications, not because they are the best choice. In fact, there is no best choice that works for all system-modeling situations. A vital role for the project manager is to provide leadership in creating and implementing a selection process for each project based on what works best for that project rather than what is the most well advertised. Regardless of your preference, always keep in mind that the goal of project management is to keep the technical scope aligned with the available cost and schedule resources.

References

(**McConnell, 1996**)   McConnell, S. "Software Quality at Top Speed," *Software Development*, **4**(8), pp. 38–42, 1996.

(**DeMarco, 1987**)   DeMarco, T. *Structured Analysis and System Specification*, New York: Yourdon Press, 1987.

(**Ross and Brackett, 1976**)   Ross, D. T., and J. W. Brackett. "An Approach to Structured Analysis," *Computer Decisions* **8**(9), pp. 40–44, 1976.

(Marca and McGowan, 1993)   Marca, D. A., and C. L. McGowan. *IDEF0/SADT—Business Process and Enterprise Modeling*. San Diego, CA: Eclectic Solutions Corporation, 1993.

(Warfield, 1976)   Warfield, J. N. *Societal Systems: Planning, Policy and Complexity*. New York: Wiley Interscience, 1976.

(Software Consultants International, 1998)   Software Consultants International Ltd. *Requirements Self-Interaction Matrix Database System*. Ridgecrest, CA: Project YDRA, U.S. Navy China Lake Naval Weapons Station, 1988.

(Eeles and Ericsson, 2003)   Eeles, P., and M. Ericsson. "Modeling for Enterprise Initiatives with the IBM Rational Unified Process. Part I: RUP and the System of Interconnected Systems Pattern," *The Rational Edge*, 21 June 2003.

(Deutsch, 1988)   Deutsch, M. "Focusing Real-Time Systems Analysis on User Operations," *IEEE Software*, **5**(5), pp. 39–50, 1988.

(Coleman, 1998)   Coleman, D. "A Use Case Template: Draft for Discussion," *Fusion Newsletter*, April 1998.

(Chapin, 1970)   Chapin, N. "Flowcharting with the ANSI Standard: A Tutorial," *ACM Computing Surveys* **2**(2), pp. 119–146, 1970.

(Peters, 1981)   Peters, L. J. *Software Design: Methods and Techniques*. New York: Yourdon Press, 1981.

(Warnier, 1976)   Warnier, J. D. *Logical Construction of Programs*, 3rd ed. New York: Van Nostrand Reinhold, 1976.

(Jackson, 1975)   Jackson, M. *Principles of Program Design*. London: Academic Press, 1975.

(McKenzie, 2001)   McKenzie, R. *The Relationship-Based Enterprise: Powering Business Success Through Customer Relationship Management*. Toronto: McGraw-Hill Ryerson, 2001.

Chapter 7
Estimating Project Size, Cost, and Schedule

A cynic is one who knows the cost of everything and the value of nothing.

—Oscar Wilde

Determining how long a software development effort will take and cost is a multistep process. It involves estimating the magnitude of the effort, establishing a schedule, and then computing the cost of the project using labor and other costs appropriate to your firm. This process is repeated almost continuously throughout the project's lifecycle as the requirements and other factors change.

In this chapter, I examine and demonstrate methods for estimating the magnitude of the effort in terms of number of lines of code. We look at system size initially because the sizing and estimating methods for software that have developed over the years require code estimates as input. This is similar to costing methods used in other fields such as the construction industry. For example, in that industry, once the size of a single-family home has been estimated in terms of the number of square feet, the type of construction, and some desired finish features, most contractors can quote a construction fee for typical quality construction, and they can also provide a high and low price range to accommodate the most economical choices and more expensive levels of fit and finish.

Viewing Cost Estimation as a Process

Like other projects in the engineering world, software projects involve estimating, reestimating, and adjusting estimates throughout the execution of the project plan. For those who have not run a software project before, the reason for the seemingly continuous reestimating of the project is that projects rarely go according to plan. The setbacks you can expect include people leaving the project and/or company, complex technical issues arising, the target market changing, the competition releasing a better product, the customer changing requirements, funding for the effort being reduced or, rarely, increased, and other factors beyond your ability to foresee and control.

The basic software project estimation process is presented in Figure 7-1. Although this chapter focuses on the earliest stages of project estimation, note that revisions of the initial estimate(s) are missing from the model. In fact, the process in Figure 7-1 is a continuous one. That is, you begin on the left and proceed to the right over and over again throughout the project, ending with project completion and the archiving of relevant data for the next project and project manager to use in making estimates.

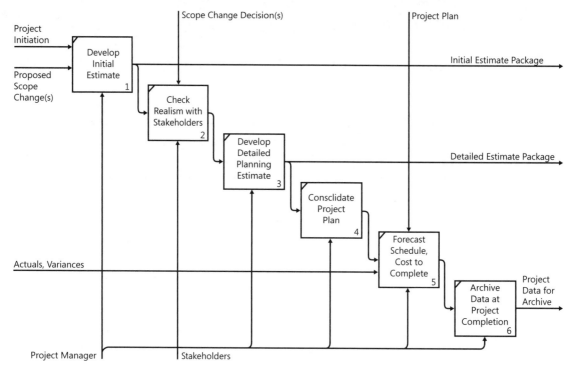

FIGURE 7-1 Software estimation as a lifecycle process.

Archiving Project Data

A brief advisory regarding archiving of project data is in order here. Although some very large firms carefully document all cost and estimation aspects of development efforts, office reconfiguration, and the like, they tend not to record detailed costing data, changes, revisions, and other factors associated with their internal and external software projects. Why? Perhaps it is the physical versus the virtual view, as discussed earlier in Chapter 2, "Why Is Software So Difficult?" or ignorance or lack of understanding of the value such information might have for the company.

Whatever the reason, many prominent firms still do not collect and maintain databases containing such information. In other engineering fields, such data is saved and used in subsequent, similar efforts. This body of knowledge enables the firm to draw on historical knowledge and refine its estimating process and the accuracy of the estimates over time, giving the firm a competitive edge over those who do not maintain historical data.

Estimating Variability as a Function of Project Flow Time

In all projects, the farther along you are, the more accurate will be your estimates of when you will be done, how large the final deliverable will be, how much effort will be involved, and what the final cost will be. Boehm, McConnell, Deutsch, and others have captured this concept graphically, as shown in Figure 7-2 (Boehm, 1981; McConnell, 1996; Deutsch, 2003).

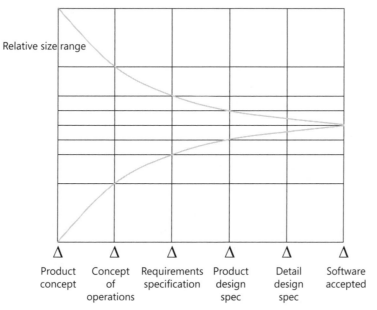

FIGURE 7-2 Variability in key estimates through the lifecycle. (Adapted from Deutsch, 2003. Used with permission of M. Deutsch.)

If you look at the Effort And Size and Schedule sections in Table 7-1, where percentages are expressed as a decimal regardless of the units involved, note the range of variability at the start of the project versus the range at the end. This *cone of variability* is what all projects— software, hardware, home and commercial construction—have to deal with. Yes, commercial construction projects (Amos, 2004) have experienced and reported on the same type of variability curve for more than 50 years.

TABLE 7-1 Variability in Estimate Data Through the Lifecycle

Phase	Effort and Size		Schedule	
	Optimistic	Pessimistic	Optimistic	Pessimistic
Initial product definition	0.25	4.0	0.60	1.60
Approved product definition	0.50	2.0	0.80	1.25
Requirements specification	0.67	1.50	0.85	1.15
Product design specification	0.80	1.25	0.90	1.10
Detailed design specification	0.90	1.10	0.95	1.05

Source: Adapted from Deutsch, 2003, and used with the permission of M. Deutsch.

The primary goal of the estimating methods discussed in this chapter is to reduce estimate variability as much as possible. Each method takes a different approach to predicting cost, size, and schedule. These range from relatively simple formulations focusing on the code, such as IBM's approach, the function point method, and others presented here, to more comprehensive, almost holistic approaches that characterize the development environment and the nature of the product. One of the first methods to significantly contribute to achieving this goal was the Constructive Cost Model (COCOMO), developed and published in 1981 (Boehm, 1981). It represents a milestone in the industry in that, to the best of my knowledge, no one had ever collected and analyzed such a large volume of data on so many projects and then tried to make sense out of what that information implied.

Since then, other methods also discussed herein took a similar route and employed a variety of procedural and mathematical techniques to wring from the data some patterns and trends. However, over the more than 20 years since COCOMO and other methods were published, the software industry has changed considerably. For example, the use of the PC, the Internet, a preference for the use of commercial off-the-shelf software (COTS) for constructing systems, improvements in development environments, and increased knowledge and use of quality practices all changed the underpinnings of software project estimation methods, resulting in the need for new ones.

Costing and Sizing Software Projects

For more than 40 years, the software engineering profession has attempted to create a means of estimating software costs that is accurate, reliable, and consistent. The lack of repeatability or sameness from one software project to the next makes this a seemingly daunting task.

But don't be misled into believing software development is unique because each project is different from the previous one. I have consulted on IT systems related to new commercial construction and can assure you that the construction industry experiences the same phenomenon. Much of the success of that industry has been the result of capturing relevant data, standardization, and emphasizing the importance of competent project managers as the keys to successful projects.

What most software researchers have opted for has been to find ways of characterizing software projects in terms of difficulty, risk, complexity, and other factors and characterizing the skill of the people who will do the work. Again, the project management aspect has been largely ignored by software researchers, but this is to be expected from such technically oriented treatises. Even so, one study shows estimation techniques to have an error rate of 85 percent to 610 percent before calibration to the specifics of an organization and an error rate of 50 percent to 100 percent after calibration (Shepperd, 1992). Obviously, calibration helps, but the error rate the software industry is experiencing is still unacceptable.

A common characteristic of the most popular estimation models is the requirement of having an initial "guesstimate" of the number of lines of code the proposed effort will produce. A colleague once commented that using the number of source lines of code (SLOC) as a key parameter in estimating cost is like using the estimated weight of a building to project the cost of its construction. This is not a viable practice in other industries, so why should it be considered useful in the software industry? Another important difference between software estimation and other industries (such as construction) is that other industries estimate cost based on a blueprint or, in our terms, a detailed (that is, "build to") design. This practice might result from the fact that we do not physically experience software, the nature of the people who develop it, the kind of rush to market environment software exists in, or some combination of these and other factors. But the fact remains that as a matter of standard practice, software development teams estimate flow time, size, and cost from little more than experience, limited understanding of the requirements, and a drive to be successful. Not having a "build to" design to estimate from makes accurate software system cost, size, and delivery date estimates an unlikely proposition.

Some researchers have suggested that estimating by phase can help improve estimation accuracy. That is, for software projects we should estimate and commit only to the next phase rather than the entire effort. Although this might be effective, it is not practical. Stakeholders want to know early on what the entire project will cost and how long it will take. (They have become accustomed to having this information early from dealing with other vendors such as construction managers.)

Another issue involved in software estimation is the programming language. The higher the level of the language, the lower the SLOC. Current estimating schemes take this into account. SLOC has proved to be a surrogate for the entire stream of work resulting in code as a product.

Keys to Estimating

Following are some key points to remember about estimating:

- The estimate is *not* the project plan, only an input to it.
- A variance (as discussed in this chapter) should be attached to any estimate.
- Adjusting factors to get the desired answer leads to trouble.
- Partner with your client to mutually share risks and concerns as adults.
- Be honest—if the schedule appears impossible, it probably is.
- In adjusting the project plan, incorporate the client's priorities regarding what must be done first and so forth.

Above all, try to achieve a win-win situation, where the project team and the client feel that the project has been mutually beneficial.

General Form of Schedule Estimation Formulas

The published and accepted estimation schemes all take the following general form:

*Person-months of effort required = p * S*

Where

p = a productivity constant that varies, depending on the author, representing lines of source code per person-month

S = size of the system in thousands of lines of source code (KLOC)

Using the preceding formula, if a group averages about 500 SLOC per month,

p = 1 / 500 = 0.002

and the estimated size of the system is 7,000 SLOC, then

*Effort = 0.002 * 7,000 = 14 person-months*

Note that the SLOC rates we are talking about all assume that some reasonably consistent and controlled development environment is in use from one project to the next. Otherwise, in a single firm, we would effectively be making ill-advised comparisons (that is, apples to oranges).

IBM's Findings at the Federal Systems Division

A study of 60 projects at IBM produced a sizing model reflective of the types of software IBM builds, their personnel, development environments, and so forth (Walston and Felix, 1977). Their model takes the following generic form:

Effort = 5.2L $^{0.91}$

Where

L = size in KLOC (thousands of lines of source code)
5.2 = a scaling factor

Table 7-2 demonstrates their findings' scaling factor values.

TABLE 7-2 IBM Early Scaling Factor Approach Values

Effort (Person-Months)	Size (Thousands of Lines of Source Code)	Productivity (Effort/Size)
36.44	10	3.64
296.18	100	2.96
2407.48	1000	2.41

Note how slowly the values in the right-hand column change with respect to the values in the left-hand column, resulting in less than a linear relationship with respect to the values in the center column. The issue of scaling factors with respect to project size in KLOC is an important one and is discussed in more detail in Banker and Kemerer (1989). Also, Table 7-2 indicates that there is an inverse relationship with respect to economy of scale associated with this data. This conclusion is consistent with that of COCOMO II, which indicates that the larger the system, the lower the KLOC rate per person per month. The inverse nature of these two results is not explained in IBM's results.

Software Lifecycle Management

Software Lifecycle Management (SLIM) employs a modified form of a Rayleigh distribution and is supported by an automated tool (Putnam, 1978). It supports software cost estimation in several ways. The algorithm used in the SLIM approach is as follows:

$S = C * K^{(1/3)} t^{(4/3)}$

Where

S = the estimated size of the software system in KLOC
C = technology constant
K = total lifecycle effort in programmer years
t = development time in years

This offers a different perspective in that it tries to address the issue of whether the use of more programmers right from the start will really reduce the total development time linearly. Also, the coefficient C takes on different values for different types of projects. The recorded values by project type are represented in Table 7-3.

TABLE 7-3 Factors Used in the SLIM Method

Project Type Descriptor	Value of C
Real-time embedded	1,500
Batch development	4,894
Supported and organized	10,040

One issue with this estimation approach is that its applicability is mainly for large development efforts. From the equation, you can see the extreme sensitivity the results have to the value of the technology coefficient C. Because many projects are made up of multiple pieces that can each be classified differently using the preceding scheme, some care must be taken in applying this approach.

Function Point Estimation Method

A required input to many cost estimating methods is an estimate of the number of lines of source code in the final product. The function point method can be used to obtain just such an estimate (Kemerer, 1993).

The function point method estimates source code size by using an intermediate variable called function points. After a value for the number of function points has been computed and adjusted for factors I discuss later and a programming language has been selected, you can compute an estimate for the number of lines of source code. This method focuses on estimating the number of unique functions (function points) in the final system and then using that to develop the coding estimate. What is counted is the number of unique function types, as listed in Table 7-4.

TABLE 7-4 Descriptions of Function Types

Type	Example
External inputs	Filenames
External outputs	Messages
Queries	Inputs from a user of an interactive system requiring a response
External files or interfaces	Files shared with other software systems
Internal files	Files not visible outside the system

Estimates are developed by analyzing the requirements and spelling out the functions called for by using the list in Table 7-4. The function points are classified as simple, average, or complex, and a relative weighting factor is applied, as listed in Table 7-5.

TABLE 7-5 Values of the Coefficients Used in Function Point Estimation

| Function Point Type | Characterized As: | | |
	S–Simple	A–Average	C–Complex
External inputs	3	4	6
External outputs	4	6	7
Queries	3	4	6
External files	5	7	10
Internal files	7	10	15

The results of the application of weighting factors is called the *raw, unadjusted function count*. This is refined using the 14 project complexity factors listed in Table 7-6.

TABLE 7-6 Technical Complexity Factors for Function Point Analysis

Complexity Factors	
Data communication	Online update
Distributed data processing	Complex processing
Performance	Reusability
Heavily used configuration	Ease of installation
Transaction rate	Ease of use
Online data entry	Multiple sites
End user efficiency	Facilitate change

As most of us have experienced, more complex problems take more time and more work to solve. The same is true with software, and the function points method takes this into account. Here's how: Each technical complexity factor is assigned a value from 0 to 5, where 0 equals no influence on the project and 5 equals a high degree of influence. The overall technical complexity factor T_{cf} is given by the following equation:

$$T_{cf} = 0.65 + SUM\ (i = 1\ to\ i = 14)\ (T_{cfi})\ /\ 100$$

$$FP = UFC * T_{cf}$$

Where

UFC = unadjusted function count, a count of the number of different user visible functions in the system specification

T_{cf} = technology complexity factor

i = *the ith complexity factor*

T_{cfi} = the value of the ith complexity factor (assigned a value of 0 to 5)

With the function point value (FP), the user of this method can estimate program length in SLOC using the simple conversions shown in Table 7-7 and multiplying FP by the appropriate source statements per function point factor.

TABLE 7-7 Conversion Factors from Function Points to Language Statements

Programming Language	Source Statements per Function Point
Assembler	320
C	150
COBOL	106
FORTRAN	106
Pascal	91
Smalltalk	21
Query languages	16
Spreadsheet languages	6

Overview of the Process

Figure 7-3 shows an overview of the function point process needed to compute the function point estimate of source code.

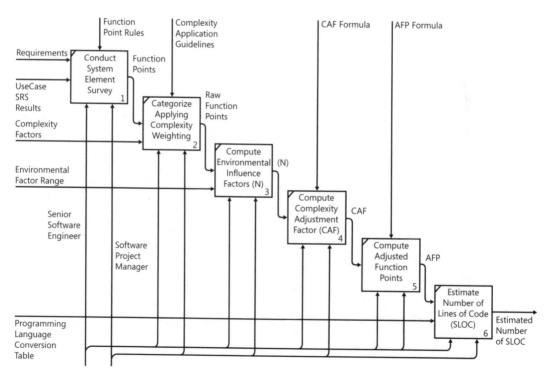

FIGURE 7-3 The function point method as a process.

An Example

To demonstrate the use of the function point method, I use a hypothetical Patient Drug Control and Administration System. This system is used to administer drugs automatically to patients in the intensive care unit precisely as prescribed by their attending physician. It monitors the level of specific drugs in the patient's system; adjusts the dosage to achieve physician-recommended levels; automatically produces reports; notifies personnel if there is a malfunction; monitors patient vital signs, producing an alarm if a life-threatening condition occurs; and provides information over the Internet to authorized medical personnel any-where in the world. Assume that we have developed a use case model, a Stimulus-Response scenario (SRS), or other means of establishing what goes into and out of the system as well as where information will be stored. As shown in Figure 7-3, this is a six-step process.

1. **Conduct (function point) component survey**   This information is presented in Table 7-8 using the conventions established in this method and based on the requirements statement.

TABLE 7-8 First Catalog of Function Points for Drug Monitor

Function Point Type	Description		
External inputs	User logon Main menu choice Patient health data	Patient drug prescriptions Patient drug level readings Patient vital signs	AMA database update
External outputs	Drug flow display Drug level(s) display Vital signs display	Drug flow adjustment Medical staff notification Administration notification	Notify Security Alarm (sound) Activate warning light
Queries	Prompt for user logon Verify patient data Verify drug dosage	Approval by second doctor AMA database update	
External files	Event log Patient data file Authorized personnel list		
Internal files	AMA drug limit database AMA update schedule Self-diagnostic schedule		

2. **Categorize (each function point), applying complexity weighting**   The complexity categories are Simple (S), Average (A), and Complex (C). They have been applied to the information in Table 7-8 and are presented in Table 7-9. Note that the categorizations are judgmental in nature and subject to review and discussion among those involved in the project. The key is that we are attempting to obtain an estimate—not necessarily an exact value. If you are concerned about the category decisions, try revising the values, computing your own results, and comparing them with the results of this example. A summary of the population in each category arranged by complexity level is presented in Table 7-10. By using the complexity weighting factors that were presented earlier in Table 7-5, we can compute the weighted value, as shown in Table 7-11.

TABLE 7-9 Categorization of Initial Function Point Elements

Function Point Type	Description with Category (S|A|C)		
External inputs	User logon **S** Main menu choice **S** Patient health data **A**	Patient drug prescriptions **A** Patient drug level readings **C** Patient vital signs **C**	AMA database update **A**
External outputs	Drug flow display **A** Drug level(s) display **A** Vital signs display **A**	Drug flow adjustment **A** Medical staff notification **S** Administration notification **S**	Notify Security **S** Alarm (sound) **S** Activate warning light **S**
Queries	Prompt for user logon **S** Verify patient data **S** Verify drug dosage **S**	Approval by second doctor **S** AMA database update **C**	
External files	Event log **C** Patient data file **A**		
Internal files	AMA drug limit database **A** AMA update schedule **S** Self-diagnostic schedule **S**	Authorized personnel list **C**	

TABLE 7-10 Summary of the Categories and Complexity Rankings

Function Point Type	Simple (S)	Average (A)	Complex (C)
External inputs	2	3	2
External outputs	5	4	0
Queries	4	0	1
External files	0	1	1
Internal files	2	1	1

TABLE 7-11 Results After Applying the Complexity Values

Function Point Type	Simple (S)	Average (A)	Complex (C)	Σ
External inputs	2 × 3 = 6	3 × 4 = 12	2 × 6 = 12	30
External outputs	5 × 4 = 20	4 × 6 = 24	0 × 7 = 0	44
Queries	4 × 3 = 12	0 × 4 = 0	1 × 6 = 6	18
External files	0 × 5 = 0	1 × 7 = 7	1 × 10 = 10	17
Internal files	2 × 7 = 14	1 × 10 = 10	1 × 15 = 15	39
			Total (UFC)	**148**

3. **Compute environmental influence factors** (N)   As discussed earlier, this method incorporates several different kinds of adjustments to the function point estimates to accommodate specific issues in your system. The technical complexity factors are listed in Table 7-12. Included in that table are the values assigned for each factor in this example. The values range from 0 (not a relevant issue) to 5 (definitely a relevant issue).

TABLE 7-12 Results After Applying the Complexity Values

Item	Assigned Value
Data communications	5
Distributed data processing	3
Performance	5
Heavily used configuration	3
Transaction rate	4
Online data entry	5
End user efficiency	5
Online update	5
Complex processing	4
Reusability	1
Ease of installation	5
Ease of use	5
Multiple sites	1
Facilitate change	3
Total (N)	**54**

4. **Compute complexity adjustment factor**   As you might recall, the function point method includes an adjustment factor to apply to the raw or unadjusted function point (UFC) count. This factor is computed using the formula presented earlier:

$T_{cf} = 0.65 + (0.01 * N)$

Substituting the value for N, we obtain

$T_{cf} = 0.65 + (0.01 \times 54) = 1.19$

5. **Compute adjusted function points**   This calculation involves applying the technology complexity factor (T_{cf}) to the unadjusted function point count (UFC) using the formula presented earlier:

$FP = UFC * T_{cf}$

Substituting for both variables, we obtain

$FP = 148 \times 1.19 = 176.12$

6. **Compute the estimated number of lines of source code**   Using the values presented in Table 7-7 and selecting C as the programming language for this project, we can compute an *estimate* of the total number of lines of code using the following formula:

$SLOC = FP \times Source\ Statements\ per\ FP\ Conversion\ Factor$

In this case, FP = 176.12 and the conversion factor is 150, yielding

$SLOC = 176.12 \times 150$

$SLOC = 26,418,\ or\ 26.418\ KLOC$

Automated Assistance for Function Point Computation

You can use several commercially available software packages to compute function points. We employ one of the tools available on the Web free of charge from the University of Southern California (USC) (University of Southern California, 1999). As noted earlier, different authors differ in how they weight factors. This can result in a different value for the unadjusted function point count. Using the USC tool and the same values we employed in the previous example in Table 7-10, we obtain an unadjusted function point count of 144, as shown in Figure 7-4. This differs from the earlier result. However, keep in mind that we are using this method for obtaining an estimate—not an exact value, an estimate. Hence, given the ease with which a software tool like this can be used and its reliability, it represents a valuable asset in computing function points.

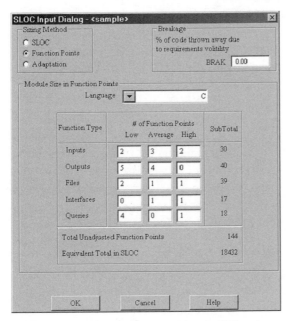

FIGURE 7-4 A function point count using the USC tool.

Function Points: A Summary

The function point method might be the most consistent and, possibly, most accurate estimation method available today. In fact, Gartner Research indicates that the function point method has a .8 probability of success (Gartner Research, 2002). Given the success rate of other methods, an 80 percent (.8) success rate is impressive. However, to yield viable results it requires the project team to have enough experience to be accurate, the project manager to apply consistent judgment, and all participants to be honest. This includes selecting appropriate programming languages. For example, in the sample computation, it might have been tempting to select a programming language that had a lower conversion factor (such as Smalltalk). It stands to reason that if fewer lines of source code have to be generated, the cost formulas discussed later in the text will show shorter development times and lower costs. But the matter of cost and schedule cannot be so simply brought under control. The utility of the language, the team's knowledge of and experience with it, and so forth are all in play. For example, as of a couple of years ago, the Smalltalk programming language, although strongly object oriented, did not include methods for enforcing strong data typing. As a result, any data entry situation involved writing such code from scratch or purchasing it from a third party, thereby increasing cost and affecting reliability and, potentially, development flow time.

Keep in mind that the function point method yields an estimate, not a precise computation of the number of source lines of code that will be needed to meet the requirements. Its successful use will provide reasonable guidance as to the order of magnitude of an effort with some uncertainty regarding the final size of the project.

3D Function Point Method

A seldom discussed aspect of the function point method is that it was developed based on business application software experience. Software engineers who develop real-time embedded systems were concerned about this (Whitmire, 1992) and subsequently developed an approach to estimating the number of source lines of code that extends the function point method to the scientific and real-time embedded software community. It is called 3D.

The three dimensions of the 3D approach are as follows:

- **Data**   User interfaces and data as in the original method
- **Function**   Internal processing
- **Control**   Real-time behavior(s)

Each of these dimensions is described in the following subsections.

Data Dimension

The data dimension is most clearly related to the original function point method. It concentrates on user interfaces and the characteristics of the data being processed. This dimension retains the same elements as the original method—internal files, input, output, queries, and external files. The same conventions are used for evaluation of this dimension as in the original method.

Function Dimension

The focus of the function dimension is on processing that occurs in the system. It is called internal processing and includes the individual processing steps that might involve mathematical computations (for example, related to targeting, navigation) as well as semantic statements. This second category includes the classic real-time programming practices of confirming preconditions, postconditions, and invariants vital to the proper functioning of a real-time system.

Measurements in this dimension deviate from the original function point method in that they focus on the number of internal operations that must be executed to transform inputs into outputs. The working definition of a *transformation* is a series of steps with semantic constraints that are achieved by using an algorithm. Evaluation of this dimension can use one of the schemes shown in Table 7-13.

TABLE 7-13 Semantic Evaluation Schemes for 3D Function Points Method

	Number of Semantic Statements		
Processing Steps	1–5	6–10	> 11
1–10	Low	Low	Average
11–20	Low	Average	High
≥ 21	Average	High	High

Control Dimension

The control dimension focuses on the state-based aspects of the real-time system. Factors included in this dimension are concurrency, events, time, and other real-time properties. A value for this dimension is obtained by estimating the number of state transitions that will occur, which can be done by using any of several means of documenting expected state transitions, including state transition diagrams (STDs) (Peters, 1988).

Computing Real-Time (3D) Function Point Estimates

The process for computing an estimate of function points using the 3D approach is much like the one used in the original method with one important exception: Table 7-5 (shown earlier) is replaced by Table 7-14. The remainder of the process is the same.

TABLE 7-14 Complexity Weighting Factor Set Used in 3D Function Point Method

	Complexity Level			
	Simple	Average	High	Total
External inputs	3	4	6	
External outputs	4	6	7	
Queries	3	4	6	
External files	5	7	10	
Internal files	7	10	15	
Transformations	7	10	15	
Transitions	—	10	—	
		Total 3D UFC		

I use the data from our previous example to demonstrate the differences between that approach and the real-time-oriented one used in this example. Assume that the system is identical to the one in the previous example with the addition of 18 transformations (4 simple, 4 average, 10 complex) and 10 state transitions (all of average complexity). Table 7-15 shows complexity levels of the example values.

TABLE 7-15 Example Values Embellished Using the 3D Function Points Method

| | Complexity Level | | | |
	Simple	Average	High	Total
External Inputs	2 × 3 = 6	3 × 4 = 12	2 × 6 = 12	30
External Outputs	5 × 4 = 20	4 × 6 = 24	0 × 7 = 0	44
Queries	4 × 3 = 12	0 × 4 = 0	1 × 6 = 6	18
External Files	0 × 5 = 0	1 × 7 = 7	1 × 10 = 10	17
Internal Files	2 × 7 = 14	1 × 10 = 10	1 × 15 = 15	39
Transformations	7 × 4 = 28	10 × 4 = 40	15 × 10 = 150	218
Transitions	—	10 × 10 = 100	—	100
			Total 3D UFC	466

Using the same adjustment factor to compute SLOC and selecting the C programming language as before, we obtain

SLOC = 466 × 150

or

SLOC = 69,900, or 69.9 KLOC

Note the significant difference between this result and the earlier one. Even this simple example demonstrates how challenging real-time systems can be to estimate and build.

Pseudocode-Based Estimation Method

As you have seen, a key element of the previously presented methods and others is obtaining a reasonable estimate of the number of lines of source code. One scheme for doing this that I have used in an informal way is to develop a design and accompanying pseudocode as early in the software project as is practicable. After a very short period of experimentation, you can create a conversion table of pseudocode statements to actual statements in the language to be used. For example, an *IF-THEN-ELSE* in the pseudocode might convert to four lines in the target language, simple computations might convert on a one-to-one basis, *DO WHILE* might convert to six lines, and so forth. A simple program was written to convert and account for each function and subroutine in the pseudocoded system. The results were fairly accurate, but, more important, they gave us insight into the overall amount of code we would have to deal with and the relative size (we already obtained this from the pseudocode) of each routine.

The key advantage of using this approach is that there is little or nothing to learn, no software tool to purchase, and no delays. If your team finds itself in the same situation, you might try this or something similar.

Cost and Schedule Estimating: An Advisory

So far, I have described several methods you and your team could employ to obtain cost and schedule estimates. Each method is more or less appropriate for you, your team, and the project you are estimating. If you were to stop right here, you might feel compelled to adopt one method or another. I have found the most effective means of assessing cost and schedule is to use more than one method followed by a "sanity check" (that is, asking if the results make sense). This approach gives the team a range of values. The real result of the effort will most likely fall somewhere between the extremes, but most often the development team tends to err on the side of safety, so estimates tend to be biased toward the high side. Besides, reestimating occurs throughout the project lifecycle.

You have already seen how a relatively small change in an assumption or judgment call on a parameter can have a high impact on an estimate. In the next section, I describe a formulated means of computing the estimate variability based on the initial estimate and the expected number of changes.

Constructive Cost Model

The Constructive Cost Model (COCOMO) is a very popular method but might not be the most widely used one. Its original development (COCOMO I) was based on 63 projects and a large volume of data from a broad range of sources (Boehm, 1981). It has been refined recently and repackaged as COCOMO II (see the section titled "COCOMO II" later in this chapter), which reflects many years of use and experiences with COCOMO as well as many refinements. In COCOMO II, three levels for the COCOMO model were proposed: basic, intermediate, and detailed. We focus on the basic level. The others are all well documented in the referenced text.

COCOMO is based on two equations:

$MM = a * KDSI * b$

And

$TDEV = c * MM * d$

Where

MM = the estimated effort in person-months

KDSI = thousands of deliverable source instructions (excluding test drivers and other nondeliverable code)

TDEV = development time in person-months

Coefficients *a*, *b*, and *c* are set values. Coefficients *a*, *b*, *c*, and *d* are based on the mode of development. The values of these coefficients are presented in Tables 7-16 and 7-17.

TABLE 7-16 Coefficients Used in COCOMO

Development Mode	Value of *a*	Value of *b*	Value of *c*	Value of *d*
Organic	3.2	1.05	2.5	0.38
Semidetached	3.0	1.12	2.5	0.35
Embedded	2.8	1.20	2.5	0.32

Table 7-17 Descriptions of Classification Terms Under COCOMO

Development Mode	Description
Organic	The project involves known problems (for example, inventory control); uses small teams in a stable environment.
Semidetached	Project involves broader, mixed range of knowledge and experience on project team(s) with tighter constraints than organic projects but not as tight or demanding as embedded projects.
Embedded	Development occurs under tight constraints; project is very complex with high likelihood of requirements changes (for example, device drivers, some defense systems, development for new hardware, fixed release date).

The process involved in using COCOMO consists of four steps:

1. Establish the project mode (that is, organic, semidetached, or embedded).
2. Estimate the size of the project in KDSI (that is, the "nominal" effort estimate).
3. Compute the project effort estimate (MM).
4. Compute the project development time (TDEV).

For example, if we estimate the size of a device driver (an embedded project) at 5 KDSI,

*MM = 2.8 * 5 * 1.20 = 16.8 person-months*

*TDEV = 2.5 * 16.8 * .32 = 13.44 months*

In this example, the original COCOMO method estimates that it will take 1+ persons almost 14 months to produce the driver. For those of you who have written driver software and are smirking right now, the flow time you experienced might have been considerably shorter or longer because a significant portion of the code was adapted from earlier drivers or major portions of the driver had to be written from scratch. Code reuse can significantly reduce development if the previously developed code is worth reusing. COCOMO II addresses this and more.

COCOMO II

The COCOMO II method (Boehm et al., 1995) is more than just a refinement of the original COCOMO model (Boehm, 1981). It represents a rethinking of the problem of software project estimation together with an upgrade to reflect developments that have occurred in software engineering over the last 20 years. One concept this method is built on has been around for a couple of millennia: The closer you get to the end of a journey (or project), the more accurate will be the prediction of your arrival time (or total project cost).

COCOMO II treats the problem in three stages:

- Application composition model
- Early design model
- Postarchitecture model

This approach employs parametric equations. The earliest form of this type of equation might have been used during the Industrial Revolution. The problem engineers had then was similar to the problem COCOMO II's architects are trying to solve now. At the start of the Industrial Revolution, engineers found out very quickly that they could neither explain in detail what was going on inside a steam engine nor explain the physics of what was happening. What we now know is that, among other things, free radicals exist in a steam engine and they recombine and decompose in a dynamic way, making prediction and explanation impossible. The plumes from today's booster rockets exhibit many of the same impossible characteristics.

Following is the approach that was used to create parametric equations of the form

Desired Value = aX + bY + cZ + dT + . . .

That is, to string together a set of constants (represented by *X*, *Y*, and *Z*) and to multiply them by scaling factors (represented by *a*, *b*, and *c*). At first, this approach yielded poor results, but over time, the measurements became better, the scaling factors adjusted, and the constants revised. For example, the concept of enthalpy, which is a man-made factor, proved useful in many industries and resulted from such a formulation.

A major difference between the type of work done by engineers working on steam engines and that of COCOMO II is that software organizations are not nearly as stable and predictable as the physics and chemistry that govern what goes on inside a device like a steam engine. Similar to the physical world, the developers of the COCOMO II method have collected data from a wide range of software projects, analyzed and characterized the projects, and established categorizations and guidelines for developing estimates.

In this discussion of COCOMO II, I focus on development effort estimating and development schedule estimating because these are the predominant concerns among software project managers. Much of this discussion is adapted from Putnam (1978), which contains additional details and discussions of other aspects of COCOMO II related to estimating.

Estimating Development Effort as a Two-Phase Process

Estimating takes place throughout the development effort. It takes two distinct but necessary forms over time: initial and detailed, as shown in Figure 7-5 and Figure 7-6. These correspond to the early and architectural stages in COCOMO II. The processes described here could be used with other estimating techniques.

- **Initial planning estimate**   Figure 7-5 describes this process graphically. Each of the six steps in the process is detailed as follows:
  - ❑ Identify software activities and components
    - ◆ Review product requirements
    - ◆ Create a Work Breakdown Structure (WBS), and analyze it
    - ◆ Review and understand project goals and constraints (such as schedule, other limitations)
  - ❑ Estimate software size
    - ◆ Time permitting, decompose product structure
    - ◆ Using the guidelines discussed in the next section, create source lines of code (SLOC) estimates for
      - ❑ New components
      - ❑ Adapted/reused components specifying adaptation parameters
    - ◆ Estimate SLOC with most likely, maximum, minimum values
  - ❑ Set model cost parameters
    - ◆ Set scale factors, effort adjustment factors
    - ◆ Identify unfavorable cost driver parameters for improvement

❑ Generate probability distribution of schedules and costsq

  ◆ Using a software tool or manual computations, develop set of efforts, schedules, and associated achievement probabilities

  ◆ Temper the preceding work with project-imposed constraints

❑ Review options versus constraints and "what-if" scenarios

  ◆ Consider schedule versus cost tradeoffs, cuts in features, different personnel mixes, and other ways to achieve a mix that works

  ◆ Review alternatives with stakeholders

  ◆ Select baseline approach

❑ Add other efforts as a percentage of development effort

  ◆ Use WBS as checklist; examples of other costs:

    ❑ System requirements analysis

    ❑ Field testing

    ❑ Maintenance

    ❑ COTS components

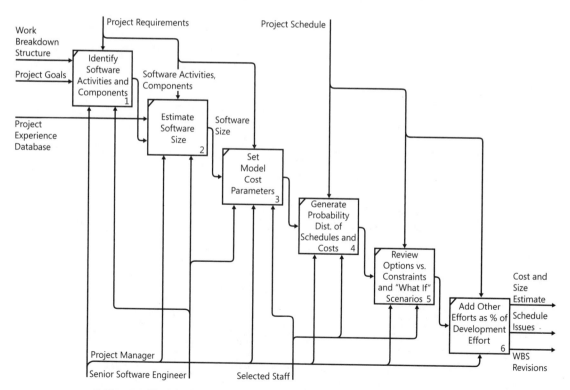

FIGURE 7-5 The initial estimating process.

- **Detailed planning estimate**   Figure 7-6 describes this process graphically. Each of the five steps in the process is detailed as follows:

  - ❏ Estimate the size of each component

    - ◆ Refine earlier size estimate with current information

    - ◆ Assign SLOC estimates for

      - ❏ New components

      - ❏ Adapted/reused components specifying adaptation parameters

    - ◆ Estimate SLOC with most likely, maximum, minimum values

  - ❏ Set model cost driver parameters

    - ◆ Refine information using the latest data

    - ◆ Where unfavorable ratings exist, consider alternatives in approach that will improve the situation

  - ❏ Generate probability distribution of possible schedules and costs

    - ◆ Lay out component development timelines within master plan

    - ◆ Use nominal schedules initially

  - ❏ Fill in other activities in the master plan, noting conflicts

    - ◆ Lay out system integration patterns, dependencies

    - ◆ Estimate other WBS activities as a percentage of development cost

    - ◆ Compare with initial estimate

    - ◆ Identify conflicts and tradeoffs to resolve

  - ❏ Converge on final plan and prepare estimation package

    - ◆ Revise estimates and resolve conflicts

    - ◆ Review options with stakeholders

    - ◆ If required, obtain management approval for estimation package

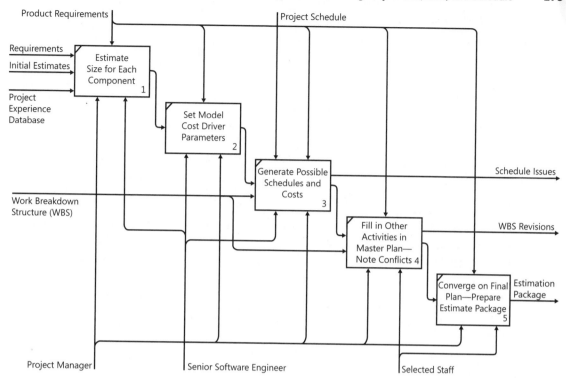

FIGURE 7-6 The detailed estimation process.

Development Effort Estimates

Software development effort in COCOMO II (referred to herein as *development effort*) is es-timated in person-months. A person-month is one person working for 1 month. As with the standard in the industry, the person-month estimates exclude weekends, holidays, vacations, and personal time off. In addition, COCOMO II uses a separate formula to compute the flow time for the project. (See the section titled "Development Schedule Estimates" later in this chapter.) For example, a project might be estimated to require 120 person-months using the development effort estimation formula and requiring 12 months flow time to complete using the development schedule estimate, implying that approximately 10 people are required for that effort.

The development estimate formula is the following equation:

$$PM_{nominal} = A \times (Size)^B$$

Where

PM = the required effort in person-months

A = a constant

B = a scale factor

$Size$ = estimated size of the project in KSLOC (thousands of source lines of code)

Just to make sure you understand what a source line of code (SLOC) is, look at a classification scheme presented by some of the authors of COCOMO II (Banker and Kemerer, 1989; Putnam, 1978). Tables 7-18 through 7-20 list the categories and whether or not lines of source in those categories are counted as part of SLOC.

TABLE 7-18 Counting Conventions Used by Statement Type in COCOMO I

Program Statement Type	Order of Precedence	Include	Exclude
Executable	1	X	
Nonexecutable			
Declarations	2	X	
Compiler directives	3	X	X
Comments			
On their own lines	4		X
On lines with source code	5		X
Banners and nonblank spaces	6		X
Blank (empty) comments	7		X
Blank lines	8		X

Note When a line or statement contains more than one type of source statement, classify it at the highest precedence level present in that line.

TABLE 7-19 **Production Conventions for Counting SLOC in COCOMO II**

How Produced	Include	Exclude
Programmed	X	
Generated using a source code generator		X
Converted with automated translators	X	
Copied or reused without change	X	
Modified	X	
Removed		X

TABLE 7-20 **Source Line Origin Conventions Used in COCOMO II**

Origin of the source lines	Include	Exclude
New work, no prior existence	X	
Prior work, taken from:		
A previous version, build, or release	X	
Commercial off-the-shelf software (COTS) other than libraries		X
Government-furnished software (GFS) other than reuse libraries		X
Another product		X
A vendor-supplied language support library (unmodified)		X
A vendor-supplied operating system or utility (unmodified)		X
A local or modified language support library or operating system		X
Other commercial library		X
A reuse library (software designed for reuse)	X	
Other software component or library	X	

A Simple Example

Continuing the example used in the function point discussion earlier, we can employ the same software tool (Kemerer, 1993) to compute a project estimate using COCOMO II. The results are presented in Figure 7-7. Note that these results have not been adjusted using any of the various estimate adjustments that are part of COCOMO II. Adjustments are discussed in the next section.

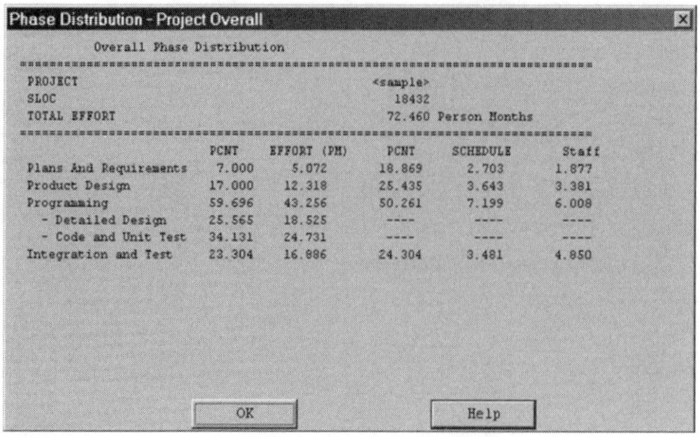

```
┌─ Phase Distribution - Project Overall ─────────────────────────────────[X]─┐
│          Overall Phase Distribution                                         │
│ ===========================================================================│
│  PROJECT                                    <sample>                        │
│  SLOC                                        18432                          │
│  TOTAL EFFORT                                72.460 Person Months           │
│ ===========================================================================│
│                         PCNT    EFFORT (PM)   PCNT    SCHEDULE    Staff      │
│  Plans And Requirements  7.000     5.072     18.869    2.703     1.877       │
│  Product Design         17.000    12.318     25.435    3.643     3.381       │
│  Programming            59.696    43.256     50.261    7.199     6.009       │
│   - Detailed Design     25.565    18.525      ----      ----      ----       │
│   - Code and Unit Test  34.131    24.731      ----      ----      ----       │
│  Integration and Test   23.304    16.886     24.304    3.481     4.850       │
│                                                                             │
│                                                                             │
│                                                                             │
│                                                                             │
│                                                                             │
│              ┌──────────┐              ┌──────────┐                         │
│              │    OK    │              │   Help   │                         │
│              └──────────┘              └──────────┘                         │
└─────────────────────────────────────────────────────────────────────────┘
```

FIGURE 7-7 COCOMO II estimate for the example.

In this example, the total effort has been estimated at about 72.460 person-months.

Estimate Adjustments in COCOMO II

The COCOMO II method includes several adjustments to the basic computation of PM as shown in Figure 7-7. The five adjustments, breakage, reuse, reengineering, applications maintenance, and person-month, were developed to address issues related to each of these factors, which can affect the effort required to complete a software project.

The details of the parametric equations and the values used to evaluate them are presented in the sections that follow.

- **Adjustment for breakage**   Some amount of code will be developed but not used (*breakage*). Breakage can affect estimates but is not incorporated into the Applications Composition model.

- **Reuse adjustment**   For more than a decade, firms have been pressing developers to reuse modules that already exist. The advantages of this include the fact that existing code, if it is being used, is more mature and less likely to contain significant errors than newly created code is. The disadvantages include the fact that the developers of the new system include the developer(s) who developed much of the code to be reused. Hence, there will be some form of learning curve for those new to the existing code and, to a lesser extent, those familiar with the code who must adapt it. This learning effort could be significant. COCOMO II addresses this issue in four ways:

  - **The software understanding increment (SU)**   You can evaluate the SU by using the valuations in Table 7-21. The better, more cohesive, and understandable the code to be reused, the less the penalty for reusing it.

TABLE 7-21 Valuations for the Software Understanding Increment

Characteristic	Very Low	Low	Nominal	High	Very High
Structure	Very low cohesion, high coupling, spaghetti code	Low cohesion, high coupling	Reasonably well structured with some weak areas	High cohesion, low coupling	Strong modularity, information hiding in data and control structures
Application clarity	No match between program and application	Some correlation between program and application	Moderate correlation between program and application	Good correlation between program and application	Clear match between program and application
Self-descriptiveness	Obscure code, documentation missing or obsolete	Some code comments and headers, some useful documentation	Moderate level of code commentary, headers, documentation	Good code commentary, headers, useful documentation but some weak areas	Self-descriptive code, documentation is current, well-organized containing design rationale
SU increment to equivalent source lines of code (ESLOC)	50	40	30	20	10

❑ **Assessment and assimilation increment (AA)**   This increment adjusts the estimate to account for the appropriateness of the reused module to the application it is being incorporated into. You can calculate the values for this increment by using the information in Table 7-22.

TABLE 7-22 Assessment and Assimilation Increment Valuation

AA Increment	Level of AA Effort
0	None
2	Basic module search and documentation
4	Some module test and evaluation (T & E), documentation
6	Considerable module T & E, documentation
8	Extensive module T & E, documentation

❑ **Programmer's relative unfamiliarity with the software (UNFM)**   This parameter accounts for the unfamiliarity that a programmer might have with the software to be reused. It is used to multiply the existing software understanding (SU) factor. Values for UNFM are shown in Table 7-23.

TABLE 7-23 **Relative Unfamiliarity with the Software**

UNFM Increment	Level of Unfamiliarity
0.0	Completely familiar
0.2	Mostly familiar
0.4	Somewhat familiar
0.6	Considerably familiar
0.8	Mostly unfamiliar
1.0	Completely unfamiliar

❑ **Adaptation adjustment factor (AAF)**   This is a measure of the amount of modification of the existing software that will be necessary. AAF is a function of three factors:

DM   The percent design modified factor. Although this is subjective, it represents the percentage of the design of the existing code that will have to be modified to accommodate the new application.

CM   This is the percentage of the existing code that must be modified to accommodate the new application.

IM   This is the percentage of effort required to integrate the existing code into the application in comparison with what would be typically expected.

AAF is computed using the following equation:

AAF = 0.4(DM) + 0.3(CM) + 0.3(IM)

Finally, this gives us all the elements we need to compute equivalent source lines of code (ESLOC) using AAF as a guide.

If the value for AAF using the preceding equation is ≤ 0.5, we use

$$ESLOC = \frac{ASLOC\left[AA + AAF\left(1 + 0.02(SU)(UNFM)\right)\right]}{100}$$

If the value for AAF using the preceding equation is > 0.5, we use

$$ESLOC = \frac{ASLOC\left[AA + AAF + (SU)(UNFM)\right]}{100}$$

where ASLOC represents the total number of lines of code to be adapted.

ESLOC must be divided by 1,000 to compute KESLOC, as required when using COCOMO II.

- **Reengineering adjustment** COCOMO II addresses the issue of reengineering through either automatic translation or more labor-intensive means. The parameter AT is introduced to address automatic translation of code from one environment or language to another. This produces an additional parameter called ATPROD, which measures the level of automation involved in the reengineering effort. The nominal amount of effort PM is computed in such cases using the following equation:

$$PM_{nominal} = A \times (Size)_B + \left[\frac{ASLOC\left(\frac{AT}{100}\right)}{ATPROD} \right]$$

where *A*, ASLOC, Size, and *B* are as previously discussed and the value of AT is determined by Table 7-24.

TABLE 7-24 AT Values for Reengineering Targets

Reengineering target	AT value (% automation)
Batch processing	96%
Batch with SORT	90%
Batch with DBMS	88%
Batch, SORT, DBMS	82%
Interactive	50%

- **Applications maintenance** COCOMO II uses a threshold level of 20 percent to determine whether the effort that is going forward is maintenance or new development. That is, if the effort adds or changes 20 percent or less of the existing or "base" code. The basic formula is

$$(Size)_M = \left[(BaseCodeSize) \times MCF \right] \times MAF$$

The parameter MCF represents the maintenance change factor. It is computed using the following equation:

$$MCF = \frac{SizeAdded + SizeModified}{BaseCodeSize}$$

The following equation is used when the amount of code that was added to the base code or modified in the base code is known. Code that was removed is not counted.

$$(Size)_M = (SizeAdded + SizeModified) \times MAF$$

MAF represents the maintenance adjustment factor and is computed using the following equation:

$$MAF = 1 + \left(\frac{SU}{100} \times UNFM \right)$$

By using the preceding equations, we can compute the COCOMO II postarchitecture development model:

$$PM_M = A \times (Size_M)^B \times \prod_{i=1}^{17} EM_i$$

- **Adjusting person-months**   The amount of effort on a project is subject to many factors. In COCOMO II, 17 effort multipliers are involved. The process is first to compute the nominal effort and then to adjust this value by using the effort multipliers. There are two sets of effort multipliers. The first set is associated with the early design model. There are seven members of this set. The second set consists of 17 different multipliers and is associated with the postarchitecture model. The general form of the equation is as follows:

$$PM_{adjusted} = PM_{nominal} \times \prod_{i} EM_i$$

As described earlier, depending on the model used (pre- or postarchitectural model), the range for i in the preceding equation is either 7 or 17, respectively.

Development Schedule Estimates

The development schedule in calendar months is measured from the point when the product's requirements reach baseline status to the point in the project when the product is certified as meeting all requirements.

The estimated schedule is computed using the following equation:

$$TDEV = \left[3.0 \times PM^{(0.33+0.2\times(B-1.01))}\right] \times \frac{SCED\%}{100}$$

Where PM represents the estimated person-months required without the application of the SCED effort multiplier, and B represents the project scale factors (discussed in the next several sections).

Computing COCOMO II Scaling Factors

The variable B that appears in the preceding equation is computed using the following equation:

$$B = 1.01 + 0.01 \times \sum W_i$$

Where

B = scale factor

w_i = weighting factor associated with rating level

Table 7-25 presents the five scaling factors for COCOMO II early design and postarchitecture modes. Details of how to evaluate each scaling factor are presented in the subsections that follow.

TABLE 7-25 **Scaling Factors Used to Compute *B* in the TDEV Equation**

Weighting Factors (*W*)	Very Low	Low	Nominal	High	Very High	Extra High
PREC	Thoroughly unprecedented	Largely unprecedented	Somewhat unprecedented	Generally familiar	Largely familiar	Thoroughly familiar
FLEX	Rigorous	Occasionally relaxed	Some relaxation	Generally conforms	Some conformity	General goals
RESL	Little (20 percent)	Some (40 percent)	Often (60 percent)	Generally (75 percent)	Mostly (90 percent)	Full (100 percent)
TEAM	Very difficult interactions	Some difficult interactions	Basically cooperative interactions	Largely cooperative	Highly cooperative	Seamless interactions
PMAT	See Notes	See Notes	See Notes	See Notes	See Notes	See Notes

Notes: RESL represents % significant module interfaces specified; % significant risk eliminated.
PMAT is the weighted average of Yes answers to the CMM Maturity Questionnaire.

- **Precedentedness (PREC) and development flexibility (FLEX)**   These scale factors are provided to recognize differences among the three modes of the original COCOMO model (organic, semidetached, and embedded). Table 7-26 and Table 7-27 provide additional guidance for evaluating these parameters.

TABLE 7-26 **Details of the PREC Factor in COCOMO II**

Feature	Very Low	Nominal/High	Extra High
Organizational understanding of product objectives	General	Considerable	Thorough
Experience in working with related software systems	Moderate	Considerable	Extensive
Concurrent development of associated new hardware and operational procedures	Extensive	Moderate	Some
Need for innovative data processing architectures, algorithms	Considerable	Some	Minimal

TABLE 7-27 **Details of the FLEX Factor in COCOMO II**

Feature	Very Low	Nominal/High	Extra High
Need for software conformance with preestablished requirements	Full	Considerable	Basic
Need for software conformance with external interface specifications	Full	Considerable	Basic

- **Architecture/risk resolution (RESL)**   This factor represents the weighted average of subjective evaluation of the listed characteristics. Components of RESL rating are listed in Table 7-28.

TABLE 7-28 Details of the RESL Factor in COCOMO II

Characteristic	Very Low	Low	Nominal	High	Very High	Extra High
Risk management plan (RMP)identifies all critical risk items; establishes milestones for resolving them by preliminary design review (PDR)	None	Little	Some	Generally	Mostly	Fully
Schedule, budget, and internal milestones through PDR are compatible with the RMP	None	Little	Some	Generally	Mostly	Fully
Percentage of development schedule devoted to establishing architecture, given general product objectives	Little (20%)	Some (40%)	Often (60%)	Generally (75%)	Mostly (90%)	Full (100%)
Percentage of required top software architects available to project	20	40	60	80	100	120
Tool support available for resolving risk items, developing and verifying architectural specifications	None	Little	Some	Generally	Mostly	Fully
Level of uncertainty in key architecture drivers: mission, user interface, COTS, hardware, technology, performance	Extreme	Significant	Considerable	Some	Little	Very Little
Number and criticality of risk items	> 10 Critical	5–10 Critical	2–4 Critical	1 Critical	> 5 Noncritical	< 5 Noncritical

- **Team cohesion (TEAM)**   This scale factor is intended to address the characteristics and cohesiveness of the project stakeholders. These include the developers, the users, the maintainers, and others who are involved in the creation, maintenance, and use of the system. Problems in this area can cause serious harm to the project. Problems include different value systems, different objectives, lack of or wide variations in experience, and so forth. Components of the TEAM rating are listed in Table 7-29.

TABLE 7-29 **Details of the TEAM Factor in COCOMO II**

Characteristic	Very Low	Low	Nominal	High	Very High	Extra High
Consistency of stakeholder objectives and cultures	Little	Some	Basic	Considerable	Strong	Full
Ability, willingness of stakeholders to accommodate other stakeholders' objectives	Little	Some	Basic	Considerable	Strong	Full
Experience of stakeholders operating as a team	None	Little	Little	Basic	Considerable	Extensive
Stakeholder team building to achieve shared vision and commitments	None	Little	Little	Basic	Considerable	Extensive

- **Process maturity (PMAT)**   The evaluation of PMAT is based on the Software Engineering Institute's Capability Maturity Model (CMM). The CMM rating that the organization has at the start of the project is used in this evaluation. Two approaches are used in evaluating PMAT:

  □ **Overall maturity level**   Assessment of the development team's CMM level using details of the scheme are shown in Table 7-30.

    TABLE 7-30 **Simplified Category Descriptions for CMM**

CMM Level	Characterized By
1	Ad hoc development, chaotic development
2	Repeatable outcomes
3	Defined processes
4	Managed development process
5	Optimizing processes, results

  □ **Key process areas**   This assessment is based on the Software Engineering Institute's 18 key process areas (KPAs) documented in Paulk and associates (Paulk, Curtis, et al., 1993; Paulk, Weber, et al., 1993). PMAT is evaluated by assigning a percentage of compliance with each KPA. The approach used is similar to the multipoint Likert scale (Likert and Likert, 1976). Table 7-31 lists the process areas and their corresponding evaluation levels. Table 7-32 presents a set of guidelines for determining which level is appropriate for the organization.

TABLE 7-31 Key Process Areas (KPAs) Used in PMAT Evaluation

Key Process Area	Almost Always	Often	About Half	On Occasion	Rarely	Does Not Apply	Don't Know
Requirements Management							
Software Project Planning							
Software Project Tracking and Oversight							
Software Subcontract Management							
Software Quality Assurance							
Software Configuration Management							
Organization Process Focus							
Organization Process Definition							
Training Program							
Integrated Software Management							
Software Product Engineering							
Intergroup Coordination							
Peer Reviews							
Quantitative Process Management							
Software Quality Management							
Defect Prevention							
Technology Change Management							
Process Change Management							

TABLE 7-32 Guidelines for PMAT Evaluation of Key Process Areas (KPAs)

Checking guidelines for evaluating key process areas

Almost Always

When the goals are consistently achieved and are well established in standard operating procedures (that is, more than 90 percent of the time)

Frequently

When the goals are achieved relatively often but sometimes are omitted under difficult circumstances (that is, about 60 to 90 percent of the time)

About Half

When the goals are achieved about half the time (that is, 40 to 60 percent of the time)

Occasionally

When the goals are sometimes achieved, but less often (that is, 10 to 40 percent of the time)

Rarely

When the goals are rarely achieved (that is, less than 10 percent of the time)

Does Not Apply

When the KPA does not apply to this particular situation

Don't Know

When uncertain regarding how to respond to the KPA

PMAT is actually calculated using the following formula, with all KPAs weighted equally:

$$PMAT = 5 - \left[\sum_{i=1}^{18} \frac{KPA\,\%_i}{100} \times \frac{5}{18} \right]$$

Another Simple Example

A simple demonstration of how COCOMO II can be applied uses the following system development situation. We have a system architecture and a plan to implement it in three builds of similar size. The customer would like the system built in a total of 24 months flow time. We have already developed the scale factors listed in Table 7-33 and a preliminary size estimate of 78,750, or 78.750 KSLOC. Table 7-34 shows the effort, duration, and staffing levels we compute. The estimating model predicts that the desired project duration of 24 months is not to be. Staffing levels, feature reduction, changing the content of each build, the type of staff, and other factors could all be reviewed to reduce the estimated schedule if schedule is a primary driver.

TABLE 7-33 Scale Factor Evaluation for Example

COCOMO II Scale Factor	Level/Rating
Precedentedness	Generally familiar
Development flexibility	General conformity
Architecture/risk resolution	Some (40 percent)
Team cohesion	Largely cooperative
Process maturity	SEI CMM level 2

Table 7-34 Schedule Estimating Data for Example

Phase	Effort (Person-Months)	Duration (Months)	Staff level (Persons/FTEs)
RQ—Requirements	23.1	4.8	4.9
PD—Product Design	56.1	6.0	9.3
DD—Detailed Design	80.9	4.5	17.8
CT—Code and Unit Test	105.7	5.9	17.9
IT—Integration and Testing	87.3	6.2	14.0
Total (RQ + PD + DD + CT + IT)	353.2	27.4	63.9

The Cost Variance Method

One thing that you can count on in a software project is that the requirements will change. There are many reasons for this, including changes in the marketplace or the competition, or simply that the customer has rethought the content of the product. One factor not considered by most of the estimation schemes we have discussed is the cost, occurrence, and likelihood of requirements changes.

An approach for computing cost variance used in the construction industry can help us compute an approximate value for the variance in cost estimate caused by changes, delays, and bug fixing (Touran, 2003). First, we need to understand that, even with little or no change from the original estimate, there will be some degree of uncertainty in our estimates for total project cost. Regardless of how project cost is estimated, most successful software project managers tend to pad the estimate. This padding of estimates is politely referred to as "contingency planning." That is, the estimate includes money and, often, schedule flow time to accommodate unforeseen difficulties. On a more personal scale, this is similar to planning a 2-week vacation to Spain and figuring out the cost of airfare, lodging, transportation, food, sightseeing, all that valuable tourist stuff (junk) you have to buy, and so forth, all based on the best available information. Although the numbers you use might be accurate, experienced travelers always add in some amount for the unexpected (such as that 10-lb. pewter statuette you absolutely have to have that ends up lengthening one of your arms while you haul it around the country).

The method for estimating the cost variability caused by changes relies on assumptions about your project as well as experience with this industry group or specific client. The term *project*, as used in this context, includes efforts that create some altogether new product as well as efforts that create a new functionality set for clients.

The steps in the cost variance process are described here:

1. Determine the estimated cost of the project without any contingency costs. For example, $100,000.

2. Estimate the project duration excluding any contingency flow time. For example, 12 months.

3. Estimate the number of changes per unit time. For example, 10 changes per month from the original requirements statement. If you are dealing with a client you have dealt with before, this will be easier than for a first-time client. However, if you are working in a specific industry group (such as banking), you should have a reasonable idea of how much change will occur. Remember, this is an estimate, not an exact measurement.

4. Estimate the average cost of a change as a portion of the original estimate. For example, if the last project with this client or industry group experienced an increase in the cost from $100,000 to $200,000 and there were 50 changes, the average cost of a change was $2,000. Thus, the fraction of the total project cost represented by the average change was 0.02 of the original total estimated cost. This is even though some changes were, essentially, free whereas others were quite expensive. *Average* is the key word here.

Some other assumptions are involved in the use of the equations. One assumption is that the changes are correlated with a correlation coefficient representing the relative range of the cost of the change or error correction. For example, as mentioned in step 4 some changes are nearly free, while others can be complex and expensive. So assigning a value of 1 monetary unit (for example, a dollar or a euro) to one end of the spectrum and a value of 1,000 monetary units for complex changes or complicated error corrections yields a variability range of 1,000. This seems reasonable in the software arena because so much of the code is strongly linked so that errors in one portion of the code often lead to additional errors elsewhere.

The formula used to compute the cost variance (CV) from the original estimate is the following:

$$CV = \frac{n^2 \, f_c^2 \, \mu_c^2}{C^2}$$

Where

n = number of changes that occur during the project

f_c = coefficient of variation of cost of change (= 1.0)

μ = the average change cost as a decimal (for example, 0.01)

C = original project cost estimate

Setting f_c equal to 1,000 addresses the fact that we are using an average value for the cost of changes, and this means that there will be as much as a 1,000 to 1 variance in change costs. Note that the variance coefficient represents the ratio of the highest-cost change to the lowest. If your experience with a certain type of software, industry, or client indicates a higher or lower ratio, use it.

Let's examine an actual project. I was responsible for the technology development and project management of a system that was used for business process reengineering. It was to be licensed to a worldwide consulting firm. It was known at the outset that this product was directed at an evolving market, so there would be a large number of changes. Because the system was already in use in other venues and was being adapted for this one, we did not expect that there would be a large number of bugs to be corrected. At the time, we were not aware of the work described in this section and, in retrospect, made some unrealistic assumptions regarding the error content of the code. Although the code was well structured, organized, designed, and thoroughly tested, the new use of the code actually caused it to be exercised in a domain for which it was not originally intended. The approximate figures that we had for that effort are shown in Table 7-35.

TABLE 7-35 Values Taken from an Actual Project

Variable	Value
C	Original cost estimate, $50,000
	The number of changes over the course of the project, 1,000
n	
f_c	Coefficient of variance of cost of change, 1,000 (all changes, on average, vary over a range of 1 to 1,000)
μ	Average change cost, approximately $2,500, equating to a value for this variable of 0.05

Note that these figures are given in hindsight and would have been much lower if we had developed them at the beginning of the project. A handicapping factor was that we had never worked with this client before and did not have extensive knowledge of the domain for which this system was being developed. If we use these values and employ the preceding equation, and substitute the values from Table 7-11 into the previous equation, we obtain:

$$CV = [(1,000)^2(1,000)^2(0.05)^2] / (50,000)^2$$

Or

$$CV = 4$$

What this indicates is that the project could have ended up costing up to four times as much as originally estimated (approximately $222,000). This is remarkably close to what the overrun was. However, the main point here is not how accurate this approach is but that it focuses on the issue of uncertainty and risk rather than the more deterministic cost estimation approaches.

We actually need to approach cost estimation in three steps, not one:

1. Use one or more cost estimation schemes to arrive at a reasonable estimate or range of costs for the project.

2. Apply the Cost Variance Method (CVM) to obtain an estimate for the amount of cost variability that might occur in the project.

3. Track changes and costs for future reference.

Some criticisms of and comments about CVM are presented in Table 7-36. Keep in mind that this method gives us insight into the reliability of our estimate. Obviously, if the CVM factor turns out to be less than 1, our confidence is higher than if it was 2 or more.

TABLE 7-36 Concerns About CVM

Concern	Comment
This approach requires that we foresee how many changes (including bug fixes) we are likely to encounter.	CVM is not very different from other estimating approaches. However, with CVM we can rely on experience with a client or group to improve our estimates.
The cost range of correcting an error is difficult to estimate.	We can develop the needed profiles by collecting the required data.

Summary

Regardless of which project sizing method you use, there are limits to how accurate you can expect it to be. A successful method is one that provides you with an estimate that is in the realm of possibility. Unfortunately, you won't know if a particular method has been successfully used until the project is completed. Also, the use of Commercial Off the Shelf software (COTS) may seem like an easy way to avoid all this purchasing and modifying existing software but the record on this practice is not good (Boehm, 2002). So how can you ensure success in this aspect of project management? Try one or more of the following techniques:

- If possible, forestall committing to hard and fast dates and costs until you and your team at least have a design with enough detail to comprehend what is involved.

- Cost and schedule incrementally. That is, cost and commit to deliver only over a limited comprehensible time frame (2 to 4 weeks maximum). Although this might drive your marketing people crazy, it offers a reliable scheme for meeting commitments.

- Use more than one estimating approach, and then compare results. Results will probably vary widely but should give you a minimum/maximum range in which to work.

Also, collecting and using data regarding the size, complexity, and related issues associated with the software your organization is writing in conjunction with the use of one or more of the estimating methods are a powerful solution to this difficult problem. If your company does not collect and use such data, start doing so with your project. The insights this data provides will pay dividends for years to come, starting with your next project.

References

(Boehm, 1981)   Boehm, B. W. *Software Engineering Economics*. Englewood Cliffs, NJ: Prentice Hall, 1981.

(McConnell, 1996)   McConnell, S. *Rapid Development*. Redmond, WA: Microsoft Press, 1996.

(Deutsch, 2003)   Deutsch, M. "Software Engineer Economics: Estimating Effort and Schedule Using COCOMO II," lecture notes, Texas A & M University, Austin, Texas, 2003.

(Amos, 2004)   Amos, Scott, ed. *Skills and Knowledge of Cost Engineering*, 5th ed. Morgantown, West Virginia: Association for the Advancement of Cost Engineering, 2004.

(Shepperd, 1992)   Shepperd, M. J. *Foundation of Software Measurement*. Hemel Hemstead, UK: Prentice Hall, 1992.

(Walston and Felix, 1977)   Walston, C. E., and C.P. Felix. "A Method of Programming Measurement Estimation," *IBM Systems Journal* **16**(1), pp. 54–73, 1977.

(Banker and Kemerer, 1989)   Banker, R. D., and C.F. Kemerer. "Scale Economics in New Software Development," *IEEE Transactions on Software Engineering* **15**(10), pp. 199–204, 1989.

(Putnam, 1978)   Putnam, L. H. "A General Empirical Solution to the Macro Software Sizing and Estimating Problem," *IEEE Transactions on Software Engineering* **4**(4), pp. 345–361, 1978.

(Kemerer, 1993)   Kemerer, C. F. "An Empirical Validation of Software Cost Estimation Models," *Communications of the ACM* **36**(2), pp. 416-429, 1993.

(University of Southern California, 1999)   University of Southern California. "COCOMOII.199.0," Copyright 1990–1999.

(Gartner Research, 2002)   Gartner Research. *Function Points Can Help Measure Application Size.* Research Note SPA-18-0878, November 19, 2002.

(Whitmire, 1992)   Whitmire, S. A. "3D Function Points: Scientific and Real-Time Extensions to Function Points," Pacific Northwest Software Quality Conference, Seattle, Washington, 1992.

(Peters, 1988)   Peters, L .J. *Advanced Structured Analysis and Design.* Englewood Cliffs, NJ: Prentice Hall, 1988.

(Boehm et al., 1995)   Boehm, B., et al. "An Overview of the COCOMO 2.0 Software Cost Model," Software Technology Conference, Salt Lake City, Utah, April 1995

(Paulk, Curtis, et al., 1993) Paulk, M. C., B. Curtis, M.B. Chrissis, and C.V. Weber. "The Capability Maturity Model for Software," Version 1.1, Report CMU/SEI-93-TR-24, Software Engineering Institute, Carnegie Mellon University, Pittsburgh, Pennsylvania, 1993.

(Paulk, Weber, et al., 1993) Paulk, M. C., C.V. Weber, S. M. Garcia, M.B. Chrissis, and M. Bush. "The Key Practices of the Capability Maturity Model," Version 1.1, Report CMU/SEI-93-TR-25, Software Engineering Institute, Carnegie Mellon University, Pittsburgh, Pennsylvania, 1993.

(Likert and Likert, 1976) Likert, R., and J. G. Likert. *New Ways of Managing Conflict.* New York, NY: McGraw-Hill, 1976.

(Touran, 2003)   Touran, A. "Calculation of Contingency in Construction Projects," *IEEE Transactions on Engineering Management* **50**(2), pp. 135–140, May 2003.

(Boehm, 2002)   Boehm, B. et al, "Risky Business: 7 Myths About Software Engineering that Impact Defense Acquisitions," Program Manager Magazine, Vol. XXXI, No 3, May 2002.

Chapter 8
Tracking the Software Project Plan

A well-designed strategy can overcome poor tactics, but good tactics cannot overcome a poor strategy.

—A military aphorism

Managing a software project is a lot like successfully flying an aircraft—you have to pay attention to more than one instrument, you need to file a flight plan, and you need a pilot to make needed course corrections to ensure that you arrive at your planned destination despite obstacles along the way. The software project manager is a lot like the pilot, and the software development team the crew. In software project management, we can create a project plan, but without day-to-day involvement by the software project manager and feedback from the software development team, it is unlikely that the project will be successful. The project manager's involvement should be proactive. Just as the pilot uses instruments to determine the position and state of health of the aircraft, the software project manager needs to employ instruments to determine the state of health of the software project and the likelihood of its being successful. In both cases, course corrections are needed and occur frequently.

In Chapter 4, "Developing and Maintaining the Project Plan," I discussed how to develop a plan for your project. I also discussed the use of the Work Breakdown Structure (WBS) and a more flow time–oriented layout that employs the Gantt chart. Figure 8-1 presents a simple WBS, and Figure 8-2 presents the same information in Gantt chart format. The incorporation of costs and flow time into the Gantt chart using a software tool such as Microsoft Office Project makes the Gantt chart form far more popular than is using the classic WBS alone. Because direct labor costs combined with overhead, general and administrative expenses, profit, travel costs, hardware costs, and other expenses are included, you can arrive at an overall project cost by using function point analysis (Albrecht and Gaffney, 1983), COCOMO II (Boehm et al., 1995), or other methods.

In this chapter, I present several methods for monitoring the status of your project in terms of evaluating what needs to be done if it is behind schedule or over budget. This monitor, adjust, reevaluate activity goes on throughout the life of the project and is intended to ensure a successful outcome.

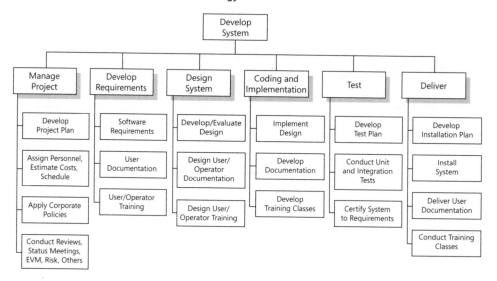

FIGURE 8-1 Example of a project plan in WBS format.

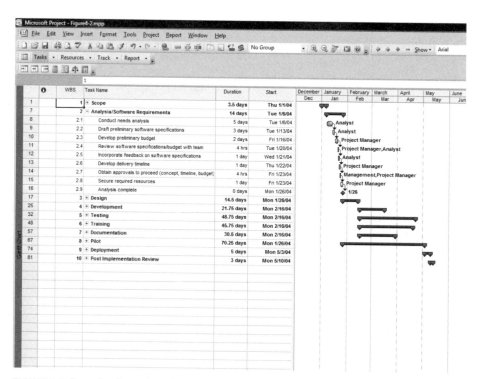

FIGURE 8-2 Example of a project plan in Gantt chart format.

Tracking Schemes

After the project starts, you can control costs, control where you focus the efforts of your people, and decide what is purchased. But the calendar is beyond your control. Eventually, the sun will rise on the morning a particular milestone is due whether you have completed the milestone or not. This issue of lack of calendar control is often ignored by software project managers because they are so focused on controlling costs. The more technical project managers are distracted by the details of some parts of the system and can get involved in developing, debugging, or testing at great risk to the project. Often, project managers ignore the calendar until it is too late.

In my consulting engagements for software projects, I commonly hear software project managers comment that because they are halfway through the schedule or have spent half of the planned budget or both, the project must be about 50 percent complete. In fact, as you shall see later in this chapter, that is rarely the case.

Questions that every software project manager must ask continually throughout the life of the project include the following:

- Do I have enough people with the appropriate skills on board or planned in the future to finish on time and on budget, and to meet all requirements? If not, which requirements do we need to forestall and with what skills do we need to supplement the team to get there?

- Is there enough money to finish the project?

- How much of the work have we completed?

- What are the project's problems?

- How much flow time and money is it likely to take to finish the project?

The first issue is one that could be addressed through examination of the current project plan, feedback from your team, and your schedule for engaging additional human resources with the needed skills. The rest of the issues can be effectively addressed using one or more tracking schemes. The most common goal-oriented tracking schemes in use today address some of these items with varying degrees of success. Let's look at a few.

Maximizing Profitability

This strategy involves tracking and controlling costs. Cost and profit are seen as the only keys to success (as in, what good does it do us if we deliver a terrific product but go bankrupt doing it?). Because cost overruns come right out of profit and the company's bottom line, the primary concern here is to prevent them. The problem with this philosophy is that it uses only one variable (money) to assess the status of the project. The underlying assumption appears to be that if you have spent all the money legitimately, the project must be complete. The philosophy is that if you control costs, everything else will take care of itself. As mentioned earlier, just spending the money might not do if for no other reason than that you can't be sure that it is enough money.

Being Task Oriented

The focus of this philosophy is just to get the work done, even if you overrun the budget. This too has some serious issues, not the least of which is corporate profits and manager credibility, plus we can't be sure the task is sufficient.

To see where this philosophy can lead, let's look at an actual project I consulted on that was undertaken by a state agency. The task involved a major revision of five report systems the state uses. As you might expect, these reports were complex. The changes in the reports were necessitated by new state and federal laws. It was estimated by the team that two people working full time could complete the task in about 6 months. Recalling the chart from earlier in this text relating resources, schedule, and scope (see Figure 2-1 in Chapter 2, "Why Is Software So Difficult?"), this project went off on its own into software's Bermuda Triangle. Each week, the two software engineers worked 40 hours but would identify more than 100 hours of new, additional work to do, as shown in Figure 8-3. In other words, more new work was being identified each week than the two software engineers were able to complete. This created an ever-increasing backlog.

Halfway through this effort, I was called in to audit the project, and I estimated this effort could go on for years. One complicating factor was that some of the work the software engineers identified included changes to the underlying system structure, databases, and related matters, all of which had an amplifying effect on the amount of change needed. Because the project manager was preoccupied with cost and schedule, the rapid expansion of scope went unnoticed until it was too late. Portions of that effort did go on for several years but under a new manager with a multiyear plan for the project. The cost overruns had a significant negative impact on that organization's budget and its credibility for years to come.

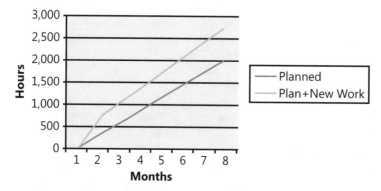

FIGURE 8-3 Example of a runaway effort.

Finding a Better Way

Some project managers have realized that there must be a better way of tracking projects and foreseeing schedule, cost, and work overruns than simply by managing cost and schedule as independent variables. What these professionals recognize is that cost and schedule are not really independent. The relationships among time, cost, and work are linked in a way that enhances the software project manager's ability to assess real progress more accurately by using a concept called Earned Value Management (Project Management Institute, 2004).

Earned Value Management

As mentioned, controlling a project requires consideration of three variables: cost, work, time. A management method that has been used for some years in other engineering fields called Earned Value Management (EVM) has proved effective in helping managers understand what is *really* happening to their projects. EVM does this by analyzing the relationships among those three variables while incorporating a new concept—value.

EVM is about calculating the *value* a project has created from the resources (money, work, and flow time) that were expended at various points in the project. To demonstrate the concept, let's look at a simple project. We will use the WBS and the Gantt chart presented in Figures 8-1 and 8-2. Let's assume that the project has gone forward and we have spent half the budget. Because we have spent half the money, we might expect that half of the work has been done. But that only occurs in an ideal situation, and projects are rarely, if ever, ideal. Figure 8-4 shows the cost versus plan situation graphically. Notice how the Actual cost line rises above the budgeted cost line (Plan) each month.

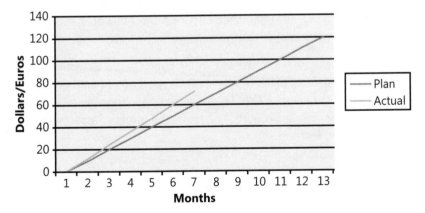

FIGURE 8-4 Plan versus actual EVM example.

At the end of 6 months, we are halfway through the schedule but have overspent the budget by about $12,000. Assuming that the work that was supposed to have been completed during this 6-month period is all finished, in effect we end up spending $72,000 for what we estimated at the start of the project would be worth $60,000. In other words, we did not get the expected value for our money: we expected to get $60,000 in value by spending $60,000 but received $60,000 in value after spending $72,000. An alternative explanation is that we might not have really understood the problem well enough from the start, so our cost estimate was low. But the fact remains: we committed to a budget and accepted it. In real software projects matters are often much worse because we rarely have the details needed to make an accurate budget and schedule, and we most likely did not complete all of the work planned for the first half of the effort. This makes the value proposition (that is, spend more than you actually receive in benefit) even more difficult to accept.

EVM addresses the preceding and other issues through the application of some simple formulas, ratios, and percentages. Its goal is to provide the project manager with a more insightful statement of the health of the project. This assessment implies what the project manager can or must do to get back on track. For example, the Cost Performance Index (CPI) is the ratio of what we expected to spend to what we actually spent at a given point in time during the life of the project, and in the situation just described, it is 60/72, or about 0.83. This means that we are getting only about 83 percent of the value we expected. Looking at it another way, from that point on, we are going to have to find a way to complete the work far enough below budget to realize a CPI of 117 percent or more for the second half of the project.

At this point, to finish the project within budget, we must become much more efficient than we have been so far. This leap in efficiency is highly improbable but not impossible. Hence, the need to monitor these and other metrics continuously from the start to prevent getting so far off the path to success. Early intervention by the project manager and the development team can improve performance relatively easily.

EVM has gotten a bad reputation because of the perception that it introduces excessive overhead. This has been a direct result of the detailed reporting required on most government projects. However, the value of EVM far outweighs these concerns when it is coupled with requirements for less-detailed reports. The terms and formulas associated with EVM are discussed in the following sections.

Using EVM: Terms and Formulas

By using EVM, project managers can scrutinize a project from several different vantage points. In doing so, we hope we can identify the issues, pinpoint the cause of problems, and take corrective action in time to save the project. In the preceding example, the project overran the budget in the first month. A key to successful project management is to track all aspects of the project in an objective and continuous manner to prevent such a situation from happening for so many months. Early tracking of that project would have detected the overrun and indicated that processes had to be fine-tuned to reduce cost going forward. This would have occurred in the first or second month, not the sixth.

The EVM method employs combinations of measurements to evaluate current status and provide insight going forward regarding the outcome of the project. The most commonly accepted set of acronyms for use in EVM is presented in Table 8-1 (Boehm and Guio, 2003). These are presented together with the newest simplified labeling scheme adopted by the Project Management Institute (Project Management Institute, 2004). In this text, I use the newer labeling scheme but present the more traditional one as a convenient cross-reference for other discussions on this topic you might find elsewhere.

TABLE 8-1 Acronyms Used in EVM

Label	Traditional Label	Description	Formula
AC		Actual Cost	None
	ACWP	Actual Cost (of Work Performed)—the actual cost during the project	
BAC	BAC	Budget at Completion—the budgeted final cost	None
EV		Earned Value	None
	BCWP	Budgeted Cost of the Work Performed—the budgeted cost of the work	
PV		Planned Value	None
	BCWS	Budgeted Cost of Work Scheduled—the budgeted cost of work as planned	
CPI	CPI	Cost Performance Index—measures the value received for expenditure	CPI = BCWP / ACWP
CV	CV	Cost Variance—% difference between work done and the cost to do it	CV = (BCWP − ACWP) / BCWP (× 100%)
EAC	EAC	Estimate at Completion—total cost to complete at current efficiency	EAC = BAC / CPI
ETC	ETC	Estimate to Complete—remaining cost to complete at current efficiency	ETC = EAC − ACWP
SPI	SPI	Schedule Performance Index—ratio of days scheduled to days worked	SPI = BCWP / BCWS

Label	Traditional Label	Description	Formula
SV	SV	Schedule Variance—% (ratio) between budgeted schedule and work done	SV = (BCWP – BCWS) / BCWS (× 100%)
TCPIB	TCPIB	To Complete Performance Index (Budget)—efficiency improvement needed to finish within budget	TCPIB = (BAC – BCWP) / (BAC – ACWP)
TCPIP	TCPIP	To Complete Performance Index (Estimate)—current efficiency extended to end of project	TCPIP = (BAC – BCWP) / (EAC – ACWP)

These acronyms and their formulas are discussed in more detail in the following sections. These are broken down into the three categories analyzed under EVM:

- Time

- Money

- Work

Cost-Related Factors

In EVM, currently eight measurements are used to evaluate software projects and their performance:

- **Actual Cost of the Work Performed (AC)**   This measurement is simply the actual cost incurred in performing the work. It is advisable to synchronize this with frequent milestones of a binary nature; that is, the milestone is either complete or not complete—no partial completion status is considered.

- **Budget at Completion (BAC)**   This is the sum of all costs approved for the project. It is the project's budget at the time of the evaluation.

- **Earned Value (EV)**   This is the amount that was budgeted for the work that was actually completed or partially completed (BCWP, or Budgeted Cost of the Work Performed). For example, let's assume that at a certain point in the project plan, three WBS items were to be complete and a fourth one 50 percent complete. If each item had a budgeted value of $10,000 but we only completed two of the first three items and did none of the work on the fourth, BCWP would have a value of $20,000 (that is, 2 × $10,000 + 0% of $10,000). This is where honesty and judgment are important. Because we could make things look better than they actually are, it is vital that software project managers be as accurate as possible in making this and the other assessments in EVM. Remember that the goal is to get as accurate a picture as possible of the state of health of the project, not to deceive ourselves and others.

- **Planned Value (PV)**   This measurement is the sum of the budgeted amounts for work as scheduled. In the preceding example, PV would have a value of $35,000 (that is, (3 × $10,000) + (50% × $10,000)). Notice that the value of PV is strictly based on the budget to the point in time when the measurement is taken—not on what was or was not done.

- **Cost Performance Index (CPI)**   The purpose of this measurement is to gauge how efficiently we are using the money spent on the project by calculating the ratio of the budgeted cost of the work (EV) to the actual cost of the work performed (AC). The formula for CPI is as follows:

$CPI = EV / AC$

Interpretation:

  - ❑ **CPI = 1**   We are right on track.

  - ❑ **CPI > 1**   We are ahead of plan in that actual cost is less than budget.

  - ❑ **CPI < 1**   We are falling behind the plan in that the actual cost of work performed is running higher than what was budgeted.

- **Cost Variance (CV)**   This measurement represents the difference between what was budgeted to do the work and the actual cost to do the work. The formula for CV is as follows:

$CV = (EV - AC) / EV \times 100\%$

Interpretation:

  - ❑ **CV = 0 percent**   We are right on track.

  - ❑ **CV > 0 percent**   Actual Cost < Budgeted Cost. It is possible to create a management reserve.

  - ❑ **CV < 0 percent**   Actual Cost > Budget, and this must be made up for by using the management reserve, increasing the budget, reducing the scope of the work, and so forth.

- **Estimate at Completion (EAC)**   This parameter represents the projected cost of the project upon completion. It achieves this by scaling the budget at completion (BAC) to account for the efficiency with which the project is using resources (CPI). The formula for EAC is as follows:

$EAC = BAC / CPI$

Interpretation:

  - ❑ **EAC = BAC**   The project is on track (that is, CPI = 1).

  - ❑ **EAC < BAC**   The project is running below budget (that is, CPI > 1).

  - ❑ **EAC > BAC**   The project will exceed budget (that is, CPI < 1).

- **Estimate to Complete (ETC)**   ETC estimates the cost remaining to complete the project. Unlike EAC, ETC estimates the cost of getting from this point in the project to completion. The formula for ETC is as follows:

$ETC = EAC - AC$

> **Note** Because EAC is adjusted by CPI, the cost to complete the project will increase if CPI is less than 1.

Interpretation:

- ❑ **ETC = remaining budget**   Project is on track.
- ❑ **ETC > remaining budget**   Project will overrun budgeted amount.
- ❑ **ETC < remaining budget**   Project will come in under budget.

Schedule-Related Factors

EVM includes two parameters related to schedule. One is an efficiency index (similar to CPI, the Cost Performance Index), and the other is related to variance.

- **Schedule Performance Index (SPI)**   Like the other indexes in EVM, this one measures efficiency, in this case, the efficiency with which we are able to perform with respect to the schedule. The formula for SPI is as follows:

$SPI = EV / PV$

Interpretation:

- ❑ **SPI = 1**   The project is right on track.
- ❑ **SPI > 1**   The project is performing above expectations.
- ❑ **SPI < 1**   The project is underperforming and likely to finish late.

- **Schedule Variance (SV)**   This measures the variance between the value of the work actually performed and the budgeted value of the work that was scheduled to be performed. The formula for SV is as follows:

$SV = (EV - PV) / PV \times 100\%$

Interpretation:

- ❑ **SV = 0 percent**   The project is performing as expected.
- ❑ **SV > 0 percent**   The project is performing above expectations.
- ❑ **SV < 0 percent**   The project is performing below expectations with a late finish likely.

Work- and Content-Related Parameters

EVM includes two parameters in this category related to work and money.

■ **To Complete Performance Index within Budget (TCPIB)**   This index computes the budget-related efficiency needed to finish the project within the allocated budget. In other words, it spells out how much more effective we must be in spending money and completing work to finish the project without going over budget. The formula for TCPIB is as follows:

$$TCPIB = (BAC - EV) / (BAC - AC)$$

Interpretation:

❑ **TCPIB = 1**   The money remaining and the work remaining are consistent with each other. By continuing in this mode, we will meet, not exceed, the budget.

❑ **TCPIB > 1**   The efficiency that we must achieve with respect to money and useful work to complete the project within the current budget is above expectations.

❑ **TCPIB < 1**   Our current efficiency at producing useful work for money spent is higher than expectations. This still represents the efficiency that we must achieve to complete the project within budget, but in this case, we could reduce our efficiency and still finish within budget. If we do not reduce efficiency, we will end under budget.

■ **To Complete Performance Index Within Projected Estimate to Complete (TCPIP)**   This work-to-money ratio involves prediction based on the current efficiency remaining constant. This index states how the project will turn out with that efficiency. The formula for TCPIP is as follows:

$$TCPIP = (BAC - EV) / (EAC - AC)$$

Interpretation:

❑ **TCPIP = 1**   Our current efficiency puts us on track to finish on budget.

❑ **TCPIP > 1**   More work is left to be done than we can complete at our current efficiency (that is, converting money into work)—an overbudget finish is likely.

❑ **TCPIP < 1**   Our efficiency is such that there is less work remaining than the money we will consume. An underbudget finish is likely.

Summary of EVM Factors

A summary of the implications of each of the EVM parameters is presented in Table 8-2.

TABLE 8-2 Summary of EVM Factors and Their Relative Desirability

Label	Related To	Desirable	Nominal	Undesirable
AC	Cost	—	—	—
BAC	Cost	—	—	—
EV	Cost	—	—	—
PV	Cost	—	—	—
CPI	Cost	> 1	= 1	< 1
CV	Cost	> 0%	0%	< 0%
EAC	Cost	< BAC	= BAC	> BAC
ETC	Cost	< Remaining budget	= Remaining budget	> Remaining budget
SPI	Schedule*	> 1	= 1	< 1
SV	Schedule*	> 0%	0%	< 0%
TCPIB	Work/Content	< 1	= 1	> 1
TCPIP	Work/Content	< 1	= 1	> 1

* This is computed based on dollars; more on this inconsistency later.

Applying EVM

In Chapter 6, "Modeling the Target System," and Chapter 7, "Estimating Project Size, Cost, and Schedule," I introduced the use of function points and the COCOMO II estimation method, respectively. The software tool for COCOMO II estimates the number of person-months that the project requires by phase. Results of this additional feature are presented in Figure 8-5.

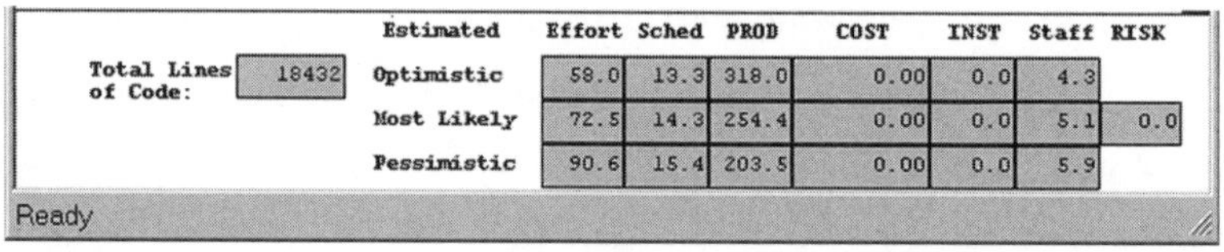

	Estimated	Effort	Sched	PROD	COST	INST	Staff	RISK
Total Lines of Code:	18432							
Optimistic		58.0	13.3	318.0	0.00	0.0	4.3	
Most Likely		72.5	14.3	254.4	0.00	0.0	5.1	0.0
Pessimistic		90.6	15.4	203.5	0.00	0.0	5.9	

Ready

FIGURE 8-5 Total flow time estimate using the COCOMO II tool.

To demonstrate the use of EVM, we can use the *Most Likely* flow time value, 14.3 months. Again, throughout this discussion, keep in mind that we are using estimates and that the numbers we employ might vary but will not affect the overall results. By referring to the results in Chapter 7 and those shown in Figure 8-6, we can lay out what the person load will be by month in Gantt chart style, as shown in Figure 8-7. The person load is obtained by taking the total flow time for the project and laying in the first phase (Plans and Requirements) and the last phase (Integration and Test), and then allowing the intervening phases to overlap the first and last phases in time. Although this amounts to a form of waterfall chart, it is employed here for simplicity and to demonstrate the use of EVM. Table 8-3 lists the duration and person loading for each phase.

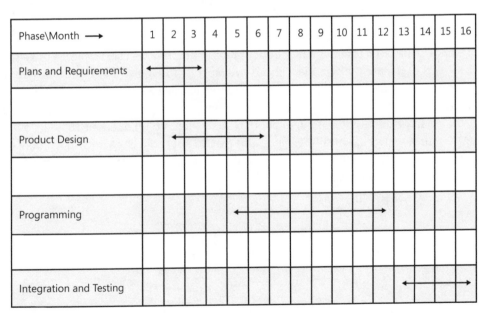

```
Phase Distribution - Project Overall                                    [X]
          Overall Phase Distribution
==============================================================================
  PROJECT                                  <sample>
  SLOC                                       18432
  TOTAL EFFORT                             72.460 Person Months
==============================================================================
                        PCNT   EFFORT (PM)    PCNT    SCHEDULE    Staff
  Plans And Requirements  7.000    5.072     18.869     2.703     1.877
  Product Design         17.000   12.318     25.435     3.643     3.381
  Programming            59.696   43.256     50.261     7.199     6.008
   - Detailed Design     25.565   18.525      -----     -----      ----
   - Code and Unit Test  34.131   24.731      -----     -----      ----
  Integration and Test   23.304   16.886     24.304     3.481     4.850




                    [   OK   ]              [   Help   ]
```

FIGURE 8-6 Flow time by phase estimate using the COCOMO II tool.

Phase\Month ⟶	1	2	3	4	5	6	7	8	9	10	11	12	13	14	15	16
Plans and Requirements	←		→													
Product Design				←				→								
Programming						←						→				
Integration and Testing													←			→

FIGURE 8-7 Project phases, duration, and person loading.

TABLE 8-3 Duration and Person Loading for the Example

Phase	Duration (Months)	Person Load
Plans and Requirements	2.7	1.9
Product Design	3.6	3.4
Programming	7.2	6.0
Integration and Test	3.5	4.8

By using simple mathematics, we can develop a spending line that shows how much money the project is costing us every month. To create the spending line, we need some estimate of the cost of the personnel assigned to the project; we use the amount of time they are on the project to compute a monthly cost. Table 8-4 gives a sample cost breakdown for a hypothetical team. These numbers are "straight time," or direct cost, and do not reflect the burdened cost as developed earlier. Which cost method you use does not matter as long as you are consistent throughout the process.

TABLE 8-4 Labor Rates for the Example

Item	Rate per Hour	Hours per Month	Hours per Year
Project manager	$45	167	2,000
Senior software engineer	$40	167	2,000
Software engineer	$35	167	2,000
Software tester	$30	167	2,000

Using the labor rates and the number of hours per month, we can develop a table showing the cost of the project by project phase. We must do this in two steps. First, we have to allocate a level of effort for each person, as shown in Table 8-5. In Table 8-5, a 1 indicates full time, or about 167 hours per month. For example, a value of 0.4 indicates that 40 percent of the person's time is committed, or about 67 hours per month or about 16 hours out of each 40-hour work week. Similarly, 0.9 indicates that 36 hours out of each 40-hour work week are committed. Using the notation in the table, for example, 0.9/1 should be interpreted as 90 percent committed, 1 person.

TABLE 8-5 Duration and Person Loading for the Example

| Phase | Level of Effort / Number of People | | | | |
	Project Manager	Senior Software Engineer	Software Engineer	Software Tester	Total Cost per Month
Plans and Requirements	0.9 / 1	1 / 1			$13,444
Product Design	0.4 / 1	1 /1	1 / 2		$21,376
Programming	0.4 / 1	1 / 1	1 / 4.6		$37,573
Integration and Test	0.4 / 1	1 / 1		1 / 3.4	$26,720

With the cost per month for each phase, the duration of phases, and the phase overlapping, we can lay out the project plan with respect to project costs, as shown in Table 8-6. With this information and the planned completion dates for each phase, we can demonstrate the use of EVM. Although this EVM example does not provide the level of detail you would typically use for a real-world software project, it suits the purposes of this explanation.

TABLE 8-6 Relationship Between Project Cost by Phase and Flow Time

Month	Plans and Requirements	Product Design	Programming	Integration and Testing	Aggregate Cost to Date
1	$13,444				$13,444
2	$13,444				$26,888
3	$12,100	$21,376			$60,364
4		$21,376			$81,740
5		$21,376	$18,787		$121,903
6		$12,826	$37,573		$172,301
7			$37,573		$209,874
8			$37,573		$247,447
9			$37,573		$285,020
10			$37,573		$322,593
11			$37,573		$360,166
12			$26,301	$26,720	$413,187
13				$26,720	$439,907
14				$26,720	$466,627
15				$13,360	$479,987

We can plot the aggregate cost of the project as a function of time to demonstrate EVM, as shown in Figure 8-8.

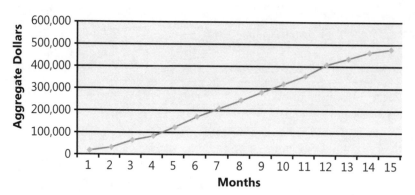

FIGURE 8-8 Cash burn rate plan for the EVM example.

If the project goes according to plan, no problem. But projects rarely, if ever, do that.

Let's assume that our project goes well through the Plans and Requirements phase and the Product Design phase. These are usually the lower-risk phases with respect to schedule and budget issues. But troubles start somewhere around 2 months into the Programming phase. Unforeseen issues are cropping up, some interface problems arise, and we are not completing the coding tasks on time. Our team has decided to work overtime, but this causes the rate at which we are expending project funds to exceed the plan shown in Table 8-6. The project hit its numbers through the first two phases, but in month 6, it is overbudget by $18,000 and an additional $18,000 in month 7, as shown in Figure 8-9. Fortunately, the project did complete the work that needed to be done by the end of month 6 and the end of month 7. We can now use those figures to employ the various elements of EVM.

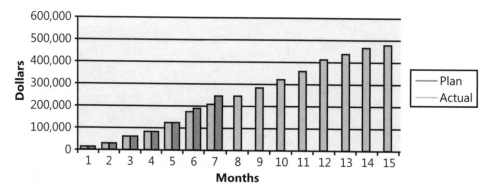

FIGURE 8-9 Planned versus actual cash burn rate for the EVM example project.

Table 8-7 shows the computed figures for our project through month 7. Some general observations about the parameters are in order:

- **AC**   As you might expect, it shows expenses are according to plan (that is, AC = EV) for the first 5 months, and then they differ in month 6 by $18,000 and in month 7 by $36,000 (that is, $18,000 + $18,000).

- **EAC**   This parameter might seem a little puzzling. In month 7, instead of showing an estimate at completion that is $36,000 higher than plan, it shows an amount of more than $80,000 higher than plan. Why not $36,000? The answer lies in the CPI parameter. Note that in month 7, CPI has a value of 0.85. This Cost Performance Index (CPI) was used to project forward with respect to the cost at the end of the project. Because the project is realizing only an 85 percent efficiency on the money spent with respect to work performed, the $36,000 in month 7 and the remaining costs through the end of the project (assuming we are on budget from this point on) are all multiplied by 1/0.85, or approximately 1.176.

- **CV**   This is the cost variance we must deal with. In the seventh month, it is running about 17 percent. The negative value means an overrun, and a positive number an underrun as described earlier (Table 8-2).

- **TCPIB**   This parameter tells us what our improved efficiency or productivity must be to complete the project within budget. It comes as no surprise that, in the seventh month, this efficiency level must be approximately 1.15.

TABLE 8-7 EVM Parameters for the Example Project Showing Cost Overruns

Parameter	Month 1	2	3	4	5	6	7
AC	$13,444	$26,888	$60,364	$81,740	$121,903	$190,301	$245,874
BAC	$479,987	$479,987	$479,987	$479,987	$479,987	$479,987	$479,987
EV	$13,444	$26,888	$60,364	$81,740	$121,903	$172,301	$209,874
PV	$13,444	$26,888	$60,364	$81,740	$121,903	$172,301	$209,874
CPI	1.00	1.00	1.00	1.00	1.00	0.91	0.85
CV	0.00%	0.00%	0.00%	0.00%	0.00%	-10.45%	-17.15%
EAC	$479,987	$479,987	$479,987	$479,987	$479,987	$530,130	$562,320
ETC	$466,543	$453,099	$419,623	$398,247	$358,084	$339,829	$316,446
SPI	1	1	1	1	1	1	1
SV	0.00%	0.00%	0.00%	0.00%	0.00%	0.00%	0.00%
TCPIB	1	1	1	1	1	1.06	1.15
TCPIP	1	1	1	1	1	0.91	0.85

Some project managers might feel that because they do not pay overtime at their firm, this type of analysis does not really apply. That is one way to look at it, but it simply masks the fact that the project is not performing up to expectations. Of course, one reason for this is that we have unrealistic expectations. Another might be that we really did not understand the complexities involved. Whatever the reasons, we have made a commitment; scoped out the work, the costs, and the potential profit; and things have not gone as expected. If your firm does not pay for overtime, make all labor estimates in terms of hours (perhaps weighted by pay rate).

Avoiding the issue by not paying overtime has some serious drawbacks. One is that the project team might go into the death march mode of development and think that they are getting things done on time, even though they are overrunning budget, only to deliver late. Several famous software firms have had this happen all too often. Why? Because the Schedule Performance Index (SPI) likely came into play. In our example, we had a simple cost overrun without any degradation in our ability to complete the tasks in the WBS on time. Usually, this is not the case. People who work long hours get fatigued, which leads to errors, resulting in additional rework and loss of effectiveness. Also, teams usually overrun budget and fail to complete some of the tasks. Just to make this point clearer, assume in our example that the work that was supposed to be completed in month 5 was only 90 percent complete, causing a cost overrun in month 6; the work in month 6 was also only 90 percent complete, causing the overrun in month 7. Although a cash flow comparison will look the same as the one shown in Figure 8-9, a more accurate depiction of the situation is represented by Table 8-8. In other words, EV would have a value of 90 percent of the value formerly listed in Figure 8-8. In the case of months 5 and 6, this amounts to $109,713 and $155,071 worth of work having been performed, instead of $121,903 and $172,301, respectively.

TABLE 8-8 EVM Parameters with Cost and Schedule Problems

| Parameter | Month | | | | | | |
	1	2	3	4	5	6	7
AC	$13,444	$26,888	$60,364	$81,740	$121,903	$190,301	$245,874
BAC	$479,987	$479,987	$479,987	$479,987	$479,987	$479,987	$479,987
EV	$13,444	$26,888	$60,364	$81,740	$109,713	$155,071	$192,644
PV	$13,444	$26,888	$60,364	$81,740	$121,903	$172,301	$209,874
CPI	1.00	1.00	1.00	1.00	0.90	0.81	0.85
CV	0.00%	0.00%	0.00%	0.00%	-11.11%	-22.72%	-17.15%
EAC	$479,987	$479,987	$479,987	$479,987	$533,319	$589,034	$562,320
ETC	$466,543	$453,099	$419,623	$398,247	$411.416	$398,733	$316,446

Parameter	Month 1	2	3	4	5	6	7
SPI	1	1	1	1	0.9	0.9	0.92
SV	0.00%	0.00%	0.00%	0.00%	−10.00%	−10.00%	−8.21%
TCPIB	1	1	1	1	1.03	1.12	1.15
TCPIP	1	1	1	1	0.9	0.81	0.85

The problems do not stop there. Look at the TCPIP parameter, which is telling us that we need to improve our efficiency by 15 percent or more. SV in month 7 indicates that our schedule performance will have to improve by more than 8 percent. This issue of schedule prompted the development of an extension of the Earned Value Management concept. This extension is called Earned Schedule.

Earned Schedule

Although EVM has been in use for more than 50 years, concerns have been voiced for some time that its schedule-oriented parameters are actually based on cost and not on time. For example, the formulas for SPI and other schedule factors use ratios of cost, not time. Although this might seem to be a minor issue, EVM schedule indicators "fail for projects executing beyond the planned completion dates" (Lipke and Henderson, 2006).

The notion of Earned Schedule (ES) was introduced about 5 years ago. Its use by some project managers has demonstrated the power of its simple, underlying principle: ES is the time in the project at which the amount of EV that has been accrued should have been earned (Lipke, 2003).

ES is calculated by projecting cumulative EV onto the PV curve, as shown in Figure 8-10. Unlike in our earlier discussion of EVM, we now can focus on the relationship between Planned Value (PV) and Earned Value (EV). There are three different values to deal with—AC, EV, and PV.

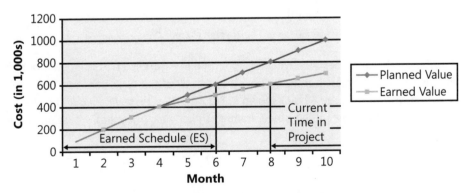

FIGURE 8-10 Projection of Earned Schedule from Earned Value.

In the figure, Earned Schedule (ES) is represented by the double-headed arrow. Its value is determined by projecting the value of Earned Value in the middle of month 8 (the current date) back to the left until it intersects the Planned Value line. Recall that this is a case where we are operating below our plan.

A formulated definition of ES is stated as follows:

The ratio of Budgeted Cost of Work Performed (BCWP) to Budgeted Cost of Work Scheduled (BCWS)

Stated as a formula:

Schedule Variance(t) = SV(t) = ES – AT

Scheduled Performance Index(t) = SPI(t) = ES / AT

where AT equals Actual Time in the base used (days, weeks, months). These are cumulative time-based measures.

We can use a revised version of our previous example (Table 8-8) and the preceding definition of ES to demonstrate the use of this concept. To facilitate the discussion, we can use a free software tool (Lipke, 2006) that will perform the various calculations for us. Let's assume that our project achieves the PV levels as scheduled for a while, then gets ahead of the plan, and finally falls behind the plan, as plotted in Figure 8-11.

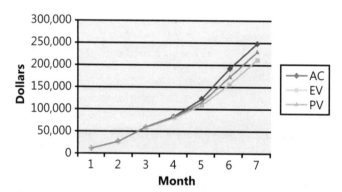

FIGURE 8-11 Plots of Actual Cost, Earned Value, and Planned Value for our example.

Here is another way to describe what is happening in Figure 8-11: Starting in month 5, we continue making progress but we do not complete all of the tasks called for in the plan. This is demonstrated in the ES plot shown in Figure 8-12. The ES line would be straight if we performed exactly as planned. Instead, it inflects positively (meaning, we go ahead of plan) with respect to project status in month 4, and then it falls behind an imaginary straight line in month 5. The SPI(t) and SV(t) show similar behaviors in the difficult months, as shown in Figures 8-13 and 8-14.

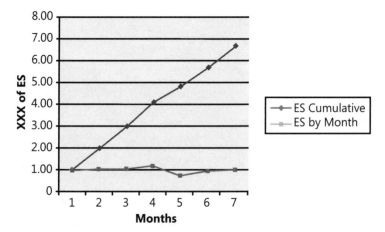

FIGURE 8-12 Changes in ES over time for our example.

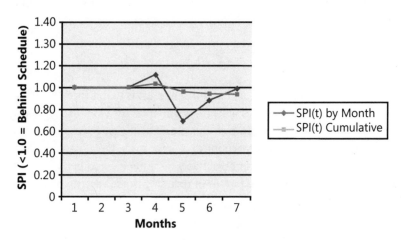

FIGURE 8-13 Changes in Schedule Performance Index (SPI(t)) over time for our example.

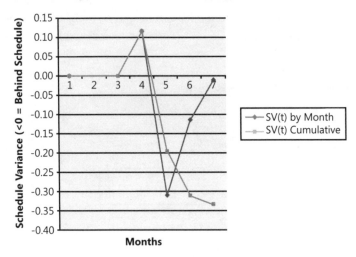

FIGURE 8-14 Changes in Schedule Variance (SV(t)) over time for our example.

Compare and contrast the ES-based plots in Figures 8-12, 8-13, and 8-14 with the results we obtained using EVM shown earlier in Figures 8-10 and 8-11. Note how your attention is drawn to the more pronounced deviation in the ES plots. This supports the notion that the project manager needs to monitor continuously and take action in a timely manner.

Summary of EVM

The real beauty of EVM (and its extension, Earned Schedule) is that it formalizes the relation-ships among work, time, and money and links these variables together in such a way that any perturbation of one affects the others. In fact, this is exactly the way real software projects work. While managing a software project, honesty is important. If we break down a project into small enough tasks for which we can objectively determine whether or not a task has truly been completed, we can avoid the pitfalls of deluding ourselves into believing every-thing is OK when it is not.

Precedence Diagramming for Cost and Schedule Control

Software project managers can use a simple method called precedence diagramming to quickly capture and maintain the essence of the project, its schedule, and its cost status in a single diagram. This method relies on the precedence relationships that exist between the major subtasks that the effort comprises. At a high enough level of abstraction, even a major software undertaking could be described in terms of a dozen or fewer tasks. One straight-forward method (Kuehn, 2006) utilizes the notation shown in Figure 8-15. Multiple passes through the project model are required to achieve the desired result. Each pass reveals im-portant details about the relationships between tasks. These details include the Critical Path, Float time, and Free Float time.

We will use a layout similar to that used earlier in Chapter 3, "Building the Software Development Team." We will use the simplest application of precedence diagramming in this example. The project starts at t = 0. This means that a task with a duration of 2 days and that starts at t = 0 is actually completed at close of business in day 1 (that is, day 0 + day 1 = 2 days total flow time). Seven different passes through the project data are made, each building upon the preceding passes to form a compact view of the entire project. I describe each pass in the order in which it is easiest to develop. Figure 8-15 describes the notation for reference.

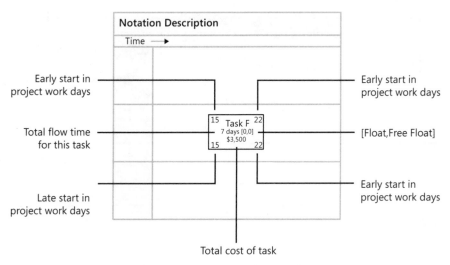

FIGURE 8-15 Notational conventions in precedence diagramming.

Forward Pass

This pass is named "Forward" because we start with the earliest activity and move forward in time to the last activity in the project. Beginning with the initial task, for example, Task A in Figure 8-16, set its Early Start to 0, add its duration, and then link it to whichever tasks depend on it (successor tasks). In Figure 8-16, Tasks B, C, and D all depend upon Task A. Because none of Task A's successors can proceed until Task A is completed, each of these successor tasks shares the same Early Start day, 5 days into the project. Similarly, apply the same process to the other tasks as shown in Figure 8-16. An important rule for constructing the Forward Pass model shown in Figure 8-16 is that the Early Start for a successor that has multiple predecessors must be equal to the latest Early Finish of its predecessors. An example of this occurs with Task F. The latest predecessor finish is Task C at 15 days, so Task F starts at 15 days.

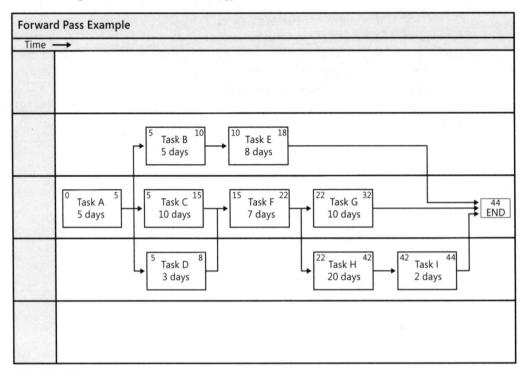

FIGURE 8-16 Forward pass example.

Backward Pass

As its name implies, this process sequence begins at the end of the project and works its way back toward the start of the project as follows.

Set the Late Finish of each predecessor task at the end of the precedence network equal to the value of the End event at the end of the network. In Figure 8-16, this means Tasks E, G, and I all will have a Late Finish of 44 days. To obtain the Late Start of each task, subtract its duration from the value of its Late Finish. For example, in Figure 8-17, Task E has a Late Start equal to day 36 (that is, $44 - 8 = 36$).

Note that the Late Finish of each predecessor must equal the earliest of the Late Start of its successor tasks. So, in the case of Tasks G, H, and F, Task F must have a Late Finish value of 22 because that is the lower of the two Late Start values in Tasks G and H.

Proceed backward through to the initial, $t = 0$ task.

Following this procedure yields the project plan shown in Figure 8-17, which includes the results of both the Forward Pass and the Backward Pass.

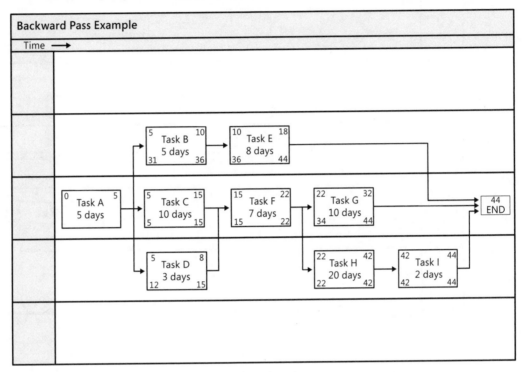

FIGURE 8-17 Backward Pass applied to the example project plan.

Incorporating Float

The term *float* is often called total slack, slack, or total float. It is a property of each task. Float refers to the amount of time a task can be delayed without affecting the completion of the project. It is computed for each task by subtracting the Early Start value from the Late Start (refer to Figure 8-15 for the location of these values). For example, in Figure 8-18, Task F has zero float (that is, 15 − 15 = 0), whereas Task B has 26 days float time (that is, 31 − 5 = 26).

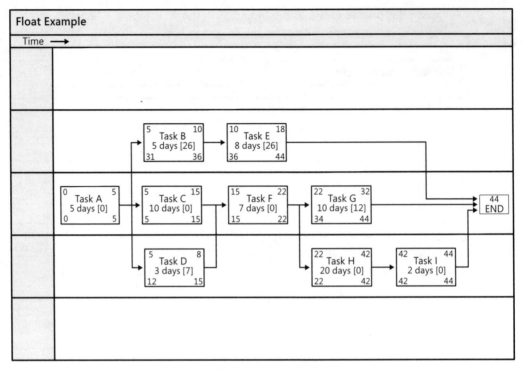

FIGURE 8-18 Float computation incorporated into the example.

Free Float

Whereas float is a useful piece of information to have regarding any task, at least as useful is *free float*. Free float is the amount of delay that a task can incur without affecting any other task in the network. It is computed using the following formula:

Free Float = Early Start(n) – Early Finish(n - 1)

Where

Early Start(*n*) = the successor task

Early Finish(*n* - 1) = the task currently being computed

Applying this approach to Figure 8-18, Task C has zero Free Float because 15 – 15 = 0. Applying this method to the remainder of the tasks in Figure 8-18 results in Figure 8-19.

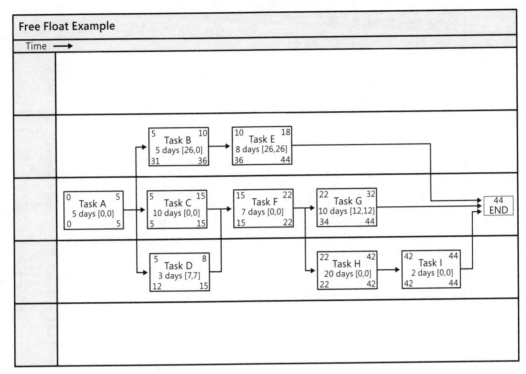

FIGURE 8-19 Free Float incorporated into the example.

The Critical Path

Recalling that float refers to the amount of time that a task can be delayed without delaying the whole project, tasks that are on the critical path all share a float value of 0. Another property of the critical path is that it is the longest path through the network with respect to schedule. Figure 8-20 highlights the tasks on the critical path by using shadowing (such as for Task A).

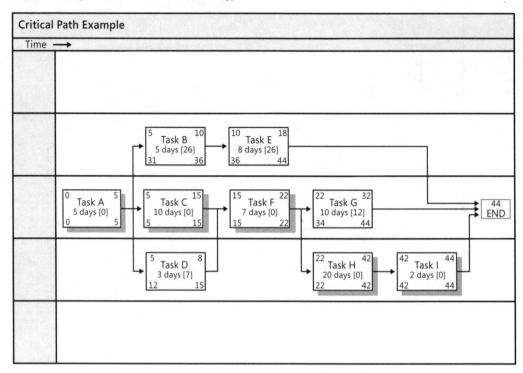

FIGURE 8-20 Critical path tasks shown with shadowing.

Cost Model

We can incorporate the cost of each task into this model as well. In Figure 8-21, I apply a simple cost computation of $500 per day for each task, but in reality, each task will have its own total cost calculated by using the concepts presented in Chapter 7.

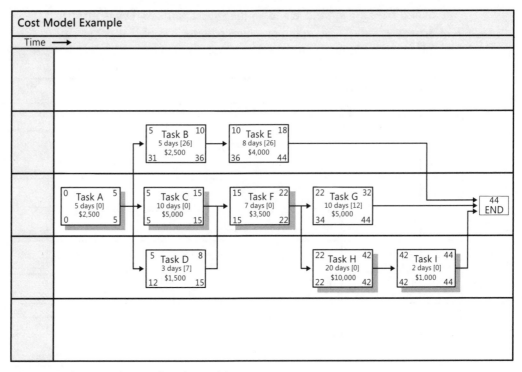

FIGURE 8-21 Incorporating cost into the model.

Schedule and Cost Model Combined

The flow times we have used so far have been days, but they could just as easily be months or even years, and dollar amounts could be in thousands. The point is that, as shown in Figure 8-21, we have a compact means of depicting our project that shows both cost and scheduled flow times. But what about the execution of the project plan and the inevitable replanning that will occur? Assuming we are at the end of day 10, certain tasks should be complete or in progress if we are on schedule. Thus, Task B should be completed, Task D should have been completed 2 days earlier, and Task C should be about two-thirds of the way complete, as shown in Figure 8-22. This is where the management of cost and schedule come together in that this type of diagram demonstrates the following in simple terms:

- Whether we are on schedule.

- Whether costs are in line with the plan and estimates.

- Where to get details using the Work Breakdown Structure, Gantt chart, or other scheme if the high-level view indicates there is a problem.

- Which tasks are in trouble and on the critical path, thereby jeopardizing the project schedule. A variation on this graphical scheme is to display actual cost to date as well as planned cost for each task to externalize project status with respect to cost.

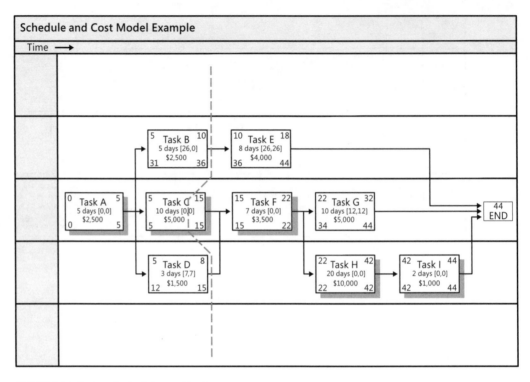

FIGURE 8-22 Cost and schedule combination.

Applying Precedence Diagramming to a Software Development Schedule

Users can download several project plans at the Microsoft Office Project Web site (*http://office.microsoft.com/en-us/project/default.aspx*) to facilitate developing their own project plans. One example project plan presents a model of a software development project. By rounding the flow times off to the nearest whole value in days used in that model, addressing only the highest-level tasks or work packages, making some changes to the names of these major tasks, and then applying the processes just described yields the plan shown in Figure 8-23. Costs were not incorporated into this model. I use shadowing to highlight those tasks on the critical path. The strategy in this downloadable project plan appears to be to ensure that tasks that have the lowest risk (such as deployment) are the most likely to benefit from additional labor resources, while the more high-risk tasks (such as development) have both float and free float to help overcome unforeseen problems while still achieving scheduled dates.

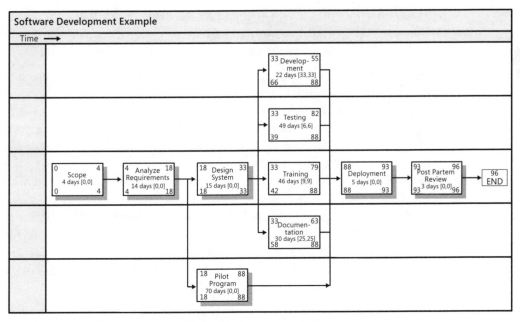

Software Development Example

Time ➡

33 Develop- 55
ment
22 days [33,33]
66   88

33   Testing   82
49 days [6,6]
39   88

0   4
Scope
4 days [0,0]
0   4

4 Analyze 18
Requirements
14 days [0,0]
4   18

18 Design 33
System
15 days [0,0]
18   33

33   79
Training
46 days [9,9]
42   88

88   93
Deployment
5 days [0,0]
88   93

93   96
Post Partem
Review
3 days [0,0]
93   96

96
END

33   63
Documen-
tation
30 days [25,25]
58   88

18 Pilot 88
Program
70 days [0,0]
18   88

FIGURE 8-23 Precedence diagrams applied to a software project plan.

Taking Remedial Action

Although EVM and other methods and techniques can tell us our project has a problem and the nature of that problem, they only imply what needs to be done to fix the situation. For example, if we are over budget, we need to reduce costs, but how?

Here are a few remedial techniques that I and others have used with some success. None is the best, and all have certain drawbacks, but I provide them as starting points from which the software project manager can create an innovative solution.

- **Prevent underestimation of the complexity of the problem**   Underestimating the complexity of a problem is the number one cause of software project estimating issues. You based your flow time, cost, and work estimates on inadequate knowledge of the problem. It will be nearly impossible to address these issues adequately once the project has begun. Although some of the remaining items in this list can help alleviate the symptoms of this problem, a positive outcome under these circumstances is highly unlikely.

   How do we prevent such underestimation from happening? There are at least two effective ways: (1) Do a better job early in the project of documenting, analyzing, and drawing out the requirements from the customer. Requirements that are added as the project progresses are often our undoing. (2) Take a cue from the construction industry.

There, fixed price bids or firm estimates are not made until a design has been created. That way, the contractor knows what must be done. Even though some changes are likely, at least the problem has been firmly bounded.

- **Use overtime**   If you are willing to trade money for a (potential) shortening of project flow time, using overtime is one way to do it. But, like other remedies, it must be used judiciously. Putting a team on overtime for more than 4 to 6 weeks increases output, but the amount of useful work and quality both begin to suffer after about 4 weeks. Also, the amount of overtime can be an issue. Almost anybody can tolerate 8 to 10 hours of overtime a week, but the 60- to 80-hour workweek almost certainly results in a death march phenomenon wherein a lot of hours are worked but not much real progress is made. Notice that I said *real* progress. Simply generating lots of lines of code or a high volume of test cases and plans does not constitute progress if these products contain errors. People can become so tired that they start making foolish mistakes and reduce the amount of work they actually do, which result in a very low return on investment for the time worked. This is even more true when you do not pay overtime but expect it to be worked.

- **Reduce scope**   I alluded to this strategy earlier in this book. This involves reducing the work part of the work-money-time equation by delaying the delivery of certain features. Through negotiations with the customer, you can agree to deliver the most vital functionality and work on the less important features later in the effort or during a follow-on effort. This is where your relationship with your customer comes into play. If you have an open, honest, and trusting relationship, the customer will likely understand the situation and agree that neither party truly understood what the project would entail at the start. If the relationship is anything but trusting, this strategy is going to involve discussion of contract cancellation, reduction in the contract fee, or even a lawsuit—all the more reason to be honest and open with your client right from the start.

- **Selectively add labor resources**   The adage that adding people to a late project makes it later is, generally, true. However, some techniques can be used that disprove that statement. It is usually true that adding people late to a project makes the project later because adding contract labor to do programming on a project can cause the team to pull valuable resources offline to instruct the new programmers (on such topics as where key libraries are located, permissions, programming standards in use, and so forth). So what you want to do is to divest the programming team of any tasks that could be done by others who do not have programming expertise. Baby-sitting the overnight build, regression testing, and so forth might work for contract laborers depending on the complexities of your project. The best way to find out just what can be offloaded from the programming staff is to do what I do—ask the staff. Be prepared to get an earful about things programmers find tedious, and be able to defend those tasks that must remain programmer responsibilities regardless of the number of contractors brought in to help.

- **Reduce labor costs** Some schemes that have worked in this regard include judiciously reducing the number of senior (and presumably higher-priced) personnel on the project and replacing them with less experienced people. Alternatively, you could reduce the hours the senior people work on the project. If the project is far enough along that their contribution is not as vital as it was in the beginning, this strategy can work. If the project is still struggling with issues only a more senior software engineer can address, you can't employ this strategy.

Certainly, many other techniques are available, but a key to fixing a project's problem is to ensure that the product being produced possesses a quality level that will retain customers and motivate the product development team through to finish. Quality is free, and more important, insisting on quality results in improved productivity because people are motivated to produce quality results that reflect well on themselves (Crosby, 1979). This is discussed at greater length in Chapter 9, "Improving Team Performance."

Avoiding Cost and Scheduling Problems in the First Instance

When working with your team to come up with an estimated cost and schedule, you might be subjected to pressure to commit to a schedule dictated by political or market factors. Most often, these forces target dates and/or costs that are unrealistic. The source of the pressure is usually the person you report to and perhaps even someone higher in the organization. So you have some choices—none of which are ideal.

At issue is whether or not your boss will accept your team's more realistic estimate, commit to the impossible schedule for your team dictated by upper management, or simply attack you, the messenger, and replace you as team leader. There are a lot of other scenarios, but you get the idea. Often, the message we get from our bosses is, "Tell me what I want to hear, even if it disagrees with perceived reality." What I and others have done in such situations is to come up with estimates that we and the team can stand behind.

For example, if your team's realistic estimate will not work for upper management, do some research, find out what functionality is absolutely essential for the initial release, and then create an estimate for that scenario and other feature mixes. The message you send to management is that the fully functional product is possible but not on the schedule they want. Note that several alternative mixes of features could be completed, which could get the product into the marketplace and meet the strategic initiative, with more enhancements to come.

The key point is that if a schedule to which they did not commit is imposed on the team, the likelihood of the team meeting that schedule is very low. Why? Because the imposed schedule is management's schedule, not the team's schedule. Remember that the psyches you are dealing with are oriented toward control and outcomes. Team members like challenges, but they also need to pick them. If the team makes a commitment to a particular schedule and feature set, the chances of meeting that schedule are excellent because it is *their* schedule, not management's.

It seems that no matter what a software project manager does to prevent it, at some point in most software projects overtime is required. Based on my experience and that of others, some guidelines are in order when employing overtime:

- Twenty percent overtime (that is, working 48 hours in a standard workweek) is effective for about 4 to 6 contiguous weeks. After that, performance tends to drop off so that after 10 or more weeks, 48-hour weeks produce the same or less useful work than the work achieved previously in 40 hours.

- In just 4 weeks, possibly less, requiring 40 percent or more overtime (that is, working 56 or more hours in a standard workweek) effectively decreases productive work output to equal or less than the work done during a standard 40-hour workweek.

- When you track the number of errors or bug reports versus the number of hours of overtime worked as a function of time, you will notice that the number of bug reports begins to fall and then later begins to rise fast. The point at which it starts to rise is the point where the effectiveness of overtime has worn off. Have the team take a weekend off, or better yet give them a 3-day weekend and see what that does to the rate of error production. Remember that fatigue results in increased error rates. Be sure to establish a baseline error rate *prior* to the institution of overtime.

About Complexity and Project Success

As mentioned earlier, simplifying the project effort can increase a project's chances of being completed on time. The literature contains large amounts of data about complex, ambitious software projects that consumed a lot of resources but really produced very little other than another grim tale of software project failure. Jones provides information that can assist the software project manager in determining the likelihood of success of the team's efforts (Jones, 1996). He uses the function point method discussed in Chapter 7 to categorize project successes and failures, as shown in Table 8-9.

TABLE 8-9 Software Project Success Statistics by Project Size

Function Points	Early Delivery (%)	On-Time Delivery (%)	Delayed (%)	Canceled (%)
1	14.7	83.2	1.9	0.3
10	11.1	81.3	5.7	2.0
100	6.1	74.8	11.8	7.3
1,000	1.2	60.8	17.7	20.3
10,000	0.1	28.0	23.8	48.0
100,000	0.0	13.7	21.3	65.0
Average	**5.5**	**56.9**	**13.7**	**23.8**

The watch phrase here is, Keep It Simple. Keeping it simple might be part of the reason why so many software efforts today are smaller, less ambitious, and potentially more successful.

Summary

It is easy to see why many project managers fixate on project costs. Business and economic climates are not conducive to letting projects stray off their planned timelines and spending plans. But we have to keep things in perspective. If we are overrunning budget but are close to maintaining our schedule, that may not be all that bad if it means we are first to market with a high-technology product or a product with a long market life. Granted, the overrun affects profits early on, but delivering on time in many cases is vital to product success.

As you have seen, even if a project manager tracks the project's spending plan closely, some problems might still be unforeseen. The advantage of using a method like Earned Value Management is that it enables the project manager to drill deeper into what is happening in the project and detect problems early on, before they become insurmountable. And EVM offers much more than that. With EVM, you can provide meaningful feedback to senior executives in the firm in terms they can understand. This improvement in communication alone makes EVM an excellent value proposition.

References

(Albrecht and Gaffney, 1983)   Albrecht, A. J., and E. Gaffney. "Software Functionality, Source Lines of Code and Development Effort Prediction: A Software Science Validation," *IEEE Transactions on Software Engineering* **SE-9**(6), pp. 638–648, November 1983.

(Boehm et al., 1995)   Boehm, B., et al. "An Overview of the COCOMO 2.0 Software Cost Model," Software Technology Conference, Morgantown, West Virginia, April 1995.

(Project Management Institute, 2004)   Project Management Institute (PMI). *A Guide to the Project Management Body of Knowledge (PMBOK® Guide)*. 3rd ed. Newtown Square, PA: Project Management Institute, 2004.

(Boehm and Guio, 2003)   Boehm, B., and L. Guio. "Value-Based Software Engineering: A Case Study," *Computer*, pp. 33–41, March 2003.

(Lipke and Henderson, 2006)   Lipke, W., and K. Henderson. "Earned Schedule: An Emerging Enhancement to Earned Value Management," *CrossTalk*, pp. 26-30, November 2006.

(Lipke, 2003)   Lipke, W. "Schedule Is Different," *Measurable News*, pp. 10-15, March 2003.

(Lipke, 2006)   Lipke, W. "ES Calculator," EarnedSchedule.com, 2006. *http://www.earned-schedule.com*.

(Kuehn, 2006)   Kuehn, U. *Integrated Schedule and Cost Control*. Management Concepts, Vienna, VA, 2006.

(Crosby, 1979)   Crosby, P. *Quality Is Free*. McGraw-Hill, New York, 1979.

(Jones, 1996)   Jones, C. *Patterns of Software Systems Failure and Success*. Radnor, PA: International Thomson Press, 1996.

Part IV
Managing Software Professionals

Chapter 9
Improving Team Performance

It's not about the money, Charlie. I could have been somebody, I could have had a shot at the title...

—Marlon Brando, in On the Waterfront

One of the most important skills a software project manager needs to develop to be successful is the ability to motivate a team. While some management experts see motivation as a leadership responsibility, I see it as being the responsibility of the software project manager as well, because so many software project managers unwittingly take actions that significantly de-motivate one or more team members. But this kind of de-motivating behavior is not reserved for software project managers alone. Companies themselves can engage in it with the best of intentions. Some firms have policies that favor the company so much that they have a de-motivating effect on nearly everyone. For example, when frequent flyer mileage programs were first introduced, some companies announced that if an employee flew on an airline that awarded miles, the company would get the credit, not the employee. Here was a golden opportunity to motivate those who had to travel on nights and weekends on company business—in effect, by saying thank you. But the message that was sent was that the company was again taking advantage of the employees. Almost overnight, nobody could see their way clear to travel nights and weekends.

In this chapter, we will examine some not-so-obvious opportunities to motivate software professionals as well as actions that should be avoided. These examples will be based on a wide range of models of why people work and why they will and will not do their best work for a firm or an individual. These models differ and might challenge your beliefs and experience, but they have several themes in common. All of them attempt to explain why, with a limited amount of time available to them, people will give up being with friends and family to go to work. As we will see in this chapter, people do not work for money alone. While money might be sufficient to get them into a job, it does not keep them there. Something else does—some intangible is at work. Multiple models of what that intangible is and how it works are presented to provide you with a broad viewpoint.

In reading this chapter, bear in mind that one of your keys to success, whether or not you realize it, is how successful your people are at what they do, and their success depends in large part on their motivation. Hence, motivation is the key to success for you both.

What Research Reveals

Motivating software engineers is not as complex as you might think. This is not to imply that software engineers are simple. They are anything but. Because it is the software project managers who create and maintain the environment within which software engineers flourish or wither, let's look at what we know about them.

Studies have shown that software engineers' job satisfaction has a high correlation to high performance and motivation (Linberg, 1999). In a study of 60 professions, software engineers differed significantly from all other professionals in that they exhibit high Growth Need Strength (GNS) and low Social Need Strength (SNS) (Couger and Zawacki, 1980). What a high GNS means is that software engineers need to be challenged. They are problem solvers. If they are not engaged in solving a challenging problem, they get bored and begin looking for other things to do. Since there is no telling where that might lead, it is best to keep them meaningfully occupied. What low SNS means is that software engineers exhibit a strong tendency to face challenges alone, rarely asking colleagues for assistance. This reinforces a concept from Chapter 3, "Building the Software Development Team"—that the highest performers exhibit tendencies similar to those associated with Attention Deficit Disorder (Ratey interview, 2001). Specifically, these individuals tend to be easily bored or distracted. What all this means to software project managers is that we are dealing with people who like to be challenged, work independently, and move quickly from one assignment or problem to the next. Not exactly the ideal makeup for people you might want to direct and organize. But these traits are especially well suited to the needs of software projects with respect to the need for key individuals to rapidly respond to unpredictable changes in direction, emphasis, and requirements. As I related in Chapter 3, one software project manager I know has likened managing software developers to "herding cats."

At the other extreme, successful projects also engage people with traits bordering on obsessive compulsive behavior (OCB) as vital assets. For example, persons in charge of configuration management had better be somewhat obsessive about what each build and shipping product version contains and about closely following the rules for admitting new code into them, or we will never know for sure just what we are building and shipping.

Table 9-1 lists management practices and their positive impact on job satisfaction when they are used. Note that the data represents the percentage of improvement over not engaging in that practice. Hence, there can be improvement of more than 100 percent because job satisfaction might go from a very low value to one more than double the original level.

TABLE 9-1 **Relative Importance of Management Practices to Job Satisfaction**

Management Practice	Improvement over Not Employing the Practice
Allowing involvement in decision making	127%
Establishing a sense of accomplishment	75%
Defining a clear path to advancement	184%
Providing frequent, positive feedback	134%
Providing opportunities to share lessons learned with colleagues	139%
Allowing participation in establishing schedule and feature list for products/projects under development	125%
Allowing participation in deciding reward system and/or recognition for achievements	116%
Ensuring satisfaction with compensation	126%
Allowing involvement in deciding when to ship what they have developed	120%

The values in Table 9-1 are based on a study of software developers within a particular geographical region, but the results are consistent with work done in other regions. The point is that these results highlight the need for changes in how most companies operate with respect to software development. For example, most firms do not give people an opportunity to participate in deciding their reward system, project schedule, product features, and so forth. These decisions are generally reserved for software project managers, program managers, and others in the power structure. The practice of sharing this power with software engineers marks an important difference between high-performance groups and everybody else. Note that the availability or use of software tools, methods, and techniques were not part of this list, although these elements have been the major focus of the industry for several decades.

More Recent Results

A study of what drives the performance of teams working in technology-intensive projects bears significant similarities to what drives software projects (Thamhain, 2008). This study involved 80 project teams and 27 companies. It examined and statistically correlated the factors in the project and company environment that positively affected high-performance project teams. These factors were separated into those that were most positive and those that, while still positive, had the least positive effect. The project team environment factors that were found to have the strongest positive influence on high-performance teams are as follows (in decreasing order of effectiveness):

- Professionally stimulating and challenging work

- Opportunity for accomplishments and recognition

- Ability to resolve conflict and problems

- Clearly defined organizational objectives

- Job skills and expertise of the team members appropriate for the project work

- Overall direction and team leadership

- Trust, respect, and credibility among team members and their leaders

- Effective and user-friendly business processes reflected in cross-functional cooperation and support

- Effective communications

- Clear project plans and support

- Autonomy and freedom of actions (that is, empowerment)

- Career development and/or enhancement

- Job security

A total of 21 factors were identified. The 13 factors in the preceding list were deemed to have the strongest positive affect on high-performance project teams. The 8 factors in the following list were deemed to have the weakest, but still positive, effect on these high-performance project teams:

- Salary increases and bonuses

- Compensatory time off

- Project visibility and popularity

- Team maturity and tenure

- Project duration

- Stable project requirements

- Stable organizational processes

- Project size and complexity

Similar to the results presented earlier in this chapter, salary increases, which might be the project manager's most trusted ally, have only a moderately positive effect on high-performance project teams.

This study focused on how the project environment affected high-performance project teams as well as individuals on those teams (Thamhain, 2008). It found that the positive project environmental factors had a positive effect on individual team members in three areas of individual performance that affected the overall performance of the team:

- Ability to deal with risk

- Increased effort and commitments to results

- Overall performance as a member of a team

From this, we can conclude that the environment that is present for a software project can positively affect the performance of the project team *and* will have a positive affect on individual team members. In a way, this becomes an evolutionary lifecycle process in that the high-performance team performs better under the right conditions, and those conditions lead to individual team members improving their skills, which in turn leads to improved performance by the team, and so forth. This begs the question, "What should a project manager do to set up and maintain the kind of environment within which high-performance teams will be just that—high performance?" We'll address this issue at the end of this chapter. But first, we need to better understand the forces at work that we will be dealing with.

The Basics

Without getting into the details of motivational theory, we can assume that some phenomena that are part of software projects are de-motivating to the team. You'll see later in this chapter, in the section "Why People Work," why these factors have such a detrimental effect, but for now, Table 9-2 simply presents them with brief explanations (Linberg, 1999).

TABLE 9-2 Factors That De-Motivate the Development Team

Phase: Development Factor	Comments
Technically high-risk requirements	Unrealistic, not anchored in what is possible.
High-risk schedule	Generated by market; not realistic or (often) technically feasible.
Staffing	Not just head count, but skill level and applicable experience.
Resources	Hardware, software, communications systems, and infrastructure.
Software quality	Just getting it done is not enough.

Phase: Distribution Factor	
Poor software quality	Reflects badly on the development team.
Feature reduction	Reduces importance of an individual's efforts.

The list of factors in Table 9-2 reads like a definition of what a software project is: high risk, resource (money and people) strapped, with pressure to quickly deliver some results that can be demonstrated. Quality is often seen as optional. Here's a typical statement made in this regard: "When we have time, we will engage the software development process we put together for our organization, but we are in a real crunch right now, so let's just get something out the door." But this is beginning to change as clients are demanding more robust, secure, and safe systems. Most of us know that the trouble with not engaging quality processes for the sake of flow time is that we never seem to have enough time to complete tasks correctly the first time, only to do them wrong and inefficiently over and over. In the section "Software Quality" later in this chapter, you'll learn more about why such statements are refuted by real-world evidence and how these and other practices can have such a devastating impact on motivation, morale, and productivity. For now, let's look at these factors in a little more detail.

High-Risk Technical Requirements

Whenever we push the state of the art in any field, we are asking for trouble and hoping for something of a miracle. It is leadership's job to set the vision and push the technology envelope, and it is the software project manager's job to figure out how we can achieve this goal. Everyone in the software business has been at "The Meeting"—that's the meeting where everyone looks worried while some visionary leader stands in front of the development team and, in glowing terms, presents a vision of his or her concept for a new product. No one feels confident that the product can be built, but this person has so much charisma, enthusiasm, and confidence that the group is more or less sold on attempting what their conscious minds tell them is impossible. Besides, if this effort is successful, the monetary rewards (stock options, bonuses, and so on) are incredible. One item usually missing from such meetings is anything resembling a feasibility study. Hence, everyone comes out of the meeting feeling uneasy about the prospect of having to build this product but gives it a go anyway. This sequence of events puts the software development team at a very low level of productivity and, unless some miracle happens, with a low chance of success.

High-Risk Schedule

At "The Meeting," the schedule is announced. The usual suspects grouse that there is no way that this product will get built in that amount of time, especially with the current load the team has on other work. The comeback often is that the team will be working on this exclusively. Besides, the marketplace for software is such that if we don't get to market first with this product, a competitor will, and we will be relegated, at best, to less than 20% market share. The de-motivating factor here relates to value systems. To the software engineers in the room, their reputation for producing products on time or nearly on time (yes, there are a million excuses why the others weren't on time, it just wasn't my fault!) is in danger of going south because of money. What kind of value system is that? But because the software engineers did not set the schedule, they don't consider it their fault if they don't achieve it—they never really agreed to this schedule anyway. This scenario is a de-motivator to the software development team because they had no control, their opinions or input were not accepted, and most of them have been through this before and can foresee the most probable outcome.

Staffing

Of all the challenges that drive software professionals nuts, not having enough people with the appropriate experience, knowledge, skill level, flexibility, and resilience has got to be near the top of the list. The lack of staff is most often the result of inadequate planning. This can be exacerbated by a human resources department that might be slow to respond and/or is resistive to the idea of paying top wages for top talent. Most often, the human resources department's mission is to minimize wages at the firm. Once they have prepared an offer, they will not increase it even when the candidate counters with a higher figure supported by the software development manager. In most firms, the human resource department's charter is to acquire the best talent for the lowest cost. This can also have a de-motivating effect on new hires because they're starting out with negative feelings about the company. The new hires' productivity is also negatively impacted because they will experience *cognitive dissonance*—that is, they know they need a job to survive, but the money they are being paid reflects negatively on their self-esteem. One way for the software project manager to overcome some of this is to emphasize the advanced nature of the work and possibly the stability of the project (only if this is true) and to remember that, "It is not about the money, Charlie." In other words, find some aspects of the work, the company, the geographic region—something—to make the new hire's decision a more positive one.

Resources

Not having enough resources includes more than people—it includes money and equipment. Without realizing it, leadership in many firms makes resource decisions that can drive the software development team crazy. For example, a colleague worked for a firm that spent $10,000 on new furniture for the executive meeting room. At the same time, they refused to spend $1,000 on upgrading their primary computer, which ran the build environment, when that upgrade would reduce the daily build flow time from more than 3 hours to less than 45 minutes. Rocket science is not needed to see that the $1,000 investment would have been recovered quickly, had it been spent. Software professionals are, for the most part, logical people. Telling a logical person to swallow that kind of seemingly illogical decision is a good way to lower productivity and ensure high turnover rates among the software development team.

Software Quality

Software quality might be the most powerful force for raising or lowering productivity. The way software is developed makes it psychologically identifiable to the software developers as an extension of themselves. As such, if the software is flawed, the developer is flawed, and vice versa. Let's look at the role that this phenomenon plays in software development. In order to retain what little sanity most of us have, nature has provided us with the ability to retain an image of ourselves as being OK. Not perfect, but OK. In this regard, software people are no different than everybody else—meaning that we see ourselves as not being seriously flawed. When we are forced into a situation where we are discouraged from producing high-quality results, this counteracts our internal view of ourselves as being OK. This is a de-motivating environment. For a development manager to take the position that we simply need to get something out the door without regard for its quality indicates an acute case of ignorance on the part of the manager. No one with a reasonably healthy mental outlook ever sets out to fail. So by pushing ill-conceived and poorly executed software systems out into the world, the software project manager guarantees that the software development team will be working at their lowest level of productivity with a succession of system failures.

Quality is free because people want to produce results that increase or maintain their self-esteem, their status among their peer group, and their status in their professional community overall (Crosby, 1979). If a software project manager makes it clear that the expectation is quality results, the motivation will be there and so will high productivity. While I realize that this is an act of faith and courage on the part of most software project managers because of the leadership (or lack of it) in their organizations, I have seen many organizations with a lot of software talent barely able to produce anything because the wrong goal was set by the leadership team. I have also seen the effect of a shift in attitude toward the expectation of high quality, and although there were complaints initially, the results were remarkably positive.

The Relative Importance of the Workplace

As in most discussions of motivation and productivity, the workplace itself must be analyzed and designed for the greatest benefit. By *workplace*, I mean both the physical surroundings and the interactions that occur between management and the software engineers as well as those occurring among the members of the team. Let's look at a few workplace factors that can affect productivity.

The Physical Workplace

Intuitively, we know that there is some correlation between the physical conditions one works in and the quality of their work product. In the software development arena, at least one study put some numbers in place to back up our intuition (DeMarco and Lister, 1999). Those results used a quartile (that is, breaking the entire group into four categories) system, where-in those in the first quartile were the highest performers and those in the fourth quartile were the poorest performers. Table 9-3 illustrates the impact of the physical environment. If you note that physical environment costs are less than labor costs, you can see why this chart is so valuable in justifying improving the physical environment.

TABLE 9-3 Relative Importance of Workplace Factors

Environmental Issue	Highest Performers (% Yes Answers)	Lowest Performers (% Yes Answers)
Amount of dedicated workspace.	78 square feet	46 square feet
Work area is acceptably quiet.	57%	29%
Work area is acceptably private.	62%	19%
Phone can be silenced.	52%	10%
Phone calls can be diverted.	76%	19%
There are constant interruptions.	38%	76%

In reviewing Table 9-3, notice how much more control the Highest Performers category has over their work environment as compared with the Lowest Performers category. Remember, software people are into control. So if one software engineer likes to listen to music while working and another prefers silence, both are put at a disadvantage in the commonly used open cubicle environment. There can also be privacy issues (for example, making a doctor's appointment for a specific medical condition) in such environments. Look at your software development team's working environment. How does it stack up with respect to Table 9-3?

The Relationship Workplace

If you have ever wondered what the big fuss is about the physical workplace, interper-sonal relationships, and communication when all people work for is money, think again. Take a look at Table 9-4, which shows a comparison of the value systems of managers and non-managers.

TABLE 9-4 Relative Importance of Workplace Factors

Factor	Manager's Importance Rank	Nonmanager's Importance Rank
Salary	1	5
Job security	2	4
Promotion/growth opportunities	3	7
Working conditions	4	9
Interesting/challenging work	5	6
Personal loyalty to workers	6	8
Tactful discipline	7	10
Appreciation for work done	8	1
Help with personal problems	9	3
Being kept informed as to what is going on in the organization	10	2

Note the relative importance of salary for each of these groups. Although variations of this chart have been published in other forums, this one is typical of those that have been published (Peters, 2002). Managers often wonder why software engineers who receive an out-of-sequence (that is, an increase in pay that occurs outside the regularly scheduled pay adjustments for all other employees) or extraordinary raise leave the firm within 90 days in over 60 percent of the cases (Dessler, 1997). At other times, people will join another firm for little or no increase in salary. When I have discussed this phenomenon with various colleagues, two primary causes are cited:

- They left because they kept trying to make what they viewed as a contribution, but their contributions were rejected or ignored.

- They were working horrendous hours or hated what they were doing. They had been asking the software project manager for help to no avail. When they were given a bonus or a raise, the raise simply confirmed for them psychologically that this situation was going to continue for the foreseeable future. In a sense, they saw this as being rewarded for suffering they no longer wanted to endure.

One acute example of this occurred while I was writing this section. A colleague who is widely recognized within his industry for his competence and insight into the market and the related technologies has been trying to get his employer to listen to his ideas about how the company could catch up with their competitors technically. After several years of frustration, he has come to several conclusions:

- He is accepting money, but his contributions are rejected.

- The company is on a course that will cause them to fall further behind, lose more market share, and eventually go out of business.

- The current situation simply does not make sense.

- He is not learning anything new in this position.

He has decided to resign from his firm. Repeating this phenomenon within an organization begins the process of "rotting" the firm from the inside out by losing key technical contributors due to corporate cranial atrophy (that is, making decisions that indicate lack of judgment and foresight).

How can we prevent processes like this from destroying our organization? Here are a few suggestions:

- Recognize that Table 9-4 translates into a potential communications challenge for you, the software project manager, and do something about it (that is, communicate with the team on topics that they are most concerned about, not those topics that are your highest priority).

- Alter the work environment in such a way as to recognize that change is inevitable.

- Plan, control, and focus change on improving the company and its products.

- Work to retain the best and brightest people while mentoring and developing future high performers as well as those more challenged by the work.

- Create an environment in which people are challenged and must learn new methods and techniques and can experiment with them without risk. This means that if an experiment (for example, a new method) fails or does not work out, the only repercussion is to have learned what does not work in that situation with some conjecture as to what situation would make it work.

Why People Work

If we want to get people to work more or at least more effectively, we first need to know why they work. The common wisdom among software project managers regarding why people work is that they work for food, shelter, and clothing. In other words, their view is that people work for survival and maybe the acquisition of stuff. But nothing could be further from the truth. Later in this chapter, in the section "Herzberg's Model," you'll see that people who have studied this issue have found that the common wisdom is only partly true. Although their models differ somewhat, one concept the researchers generally agree on is that people work to fulfill needs other than needs related only to survival. Take a moment and examine your own motives for working. In most cases, people do the work they love or have come to know well enough to be effective at it. This effectiveness creates a sense of familiarity and comfort with the job. In other cases, people cannot imagine themselves doing anything else. I have had more than one conversation with software developers regarding work and pay. Someone points out that some disdainful job in a nearby metropolitan area offers a salary higher than anyone in the room is making. At some point, someone else says, "You could not pay me enough money to do that job." So it isn't just money but something else that drives people to continue working and seeking something.

We'll explore some of the major models developed to explain this phenomenon in the following sections.

Models of What Motivates People

Several models of what motivates people to work were introduced during the twentieth century. To a large extent, these sought to explain or "model" how humans behaved and why they continued to work, often in spite of situations that were less than attractive to others. While each of the models had valid points, none has been accepted as being complete, correct, and universally applicable. The ones that have been most commonly applied to software professionals are described here.

Maslow's Model

Maslow's model proposes that people's needs are satisfied in a hierarchical manner (Maslow, 1971). In other words, people will work to satisfy the needs at the bottom of the hierarchy first (survival), and once those are satisfied, they will work to satisfy those at the next level up in the hierarchy, and so on and so forth, until they have addressed all levels. Although this is a "general" rule, some people might not start at the lowest level. Beginning with the lowest level and working upward, the levels are:

- **Physiological needs**   Food, shelter, and income.
- **Safety and security**   Job security, stable income, and security of a time frame varying from person to person—from a day's security to a year or more.
- **Social needs**   Companionship, interactions with fellow workers, and being successful or liked by others.
- **Esteem needs**   The need to be respected by others, to "be somebody" in the eyes of others. A promotion or money can substitute or satisfy the esteem need in some persons.
- **Self-actualization**   Living up to one's perceived potential as the individual perceives that potential; to some extent, being your own boss and doing what you want to do.

The challenge for the manager is that, at any one time, within a group of several people, some might be at one level while others are at a different level. This complicates management strategy development in that a strategy that would be appropriate for one level might not be appropriate for another. You will need to understand each member of the team well enough to interact with all of them in a way that motivates them. In other words, when dealing with a software development team, remember that one size does not fit all.

McClelland's Theory

Similarly, multiple people in a group might also be at different levels within the McClelland model (McClelland, 1961). According to this model, working people have three needs:

- **Achievement**   To do something of importance or significance as the person views it. This is particularly applicable to software engineering professionals, as you saw earlier.

- **Power**   To have control over what other people do as well as control over your own actions. Again, this is reminiscent of earlier descriptions of the nature of software professionals.

- **Affiliation**   The need for friendly relationships.

This is very similar to Maslow's model (Maslow, 1971) but simplifies that concept somewhat. People are still viewed as individuals with their own distinct needs.

Again, the software project manager needs to take each individual's characteristics into account in order to be effective at motivating him or her.

Expectancy Theory

Expectancy theory attempts to explain performance differences between individuals (Mitchell, 1974; Mitchell, 1979; Mitchell, 1982). It proposes that individuals who are motivated or highly motivated will outperform their less-motivated counterparts by exerting a higher level of effort. Although the factors that this theory comprises might seem obvious, they are not. The three primary elements of this theory as applied to motivation are:

- **Role ambiguity**   This has an inverse effect on effort. The more ambiguous one's role, the less effort they exert, and vice versa. This is partly due to a lack of clarity regarding where effort can be directed to be most effective.

- **Effort**   This positively effects performance.

- **Ability**   This also has a positive effect on overall performance and refers to the inherent skill of the individual.

- **Performance**   In terms of productivity, the result of effort and ability.

This model proposes that to improve performance, the individual needs a clear role within which to perform a task. In equation form, this theory states,

$P = f(R,E,A)$,

where R represents role ambiguity, E represents effort, and A represents ability.

The preceding equation implies that role perceptions and ability will define an individual's performance, as depicted graphically in Figure 9-1. A counterargument to expectancy theory exists based on a study of accountants (Ferris, 1977). However, more recent research revalidated it (Rasch and Tosi, 1992).

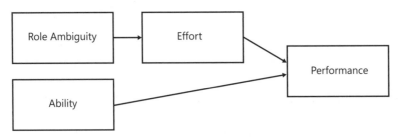

FIGURE 9-1 Elements of expectancy theory.

Goal Setting Theory

The goal setting theory model refines the concepts contained in expectancy theory and has been a popular management technique since the early 1970s (Carroll and Tosi, 1973). It is also known as "management by objectives." This model proposes that the level of success in a task is related to the difficulty of the work and the clarity of the requirements to be met. The main support for this theory is based on relatively simple tasks. In more complex task situations (for example, software development), the correlations are not nearly as strong. Since software development relates to job performance rather than task performance, the model's viability as part of this study was suspect; it was included here mainly for completeness. Perhaps due to its simplicity, this model is probably still the most widely used motivational approach in the software industry and elsewhere.

Individual Characteristics Model

Although not published under this name, the individual characteristics model relates to the work of McClelland (McClelland, 1961). Under this model, performance is theorized as being related to the individual's need for control over his or her own destiny, self-esteem, and need for achievement. It appears appropriate here due to the nature of the psyche of software professionals. The need for individual achievement has been shown to positively affect both effort and performance (Locke and Latham, 1990; Porter and Lawler, 1968). The control over one's own fate (referred to in the literature as "locus of control") has also been shown to positively affect effort and performance. High self-esteem is also seen as having a positive effect on effort and performance. There is evidence that managers with high self-esteem perform at a higher level when they are expected to achieve more difficult goals than managers with low self-esteem in the same or similar circumstances (Steers and Porter, 1983).

Herzberg's Model

I saved Herzberg's model for last because it is generally accepted as having the most widely accepted view of work and motivation. It is sometimes referred to as the "two factor theory" (Herzberg, 1966). In this model's view, there are two aspects to motivation—so-called hygiene factors and motivating factors. Hygiene factors are those that the individual needs in order to survive, including the following:

- Pay and other compensation
- Working conditions
- Respect from management and fellow workers
- Job stability and security

Hygiene factors can attract employees to a company, but they are generally not sufficient to keep them. According to this theory, managers who focus on hygiene factors as a way of keeping software engineers tend to have high turnover rates. One software project manager I had worked with basically held the opinion that "for what I am paying them, I will treat them any way I please." Yes, she had a high turnover rate both internally (that is, people transferring to other positions in other departments within the company) and externally (that is, they left the company).

Under Herzberg's model, the motivation to do a good job, stay with the company, and so forth has to do with the employee's relationship with the job itself, including the following motivating factors:

- Possibility of advancement and promotion
- Potential for higher compensation (for example, salary and stock options)
- Fair and equal treatment

Note that the first two motivating factors are about the impression that one's lot might change. This does not have to actually happen, but the potential for advancement and greater remuneration needs to be there. This model explains, perhaps to a greater extent than other models, how so many people are drawn to high-technology startups—because the startup might grow, the potential for advancement is there, and if it does grow, those stock options could be worth something significant.

Think about your own experiences. How many times have you left a company because one or more of these three motivators were violated? At least in your view, you might not have been treated fairly, the slot you were in was essentially not going to lead to anything, and the pay, both current and future, did not meet your perceived needs. You did not resign because the work was too challenging—you kept being promoted, and you could not invest enough of the money the company kept throwing at you. No, this model essentially captures what every successful software project manager and company with a stable and successful software workforce takes pride in—treating people fairly, advancing them into positions of greater responsibility, and rewarding their contributions. We should all be so lucky!

How You Can Affect Team Performance

In his keynote speech "Emerging Leadership Styles for Technological Team Leadership," presented at the International Engineering Management Conference held at St. John's College, Cambridge, UK, Dr. Hans Thamhain, recipient of the Engineering Manager of the Year award for 2000, gave the attendees a glimpse into the future (Thamhain, 2001). He pointed out that success in managing engineering professionals relies more than ever on the people management aspects of management, not the technical aspects. You've seen in this book how software project managers are selected and that, currently, people skills are not a primary criterion. One aspect of Dr. Thamhain's talk is consistent with the theme of this chapter. His talk was related to overall team performance. Significantly, his talk did not mention that a project manager's technical skills were one of the keys to teams performing at high levels. However, when we examine advertisements for software engineering project managers and more senior positions in software engineering management, there is a predominance of technical skills and a near absence of people skills. One extreme case of this occurred in a recent advertisement I found from a Fortune 100 firm that listed 26 skills and experiences (technical knowledge, experience with various programming languages, and so forth) that were required in order to apply for the position of director of software engineering—25 of these were technical, and only one was people-skills related. Furthermore, the advertisement made it clear that, in order to even be considered for the position, one had to meet all 26 criteria.

Dr. Thamhain pointed out that management needs to exhibit two types of leadership behaviors toward the teams they manage in order to develop teams that exhibit the following characteristics:

- Resource effectiveness
- Self-directed
- Cross-functional cooperation
- Market responsive

- Innovative

- Committed

These leadership behaviors can be categorized into direct behaviors and indirect behaviors:

- Direct Management Behaviors
    - Professionally stimulating, challenging work environment
    - Recognition of work done
    - Recognition of accomplishments
    - Minimal conflict, anxieties, problems
    - Clear objectives and directions
- Indirect Management Behaviors
    - Effective communication
    - Job (management) skills
    - Involvement and support by management
    - Stable work environment

When It All Comes Together or Comes Apart

A fair question to ask at this point is, "If I do all the things I should to motivate my team, what will be the effect?" To answer this, one needs only to examine the literature. The Software Engineering Institute (SEI) is a government-funded organization that, among other things, developed the Capability Maturity Model (CMM) (Paulk et al., 1993). This model is described in more detail at the SEI's Web site (www.sei.cmu.edu).

CMM describes the various stages of development in the organizations themselves, not their projects. As you saw earlier in this book, there are five levels of software project management maturity in the CMM. Each is marked by certain observable behaviors and characteristics. In evolving from the lowest stage (CMM Level 1) to the highest (CMM Level 5), software organizations proceed from producing software under chaotic conditions to well-defined, organized, and predictable conditions. This does not mean that those organizations cannot be successful at the lower levels. What it does mean is that success at the lower levels is largely a function of individual effort. This I like to call the "islands of knowledge" phenomenon, whereby specialized, highly skilled people somehow pull off getting a decent product out the door. The problem is, what happens if one of those key players ("islands") is no longer available? More than one project that I consulted on had just such a person. One project makes a good example of what can happen when relying on islands of knowledge. It was a defense project, and the island of knowledge person in question was a contractor and the only person in the organization who understood some critical aspects of the software architecture. He refused to share that information with anyone because he saw this special position as a form of job security. More than once, he had used his specialized role to obtain early promotions and generous raises. I cited the risk presented by this situation in a report to my customer and noted that risk in two ways:

- The person in question might resign or otherwise become unavailable.
- This person owned a high-performance motorcycle and refused to wear a helmet.

In either case, the project would suffer a setback that could jeopardize its outcome in a timely manner and, ultimately, cause the millions spent to that point by the Department of Defense to be wasted. The company ignored my advisory and let the situation continue, and a few months later, the island of knowledge resigned because he wanted another large increase in pay and they refused to give it to him. After much consternation and the imminent imposition of nonperformance fines for missing milestones, they rehired him three weeks later with a substantial increase in pay. This got other people on the contractor's team thinking, and a few unscrupulous ones engaged in the same activity, while others, who saw what was going on, simply left the company for other firms. As a result, the project suffered serious setbacks, the company had to renegotiate their contract with the Department of Defense, and the project was eventually canceled.

This notion of retaining knowledge as a form of job security is an old one, and its "logic" is badly flawed in at least a couple of ways:

- The company you do work for owns the product of your labor. By accepting the terms of the employment agreement that you sign upon accepting an offer, you relinquish all rights to anything you produce, maintain, or create while in the company's employment related to the work you are doing for pay. One individual I had to deal with at one company took code development more than personally. She refused to let anyone look at her source code, even though she was now on another assignment. She felt that anyone who would change the code would do a poor job and ruin this wonderful work of art she had created. She verbally stated that it was hers. The situation deteriorated to the point that we read her employee agreement to her and pointed out that she could be terminated and we would still obtain the code that way or through a court order, if necessary. This stumbling block took several weeks to undo. The firm's leadership decided not to fire her. She basically abandoned the code to the rest of the team and refused to help with questions or issues that only the author could resolve. (Of course, the code was undocumented and uncommented.)

- Being the only person who understands some aspect of the system can kill your career within the company. While other people are working on new technology and on other projects, you are continuing to be the expert on System X. At some point, System X will no longer be needed, and you will be out of date and out of work.

The long-term prospects for this type of behavior are not good.

How Much CMM Is Enough?

In striving to achieve various levels of CMM (or more recently, CMMI, Capability Maturity Model Integration), you can create an environment that increases the software development team's productivity. Progression from the lowest levels takes continuous effort to accomplish and requires considerable flow time. So a fair question for a software project manager to ask is, "Is there a point of diminishing returns?" Or, alternatively, "At what level of CMM will we have reached our maximum return on investment such that going to the next level will provide a lower return?" Let's look at some studies that might help resolve such queries.

Success at the higher levels (CMM Level 3 and higher) is largely a result of embedded processes, is repeatable, and is more dependent on systems and well-defined roles than it is on people who are "making it up as they go along."

At the lower CMM levels, software development projects are a real adventure. The rate at which "fire drills" (something serious goes wrong, requiring a massive effort to fix and lots of long hours) occur is quite high, and personnel burnout is also high. The outcome is always uncertain. As you've seen in this chapter, the higher the CMM level an organization has achieved, the higher their productivity will be, with resulting lower costs, increased quality, and so forth.

Let's look at one project as related by Steve McConnell (McConnell, 2003). The Telcordia Corporation has 3,500 technology-related people. In the last two years of the technology boom in the United States and the first year after the technology bubble burst, they went from about 2,500 to their current 3,500. They had achieved a CMM Level 5 rating. They had a product with over 1,000,000 lines of source code that was affected by a decision by the Federal Communications Commission (FCC). The decision required them to make changes to and develop more than 3,000 lines of source code. They made the changes, and no errors were reported during the use of that code for a period of one year following this event. While this might seem remarkable in and of itself, what was even more noteworthy was the fact that the more than 3,000 changes were made in just one 9-hour day. The next time someone in your organization challenges why changes have to be made to improve productivity or achieve the next CMM level, you might cite the Telcordia experience.

Managing High-Performance Teams

Earlier in this chapter, in the section "More Recent Results," I identified the kinds of environments that stimulate and nurture high-performance software development teams. Although these environments are effective, a fair question to ask is, "How can we achieve such environments?" Some guidelines that answer this question are available, and they provide a step-by-step means of addressing this issue (Thamhain, 2008). These guidelines are listed here in time-ordered sequence—that is, you should follow these steps in this order. Some of these guidelines might sound familiar and have been mentioned in various places throughout this book. I've listed them here as a convenient reference to assist you in driving high-performance teams.

1. **Ensure team involvement early in the project lifecycle.**   These early stages are crucial to the success of your project. It is understood that the team will grow over time. However, if the initial set of team members is not involved in the initial planning and scheduling stages, those team members will not identify with the project as being their own but rather will see it as belonging to upper-level management.

2. **Define the work process and team structure.**   Cross-functional teams, matrix organizations, and interorganizational transfer of technology are commonplace in today's complex software project management world. Often, however, the infrastructure and basics of the software project are overlooked. This guideline ensures that such mistakes will not happen. This step comprises five key elements for successfully driving high-performance software development teams to their highest level:

    2.1. **Project charter**   This was discussed in Chapter 4, "Developing and Maintaining the Project Plan." In the project charter, responsibilities are clearly spelled out, measures for success of the project are stated, and the important interfaces that must be established and maintained are set forth.

    2.2. **Project organization chart**   This defines the hierarchy, authority relationships, and reporting roles within the project organization.

    2.3. **Responsibility matrix**   This sets forth responsibilities within the organization.

    2.4. **Project interface chart**   This uses the Design Structure Matrix (DSM) scheme described in Chapter 4 to clearly spell out the internal and external interfaces associated with the project.

    2.5 **Job descriptions**   One of the most common complaints I have heard from software developers and sometimes from lower-level project managers is, "I do not know exactly what is expected from me—what am I supposed to be doing?" If setting forth such descriptions, including the inputs and outputs for each position, seems like an impossible task, you might not fully understand what the project is about and what is needed for it to be successful. DSM and stage gating schemes (described in Chapter 5, "Selecting a Software Development Lifecycle Model: Management Implications") can serve to make the job more tractable, but the fact remains that the project manager's vision of what needs to be done from project inception through to delivery and maintenance needs to be stated early on, reviewed, altered, and finally put into action.

3. **Develop organizational interfaces and communications channels.**   The goal here is to ensure that all team members clearly understand their roles, what inputs and out-puts they will have to work with, who they will interface with, and what information will be communicated by what means. For example, important decisions in the course of the project should not be made through a series of e-mail messages, due to the narrow bandwidth of communication that e-mail provides. Even if this means flying people to other sites, key decisions must be made through face-to-face meetings to ensure com-mitment to the decision and to ensure that this is the best decision that could be made under the circumstances. The use of DSM, stage gating criteria, and other tools that we have discussed throughout this book all come into play, as appropriate, to ensure that the roles, interfaces, responsibilities, and means of communication are all spelled out.

4. **Staff and organize the project team appropriately.**   The key to success here is to effectively match the skills and experience of potential software project team mem-bers with the job descriptions set forth earlier. It is a given that you might not always be able to get the kind of super-performing people you want for lead roles within the project, but given the constraints of time and money, do the best you can. In Chapter 3, we examined keys to team building related to personality profiles, as well as team-related experience and experience with the particular technologies that your project will be dealing with. That combined with interviewing will go a long way to successfully addressing staffing and organizing.

5. **Build a high-performance image.**   Project teams that have a clear vision of what they are tasked to do, see how the work can be done, and emote the sense that they can do it tend to perform at a higher level and are more successful than those who do not possess these traits (Thamhain, 2008). This is where your ability to motivate, encour-age, coach, stimulate the imagination of team members, and get them to think beyond their normal circumstances or outside the box is key. Whatever means you have at your disposal, such as interviews within the company's intranet or even news media, help drive home the point that this team is working on something of great importance and its members are an elite group who have been specially chosen for this task. That atti-tude must be tempered with a sense of humility on the part of the team members, but still present in the minds of others within the company is the fact that this group is a high-performance team.

6. **Stimulate enthusiasm, excitement, and professional interest.**   As you saw earlier in this chapter, factors that feed into a person's sense of self-realization and self-esteem do wonders for technical performance. Your job as project manager is to ensure that in their interactions with you, the people on the team conclude that their best interests would be served by the project being successful and by dedicating themselves to that end.

7. **Create proper reward systems.**   As you saw earlier in this chapter, salary increases and bonuses are not a very effective means of driving high-performance teams. This is a challenging task, especially when you realize that you need to reward both individuals and the team itself. By recognizing the achievements of the team and the individuals it comprises, you begin to tap into both the individuals' self-esteem and the team's collective sense of accomplishment. This process will inevitably require metrics that involve the team, the individual, and the customer relationship to measure progress and status.

8. **Ensure senior management support.**   Of all the things that can handicap the effectiveness of high-performance teams, lack of senior management support is probably the most common and most effective at driving performance toward zero. There are a lot of reasons for this, ranging from a high-performance team that is using new methods that were not adopted by senior management (akin to the "not invented here syndrome") to success by a high-performance team creating an embarrassing situation for senior management because they had not previously used processes like this, and as a result, previous projects had failed. This support is crucial also in developing and maintaining a high-performance image. I suggest that if you are unable to get senior management support for your high-performance team effort, you seriously consider abandoning the project. Why? Because even if you are successful without that support, the political "spin" put on that success will either downplay it significantly or portray it as a failure. Along the way, you and your team would certainly be made mindful of that lack of support at progress reviews, all of which will drive down performance.

9. **Build commitment.**   High-performance teams cannot perform at a high level if, as a team and as individuals, they do not support the overall project plan, the processes that will be used, the technology employed, and other vital elements of the project. If you find that some team members are not committed fully to what is going on, find out why. Talk it through with them. They might have spotted some flaw in some element of the project and could offer an important improvement in it. On the other hand, they might simply be somewhat obstructive and negative on the whole project—without being specific. If that's the case and you feel that you cannot convince them that you and the rest of the team are on the right track, you will need to replace them. If they stay, they will become a disquieting influence and might undermine all you and the team have worked to achieve to date. An important point to keep in mind here is that it is not sufficient to transfer people out of the organization just because

they disagree with what's going on. What is sufficient is that they disagree with what is being done and can't see a reason for changing their minds and can't support the project going forward.

10. **Manage conflict and problems.**   One of the primary leadership issues a project manager has to deal with is managing conflict. In fact, project activities are likely to cause conflict within the organization because they draw resources, those outside the project team might not recognize progress, and there is some disruption to the organization's activities due to the existence of the project. The key here is to identify where conflicts might come from and avoid them. If they cannot be avoided (for example, contention over transfer of a key resource from your team to another organization), negotiate as best you can for a win-win result. If someone has to be transferred out of your team, could there be a transition period where you bring another team member up to speed before the transfer takes place, could you trade for another person, and so forth.

11. **Conduct team building sessions.**   If you take a close look at high-performance teams, you will find that most constitute small social groups. They interact with each other almost as though they grew up together. They share a rapport that allows them to joke with one another and communicate almost implicitly rather than explicitly. This does not happen without significant involvement of the project manager. Social gatherings away from the workplace, the occasional on-site lunch within the workplace (for example, ordering in pizza), and so forth all contribute to a sense of camaraderie and mutual support. In spite of this somewhat easygoing atmosphere, some serious activities are taking place. The project manager, through informal discussions with team members (because people often speak more freely in one-on-one sessions with the project manager) and sometimes with the team itself, asks the following questions:

   - How are things going with respect to the efforts you are involved with?
   - Do you feel the group is truly working together as a team?
   - Are there any factors that need to be addressed or are jeopardizing the project?
   - Is there anything that is inhibiting you (or the team) from performing at its highest level?
   - What can I, the project manager, do to make things work more smoothly and reduce issues you might be encountering?

12. **Provide proper direction and leadership.**   Focus your attention on the people on the project team. The people on your team are the most important, most powerful, most innovative, and most flexible assets you have—you should treat them as such. Doing so increases the team's enthusiasm, performance, and productivity. This also means that you establish and maintain open communication with your team and its members.

They should feel comfortable bringing any issue they see as a hindrance to the project, the team, or themselves to you and expect you to take action to remedy it without repercussions. The "shoot the messenger" syndrome should never enter into these communications.

13. **Foster a culture of continuous support and improvement.**   Members of high-performance teams have a tendency to work better almost continuously. Some view this as dangerous. This is actually a healthy tendency, provided you are able to channel it toward specific goals and an inherent culture. By specific goals, I mean to ensure that change is not occurring just for the sake of change but to address some problem more efficiently or avoid the occurrence of the problem altogether. An inherent culture for improvement means that during the project and after, the team's focus is on how to work more efficiently, more effectively, and more proactively to avoid problems, reduce costs, and foster a climate of sharing lessons learned with others.

Much of the content of the 13 guidelines presented here can be found in one project management text or another or in many of the professional development classes available at universities, through private learning centers, or on the Web. The unique nature of this set of guidelines is not only its cohesiveness but also the fact that the guidelines were arrived at through significant studies with the companies and projects mentioned at the beginning of this section, were time-ordered for ease and correctness of use, and were closely scrutinized from several statistical viewpoints. They were not just arrived at empirically—significantly, they confirm much of what has gone before that *was* arrived at empirically.

Summary

Whether we use the team programming concept of the 1970s or today's Agile development method, as managers, we deal with people. This presents us with challenges far more difficult than anything we might encounter in the technical world, with far fewer ways of establishing whether we are successful. The key to success in this regard is to recognize that your people are your most important resource and to treat them like it by keeping them moving forward by challenging them to increase their skills and the quality of their work and providing them with the physical and psychological environment that makes this possible. Do this, and you will ensure that you and your team will be successful.

References

(Linberg, 1999)   Linberg, K. R. "Job Satisfaction Among Software Developers," doctoral dissertation. Walden University, St. Paul, MN, 1999.

(Couger and Zawacki, 1980)   Couger, D. J., and R. A. Zawacki. *Motivating and Managing Computer Personnel*. New York: Wiley-Interscience, 1980.

(Thamhain, 2008)   Thamhain, H. J. "Team Leadership Effectiveness in Technology-Based Project Environments," *IEEE Engineering Management Review* **36**(1), pp. 165–180, 2008.

(Ratey interview, 2001)   Interview by Steve Shirer with Dr. J. J. Ratey, KUOW Radio, Seattle, WA, 26 April 2001.

(Crosby, 1979)   Crosby, P. *Quality Is Free*. New York: McGraw-Hill, 1979.

(DeMarco and Lister, 1999)   DeMarco, T., and T. Lister. *Peopleware*. New York: Dorset House, 1999.

(Peters, 2002)   Peters, L. J. *Software Engineers and Their Managers*, doctoral dissertation. California Coast University, Santa Ana, CA, 2002.

(Dessler, 1997)   Dessler, G. *Human Resource Management*, 7th ed. Englewood Cliffs, NJ: Prentice-Hall, 1997.

(Maslow, 1971)   Maslow, A. H. *The Farther Reaches of Human Nature*. New York, NY: Viking Press, 1971.

(McClelland, 1961)   McClelland, D. C. *The Achieving Society*. Princeton, NJ: Van Nostrand-Reinhold, 1961.

(Mitchell, 1974)   Mitchell, T. "Expectancy Models of Job Satisfaction, Occupational Preference, and Effort: A Theoretical, Methodological, and Empirical Appraisal," *Psychological Bulletin* **81**(12), pp. 1053–1077, 1974.

(Mitchell, 1979)   Mitchell, T. "Organizational Behavior," *Annual Review of Psychology* **30**, pp. 243–281, 1979.

(Mitchell, 1982)   Mitchell, T. "Expectancy-Value Models in Organizational Psychology," in *Expectancy-Value Models in Psychology*, N. Feather, Ed. Hillsdale, NJ: Lawrence Erlbaum Associates, 1982.

(Ferris, 1977)   Ferris, K. "A Test of the Expectancy Theory of Motivation in an Accounting Environment," *The Accounting Review* **52**(3), pp. 605–615, 1977.

(Rasch and Tosi, 1992)   Rasch, R. H., and H. L. Tosi. "Factors Affecting Software Developers' Performance: An Integrated Approach," *MIS Quarterly*, Vol. 16, Issue 3, pp. 395–413, September 1992.

(Carroll and Tosi, 1973)   Carroll, S., and H. Tosi. *Management by Objectives: Application and Research*. New York: Macmillan, 1973.

(Locke and Latham, 1990)   Locke, E., and G. Latham. *A Theory of Goal Setting and Task Performance*. Englewood Cliffs, NJ: Prentice-Hall, 1990.

(Porter and Lawler, 1968)   Porter, L., and E. Lawler. *Managerial Attitude and Performance*. Homewood, IL: Irwin-Dorsey, 1968.

(Steers and Porter, 1983)   Steers, R., and L. Porter. *Motivation and Work Behavior*, 3rd ed. New York: McGraw-Hill, 1983.

(Herzberg, 1966)   Herzberg, F. *Work and the Nature of Man*. Cleveland, OH: The World Publishing Company, 1966.

(Thamhain, 2001)   Thamhain, H. "Emerging Leadership Styles for Technological Team Leadership," keynote speech presented at the International Engineering Management Conference. St. John's College, Cambridge, UK.

(Paulk et al., 1993)   Paulk, M. C., B. Curtis, M. B. Chrissis, and C. V. Weber. "Capability Maturity Model, Version 1.1," *IEEE Software* **10**(4), pp. 18–27, 1993.

(McConnell, 2003)   McConnell, S. "10 Myths of Rapid Development," lecture presented at Construx, Inc. Bellevue, WA, January 2003.

Chapter 10
Evaluating Software Development Teams

Crash, this is one of the toughest jobs a manager has to do.

*—Kevin Costner's manager announcing his
release by his team, in* Bull Durham

Probably the most uncomfortable job anyone has to do is judge another person. This activity is made even more difficult when one is judging another's professional performance. As you saw in earlier chapters, as in other creative professions, software professionals identify personally with the products of their labor. They psychologically see these products as extensions of themselves. So when a software professional's manager judges the product of a software professional and, therefore, his or her performance, it is personal. In this chapter, we will examine how to make the evaluation of team members and teams as a whole a positive experience, benefiting the company, the project, and the individual. We will also cover a list of dos and don'ts regarding reprimands and some labor law basics. The material presented can be used as a means of focusing your discussions with team members or, if your firm does not have an evaluation process in place, as the basis for an evaluation method that addresses the unique needs of software development teams. Remember, your success as a software project manager will be based almost entirely on your ability to interact with, communicate with, motivate, and evaluate people, and not on your technical skills.

Classic Techniques for Evaluating Individuals

The basic idea behind the personnel evaluation schemes in use today is to improve the employee's value to the company and to the employee's manager. On-the-job performance and salary are most often linked—that is, if you get a high performance rating on your annual review, you are more likely to get a raise (also known as a *merit increase*) but are not guaranteed one. The higher your rating with respect to your peer group, the larger the merit increase you are likely to receive, if you receive one.

In an effort to control labor costs, some firms have unlinked performance, wages, and status or rating. In other words, they calculate merit increases on one schedule and do performance reviews (also known as *merit reviews* in some companies) on a different schedule. This approach is most often used by firms focused more on controlling costs than on truly increasing the performance of the group via incentives. It also turns the award of merit funds into a juggling match among managers, with the manager with the most influence winning the lion's share of the available merit increase funds. Companies that use this approach (for example, aircraft and other manufacturers) most often have to deal with unionized professionals and have much smaller pools of money from which to draw raises than other industries. These companies have also often linked salary level with status or ranking. So, for example, a software engineer might have a salary of $60,000 to $90,000 per year, while a senior software engineer might have a salary range of $80,000 to $120,000 per year. In order to get a ranking of senior software engineer, you have to make a certain salary level. Other, more-forward-looking, firms seek to encourage their software professionals to improve their skills and knowledge, so they employ a different scheme. In these firms, software professionals can get promoted by taking extra course work, obtaining an advanced degree, contributing to the profession, and so forth. In this way, the software professional is in control of how far and how fast he or she can move within the firm. This relieves a lot of pressure usually placed on the software project manager, because rankings are formulated (for example, 10 years experience and a bachelor's degree in science or engineering or 5 years experience and a master's degree in science or engineering). An insidious twist on this approach that effectively short-circuits the software engineer's ability to advance through education and so forth is to specify the maximum number of slots at a certain level. Hence, even if someone is qualified for a higher ranking, he or she cannot be reclassified if no open slots are available at the higher level within the organization. Such policies destroy initiative and motivation because there is no incentive for achieving higher levels of performance.

Regardless of whether merit raises are included in or are unlinked from performance reviews, the format of the performance review invariably addresses the following themes:

- What has the employee accomplished since the last review?

- What was the employee supposed to have accomplished?

- How well or poorly do they compare, and why?

- What is the employee going to be expected to achieve during the next review period?

Often, other, longer-term, goals come into play, such as the employee's migration into a more senior technical or leadership role.

Note that the basis for the evaluation is quite local in its focus. It looks at the day-to-day activities supporting the person's manager and project, without much attention to the person's impact on the company as a whole. This lack of relevance contributes to the ineffectiveness of performance reviews and merit reviews in general (Crandall, 2001). We will revisit this point in the next section.

The Strategy-Based Evaluation Method

The need to improve retention rates among software professionals has already been established. But the current high turnover rates (that is, low retention rates) are merely a symptom of a more systemic problem. This higher-level problem stems from the fact that the annual or semiannual review communicates to the software engineer and the software engineering manager the value that the company places on each of them. A powerful means of improving low retention rates is the use of performance reviews. Some firms conduct these performance reviews on an annual basis, while others conduct reviews semiannually. Regardless of how often the reviews are done, the improved review method described in the following sections addresses multiple issues simultaneously. These issues include the following:

- Incentives for continued and improved performance

- Improved communication of how each individual's contribution helps achieve corporate goals

- Professional development

- Objectively quantifiable measure of performance

- Improved retention rate

- Improved productivity

Research into how to improve evaluation of the performance of individual software professionals has resulted in the development of a review method called the *Strategy-Based Evaluation Method*, or SEM (Peters, 2002). SEM addresses the shortcomings of other methods and better meets the needs of software engineering managers both for conducting reviews and for being reviewed by their managers. It is based in part on the *Balanced Scorecard* (BSC) method (Kaplan and Norton, 1996a), which has proven so successful at helping organizations formulate and achieve their goals. Regardless of the evaluation methods that are currently in use in your organization, the SEM approach can be used to refine and focus your evaluation activities with your team members. Starting with the basics of BSC, SEM extends the scope of that method in two important ways:

- **Ownership**   BSC does an excellent job of communicating high-level corporate goals down to the level where the work is done. In so doing, it enables employees at any level to know how they are contributing to the attainment of the corporation's goals. What it does not do is provide an explicit means of assigning responsibility, or "ownership," to each action—that is, ensuring that one or more people are responsible for executing the action. The importance of this is that execution of the listed action is required to attain the goals desired by the corporation. It's simple—no action, no goal attainment. Without a responsible person (that is, owner), no action will occur.

- **Suppliers**   The attainment of goals by breaking complex tasks down into simpler subtasks and then focusing the team or individual on achieving goals through the successful completion of these subtasks has been shown to be an effective problem solving technique since Roman times (that is, divide and conquer). However, BSC does not address situations where acquisition of the required goods and services depends on outside suppliers. SEM incorporates the issue of suppliers.

The appropriateness of an expanded method for creating and maintaining "scorecards" for software project managers and their software engineers is a significant issue. These issues are listed in Table 10-1.

TABLE 10-1 Properties of the SEM Approach

Issue	SEM
Strong link to corporate goals	✓
Ease of learning and use	✓
Automated support tools available	✓
Proven track record and effectiveness	✓
Used in broad range of corporate environments	✓
Broad scope of applicability	✓

Using SEM

As with most new or different methods, the success or failure of the initiative to introduce SEM is dependent on several related factors, including the following:

- **Ability of the corporation to set and achieve strategic goals**   SEM is oriented toward achieving corporate goals. If the corporation were currently able to set forth a strategy (note: setting sales and profit targets does not constitute a strategy) and achieve it in the desired time frame, SEM would be superfluous. In such cases, SEM is not recommended. However, this phenomenon is atypical of experience in the industry (Kaplan and Norton, 1996b).

- **Vertical support throughout the organization, meaning that there is commitment to this approach from top to bottom**   If the support for a different and improved means of doing employee performance evaluations is not present throughout the portion of the corporation affected, SEM will not work. It is paradoxical that major corporations with extensive sales and marketing forces can sell to those outside their companies but not within them. A change of this nature needs to be sold to everyone who will be affected. This means that the introduction of SEM should be scoped, planned, and executed like any other project. Otherwise, experience has shown that SEM will be introduced, be somewhat uncomfortable to use due to its differences from past practices, and then be abandoned (Peters private communications, 1985–1995; McKenzie private communications, 2000).

- ■ **Budget for SEM**   Nothing is free. This is especially true of a change of this sort. Money must be allocated for training managers at all levels on how to use this method. A budget for the process team will be needed, as well as support at the highest levels in the company. Without this support, SEM will be misused and abandoned.

All three elements (the need to realize strategy, internal support, and budget) must be present for SEM to become part of the corporate culture.

The SEM Process

The SEM process consists of the sequential steps described in this section. If your organization already has a process in place, what follows can help streamline portions of it. If it does not have a process in place, you might consider starting with this one to form your own process. In developing the SEM process, it was assumed that the director of software engineering, the software project managers, and the software engineers being reviewed all understood the use of BSC to develop corporate strategy (Kaplan and Norton, 1996b). If corporate strategy is not being developed at the highest levels, more localized strategies will be developed at the department or group level that may not necessarily be linked to overall corporate goals.

A compact means of describing the SEM process is the IDEF0 (Integration DEFinition version 0) method, whose notational conventions were described in Chapter 6. An IDEF0 model of the SEM process is presented in Figures 10-1 and 10-2. These diagrams will act as a guide to the description of each step in the paragraphs that follow.

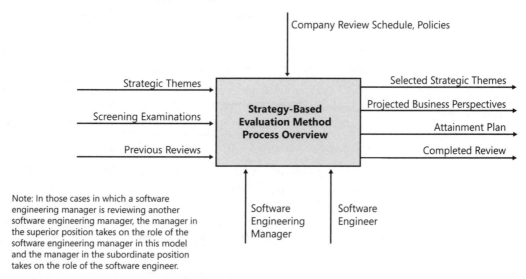

Note: In those cases in which a software engineering manager is reviewing another software engineering manager, the manager in the superior position takes on the role of the software engineering manager in this model and the manager in the subordinate position takes on the role of the software engineer.

FIGURE 10-1 A high-level view of the SEM process.

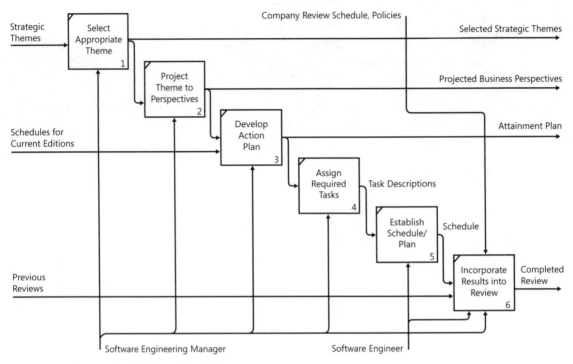

FIGURE 10-2 A more detailed view of the SEM process.

The steps involved in using SEM are described here:

Step 1: Select an appropriate theme.   Strategic themes sound a lot like goals. For example, the theme "Increase market share of consumer-based electronics" appears to be a goal, but what distinguishes it is that it is part of an overall grand scheme (or strategy) that has been developed in concert with other parts of corporate strategy. A *strategy* is a plan of action that requires multiple activities to achieve and has a measurable outcome. The higher the level in the corporation at which a strategic goal is generated, the broader the width of participation and impact it will have, and the longer it will take to achieve. Examples of strategic initiatives at the department and/or group levels include the following. (The time frames within which to achieve these have not been included.)

- Achieve Capability Maturity Model (CMM) Level 2 (Paulk et al., 1993).

- Become the premier supplier of graphics chips to the top three PC original equipment manufacturers (OEMs).

- Improve software quality.

- Reduce software development total lifecycle time.

In this context, the term *appropriate theme* per the text of step 1 refers to the selection (if it has not already been assigned) of a strategic theme that is suitable to your department or group. For example, taking on a strategic theme that is directed at improving the accounting department would be inappropriate for a software engineering group.

Step 2: Project the theme to perspectives.   There are four business perspectives: Financial, Customer, Internal, and Learning and Growth are each used as the "target" for each strategic theme. A table is the most convenient way to develop this concept. Table 10-2 shows an example of such a table for the Action section. This section states what has to be done to achieve the goals from each of the four perspectives just mentioned. The action is stated in terms with which the relevant business perspective would identify. For example, the financial perspective might be interested in an action such as "Reduce operating costs." There can be some crossover between one strategic theme and another. For example, in Table 10-2, "Reduced bug count" is an action that the customer will experience. This will contribute to the achievement of a strategic theme whose nature is to achieve a preferred status with OEMs.

TABLE 10-2 The Business Perspective/Action Table Supporting "Reduced Bug Count"

Business Perspective	Actions
Financial	❑ Lower costs.
Customer	❑ Faster bug correction/resolution. ❑ Reduced bug count.
Internal	❑ Get it right the first time. ❑ Assign, track, and follow up consistently.
Learning and growth	❑ Disciplined use of the Engineering Problem Report (EPR) system. ❑ Integration of EPR and ECP systems. ❑ Rewards based on quality of code.

Step 3: Develop an action plan.   It is in the action plan that the elements of the performance review take form. The plan consists of actions that can be measured, outcomes that are evaluated, and feedback regarding performance developed for software professionals. In general, not all of the actions listed in Table 10-2 can be expanded further into simpler actions. For example, the cost reduction action is really a result of implementing the other actions in the list. In this step, each of the actions that are suitable for expansion (that is, all of the actions except the cost reduction action) will be documented through an action plan. Table 10-3 shows an example of an action plan for the action "Rewards based on quality of code." A table similar to that shown in Table 10-3 would be drawn up for each suitable action, indicating the objective supported by the action. After these tables have been completed, we need to get buy-in from the other members of the team performing this analysis.

TABLE 10-3 **Action Plan for "Rewards Based on Quality of Code"**

Objectives/ Actions	Metric	Target Value	Initiative Title	Ownership	Supplier
Rewards based on the quality of the code produced.	Number of high-severity bugs reported by OEMs and retail customers.	No high-severity bugs are shipped to an OEM for their testing and acceptance process.	Tie in with other initiatives Tie into merit review system.	TBD (to be determined).	Not applicable.

Step 4: Assign (or get volunteers to perform) required tasks. This step involves ensuring that the tasks that have been identified actually get done. The manager of the software engineering manager or of the software engineer uses knowledge of the skills and experiences of those being reviewed to make the assignment of the task part of the review process. In some cases, it might be necessary to encourage members of the group to split up the task as a form of volunteerism. This is particularly true when the team being reviewed is understaffed or heavily overloaded with work. The key here is to establish that this task is needed to achieve an important strategic objective within the corporation or department.

Another reason for using a combination of assignment and volunteerism is that some people might volunteer who are not qualified or who would be better suited to another task or other tasks. Again, agreement from the person or persons to take ownership for achieving the task involved is crucial—even tacit agreement. Whatever form they take, these commitments are the basis for the portion of the Performance Evaluation (or "review") form (Figure 10-3 in the next section) dealing with expectations.

Step 5: Establish schedule/plan. This step involves laying out the timelines for the various tasks so that a coordinated effort will occur. Because many businesses are cyclical in nature, this also ensures that the work will be done in a manner consistent with the business cycle. A key for success here is to ensure that the owner of the task commits to the schedule. Ideally, the flow time that the owner of the task is willing to commit to is consistent with the business cycle or other time constraints. Experience has shown that this is usually not the case. The manager is then faced with some choices:

- **Impose the schedule.** This action should really be considered a last resort. Experience has shown that a significant factor in missing schedules is a lack of commitment to the schedule. The reason for this is that the control aspect of completing the task is taken out of the hands of the manager or engineer who will be held accountable. That has two negative side effects. The first is that, psychologically, the schedule is seen by the owner as being someone else's, not his or her own. After all, that person did not commit to this flow time. The second side effect is that this represents a cognitive dissonance situation that increases stress and lowers productivity (Weinberg, 1971), as was discussed in Chapter 9.

- **Adhere to the schedule that the business committed to.**   This is not always possible, but it is worth a try. Often, the business climate dictates that certain dates be met, whether or not they are possible. Also, dates are sometimes committed to without consulting those who are going to have to do the work. Schedules almost always tend to be aggressive and reflect a lack of understanding as to the amount of work involved.

- **Negotiate to a middle ground.**   A number of techniques can be used to do this. One is to reduce the task (for example, the features list). Another is to get some additional effort from the owners by stressing the importance to the company of this effort.

Regardless of which approach or combination of approaches is used, the key to success in this regard is to get commitment. Without it, the chances of success are very low.

Step 6: Incorporate results into the review.   This step is done for software professionals. The results of this effort form the basis for annual or semiannual reviews of personnel performance. The SEM plan was developed with metrics stated for each of the goals. The intent of the metric is to determine whether or not the goal was met and if only partially met, by how much? The Measurement column in Figure 10-3 contains the metrics by perspective. While this simplifies and objectifies performance evaluation (was the goal met as indicated by the metric?), it is not a panacea. For example, both the software engineer and the project manager must be sure that the goals selected were appropriate and achievable within the time frame schedule and were agreed to. Similarly, the metric must be defined in such a way as to minimize as many outside forces as possible from giving a false assessment of whether the goal was reached. For example, there can be situations in which it is politically advantageous within an organization for another manager to make it seem as though the goal was not attained. They might try to slant interpretation of the results to their advantage. They may have stated categorically that some goal could not be achieved. By achieving it, the project manager, the team, and/or the individual software engineer are proving to be embarrassing to this manager. This is why the metrics need to be objective (that is, no matter who analyzes them, they will come to the same conclusion), a baseline established, and as much as possible, results collected in a manner that leaves little room for slanting the results.

SEM—An Example

So far, I have discussed developing action plans and applying them to achieving specific goals. I have also examined the means of spelling out commitments on the part of the software engineer and/or team to achieve those goals. In Table 10-4, I extend these results to a hypothetical situation employing all four perspectives (that is, Financial, Customer, Internal, and Learning).

Part IV   Managing Software Professionals

TABLE 10-4 An example of an SEM/BSC-style Statement for Evaluation

Strategic Theme: Faster Bug Correction	Objective	Measurement	Target	Initiative	Owner	Supplier
Financial	Lower support costs.	Support resource costs (D and I).	Less than 25 percent of software costs.	Bug Cost Tracking (BCT) Task	Finance TBD by Finance Dept.	Student/ temporary help.
Customer	Rapid response. Fewer complaints.	Flow time. Customer responses.	Less than 48 hours TBD	CRM— quality and retention.	CRM director and team.	Product Develop- ment— TBD Beta sites.
Internet	Reduce bug cor- rection resources.	Flow time by severity.	Less than 48 hours.	Develop error correction process.	Product software engineering.	Not applicable.
Learning	Software team education.	Percentage of team trained over time.	50 percent in 1 year. 100 percent in 2 years.	Software engineer and manager training.	Dual role— product SWE and Education Department.	TBD— possible vendor- research availabil- ity.

Comments Regarding the SEM Process

In reviewing and applying the preceding steps in the SEM process, keep the following points in mind:

- The SEM approach is not a panacea. It is not a substitute for everything currently done in the corporation to evaluate the performance of software engineering personnel.

- If the corporation does not have a strategic plan, the SEM approach will not be any better than the techniques currently in use on a localized basis.

- The focus of SEM is not just performance evaluation but also performance management—that is, focusing valuable resources on the attainment of objectives that support corporate strategic initiatives.

Traditional Performance Evaluation Methods vs. SEM

Traditional evaluation methods have their roots in the field of manufacturing—the concept being that to get greater productivity out of people, we need to set goals for them. As they find ways to achieve those goals, the goals are increased, and so forth. This definitely benefits the company, because they get greater productivity from the factory workers without really paying them that much. Granted, some companies have productivity incentives, but productivity in software engineering is a tough thing to measure.

In Chapter 1, we looked at the alarmingly low number of lines of code that software developers were producing when productivity data was first collected. A rate of a few lines per day or even per hour is truly abysmal compared with the rates we can achieve today in modern software development environments and with the use of software libraries. Another issue that comes into play is the type and importance of the software being worked on by one person vs. another. So one person producing large amounts of high-quality code by working on one part of the system while another person who is working on the BIOS is generating very few lines of code creates a dilemma for the software project manager. Who is more productive and therefore deserves the larger raise? Actually, that is the wrong question. The question should be this: How much of a contribution did each person make to achieving corporate, department, and/or project goals? This is a tougher question to answer, but it's a far more relevant one.

It turns out that SEM helps to answer that second question far more effectively than traditional evaluation methods, as shown in Table 10-5.

TABLE 10-5 Traditional Performance Evaluation Methods vs. SEM

Characteristic	Traditional Performance Appraisal Method	SEM Performance Appraisal Method
Scope of performance evaluation	Local, task oriented	Corporate, group, and individual
Explicit linkage to strategy	No	Yes
Positive feedback in individual's need for self-worth and importance	Low	High
Explicit linkage to manager's goals	Infrequently	Always
Reinforcing of value of role within the group	Infrequently	Always
Objective evaluation of achievements	Infrequently	Always
Participation of all parties in developing goals and measurable outcomes	Low	High

The benefits that would accrue to firms using SEM to evaluate their software professionals (managers included) are as follows:

- Reduced turnover among software professionals.

- Increased motivation and performance among software professionals.

- Greater productivity at both the software engineer and software engineering management levels within the organization.

The degree to which an organization would experience these benefits would depend on the following factors:

- **The level of commitment of the organization**   Are the members of the organization willing to stick with the principles and processes of SEM even when the transition is uncomfortable? Change is difficult, and fundamental change in organizational culture is the most difficult of all (Weick, 2001).

- **The amount of patience that company personnel demonstrate during the transition**   The period of transition can take from 1.5 to 2 years while a new culture evolves within the software community at the organization. Software project managers and engineers alike have come to expect things to happen quickly. Changes of this type are no different. The issue is whether the organization will persist until significant improvement occurs or will abandon this course of action because no improvement occurs in the first few weeks or months that this approach has been in place. (For a time, the situation might even get worse.)

- **The relative stability of the business climate during the transition.**   Nothing can get a corporation to abandon a course of action that is uncomfortable or that does not have an immediate, positive impact on the bottom line as quickly as having the business climate turn sour. The excuse for not changing then becomes one of being willing to change, but not now, and not under these circumstances.

Implementing the SEM approach involves the following tasks:

- **Obtaining the support of the CEO and making that support known.**   This is probably the most important step in the process. If all managers are aware that this approach is going to be adopted and has the full support of the CEO, a lot of other intractable problems go away, including intransigence.

- **Forming a small team.**   This would consist of a group of three to six people who would work with each organization within the company to facilitate the incorporation of strategy into the criteria for evaluation and assessment. Even within a large organization, small teams are necessary in order to move swiftly and reduce the amount of coordination difficulties.

- **Defining key focal points.**   Within each group, there would be one person acting as focal point who would ensure that the changes, once made, continue in place and that the approach is not abandoned when the facilitation team is not present. A backsliding phenomenon can and will occur without top-level approval within the company and without a local facilitator.

- **Creating a short timeline.**   Depending on the size of the organization, 4 to 12 weeks should be sufficient to get the system in place and to begin tracking. Another reason for a short time frame is to reduce the time available for a backlash effort to set in. In this case, the backlash I am referring to is resistance to change in the form of either ignoring the changes or actively pushing back to get them to go away. This is different from backsliding since backsliding is more of a nonproactive push to achieve an end.

- **Providing continuity.**   This is not a one-time task. Once in place, there will be an ongoing effort to keep the process working, to improve or modify it, and to measure the benefits vs. the costs. This will be a full-time effort for one or more people, depending on organization size.

One manager I used to work for described managing managers as presenting trying challenges. These stemmed from their independence, their tendency to stick with a course of action even if it was not effective, and tending not to entertain opinions contrary to their own. This emphasizes the need for the changes and benefits that SEM offers. The potential benefit is too great to be left to chance, as is the need for ongoing support within the firm and for maintaining contact with other organizations using some form of SEM or BSC through the Web.

Evaluating the Software Development Team

The preceding section addressed the problem of evaluating software development personnel individually. A seemingly more difficult task is the evaluation of an entire software development team, but this need not be difficult. You can apply the BSC in some form just as we did earlier with SEM. As you saw in the preceding section, this will entail setting forth some objectives with the team and agreeing on some measurement criteria and target values or goals. But there are a lot of different ways in which software development teams can be measured. A key difference here is that instead of having an individual participate in setting the goals and measurement schemes, you will be working with the entire team as a group.

The five most common categories of high-technology project team performance measures have been identified and are listed here (Thamhain, 2008). Explanatory items are provided to suggest means by which measures can be established. All of these items might not be applicable to your organization or to the type of software being developed, but you should consider all of them.

- Schedule-based measures

    - How close the team came to on-time delivery of their work product or products

    - How the team's schedule performance compared with the schedule performance of other teams working on similar projects

    - How well the team adapted/responded to changes in the schedule

    - How aggressive the schedule was

- Cost/resource measures

    - The degree to which the team achieved the agreed-upon budget

    - How aggressive the budget was

    - Whether overall cost was less than the cost of similar projects

    - Achievement of a return on investment (ROI) target value

- Risk and contingency measures

    - How well risks were identified and neutralized via advanced planning

    - Addressing of uncertainties that occurred during the project

    - Degree to which the team networked with other teams to improve their own effectiveness and control risk

- Enterprise benefit measures

    - Utilization of the experiences of previous or concurrent projects

    - Creating and executing a philosophy of continuous improvement of the work product or products, processes, and practices engaged in by the team

    - Creating, adopting, and improving standard practices and policies oriented toward performance predictability and improvement

- Stakeholder satisfaction measures

    - Overall quality of deliverables and their acceptance

    - Degree to which new and/or altered requirements were addressed and ncorporated into the final product

    - Satisfaction with results as determined through interviews with a third party or a survey

    - The degree of professionalism exhibited by the software development team as perceived by the stakeholder

    - Whether or not the stakeholder would act as a reference

    - The likelihood that the stakeholder would utilize the software development team again in the future

Certainly, there's a lot to think about when selecting a specific subset of the preceding team measures. In nearly all cases, at a minimum, you and the team should be able to select one of the subordinated items in each of the five categories and come to agreement on a goal/value, a measurement mechanism, and the content of a chart for each category similar to Table 10-4.

An Alternative Scheme for Evaluating Software Development Teams

An alternative to the five-category evaluation scheme described in the preceding section is the result of some significant observations of the relationships between the software development team, the company that employs them, and their customer. The team can deliver on time and on budget, can meet or exceed all requirements, and can address and resolve risks, but still possibly not provide value to the customer. How is this possible? One aspect of the answer to this question is the *business case*. It is the business case that got the project started in the first place. The project's cost, schedule, and perceived benefit to the customer were all part of the business case, resulting in the conclusion that the project should go forward.

In case you have not been involved in the development of a business case, let's look at an abbreviated one here. Some years ago, I was consulting for an organization that was constructing a new school for its families. Throughout the design and construction of the facility, several themes dominated decision making. One of these themes was that the families wanted to act as stewards of the environment and minimize the impact on the environment caused by the school. Because the school would have several hundred desktop PCs, there was a concern that they should reduce the use of electricity by these machines when not in use. Having people turn off the machines when they were not using them had some drawbacks, in that restarting the machines took some time and would be awkward for most users (for example, instructors and office workers). I researched the matter and found that there was inexpensive software available that would take the PCs down to a very low level power state but not shut them off. This software could be used to set up any type of schedule required on a PC-by-PC basis to go to this reduced state. When needed, the system would "wake up" from this reduced state quickly as compared with powering up and then be ready for logon when the instructor arrived for class or showed up on a weekend or holiday for some unscheduled work. The cost of the software, the electricity, the impact of the systems on the HVAC (heating, ventilation, and air conditioning) systems, and other factors all had to be taken into account to determine whether this was a feasible answer for this problem. I also checked with other schools across the country and determined that they were pleased with the results and that the company was stable and had been in business for many years. In addition, I checked with the power company and found that electric rates in the area were going to go up. Installation cost of the system was minimal, as all PCs were connected via a network and the software could be installed on a "push basis" (that is, the system was installed from the server rather than from individuals installing it at each PC). Table 10-6 takes all of this into account over a five-year period.

TABLE 10-6 Business Case Computation

Item	Year 0	Year 1	Year 2	Year 3	Year 4	Total
Energy savings	$3,968	$4,167	$4,375	$4,593	$4,823	$21,926
HVAC savings	$595	$625	$656	$689	$726	$3,291
Product cost	($8,000)	0	0	0	0	($8,000)
To date totals	($3,437)	$1,355	$6,386	$11,668	$17,217	$17,217
ROI at 5 percent	$8,000	$8,400	$8,820	$9,261	$9,724	$9,724
ROI at 10 percent	$8,000	$8,800	$9,680	$10,648	$11,713	$11,713

Because money was not all that the leadership cared about, this decision resulted in providing value to them, based on their goal of being good stewards of the environment while saving them money; value to the information systems development team by providing better service and due diligence to their customer; and value to the company employing this team, which got kudos from their customer.

This case got me thinking about how high-technology teams could be evaluated. The concept was best expressed by Napier and McDonald (Napier and McDonald, 2006): the evaluation of high-technology teams needs to be focused on the stakeholders. In the view of Napier and McDonald, there are three categories of stakeholders:

- **Customers**   The customers are the ones who are paying the bills and who are the ultimate recipient of the team's work product.
- **Employees**   This is the team that is working to create the software system.
- **Owners**   The owners are the company putting forth the effort and the investment and taking the risks required to bring this project to completion.

While it is often the case that all three stakeholders are all part of the same company, they each have a vested interest in the success of the project. This model combines some of the elements of Thamhain's concept into single categories but focuses on the value proposition for all three key groups (Thamhain, 2008).

Under this simpler model, the software development team you are evaluating has just as much at risk as the customer and the company they are employed by (Napier and McDonald, 2006). This changes the nature of the evaluation to focusing on the software development team's relationship with the other two stakeholders.

Evaluating in this way requires that you look at the software development team internally (for example, learning new methods, risk assessment, and mitigation) and externally (for example, customer relationship management and documentation of lessons learned for uture software development teams). Using an abbreviated scheme similar to the BSC (Kaplan and Norton, 1996b), you can create an evaluation scorecard similar to the one shown in Table 10-7.

TABLE 10-7   EXAMPLE OF A SOFTWARE DEVELOPMENT TEAM SCORECARD

Team			Customer Relationship			Company Relationship			Total
Current	Future	Score/ Date	Current	Future	Score/ Date	Current	Future	Score/ Date	
Team has not used Agile development but has members who have successfully employed it.	Goal: Use Agile development on initial portions of system with go/ no-go decision based on progress after Phase I.	6	Not conducting intermediate reviews with customer, using "Big Bang" style (that is, system not presented until done).	Goal: Continually engage customer, with regularly scheduled reviews as system evolves.	9	No lessons learned are recorded during or after projects; no postmortem briefing to colleagues after project is delivered.	Goal: Record lessons learned as we go; conduct postmortem briefing.	10	25/30

I have inserted some numbers as though an evaluation had been conducted using a scoring system of 0 (that is, not done at all) to 10 (that is, done to the fullest extent). In practice, you will need to provide additional scoring criteria to more clearly define what constitutes an intermediate value. Other matrixes of similar form could be negotiated with the software development team. The key is to ensure that the software development team agrees to the evaluation scorecard and the scoring criteria.

Summary

Evaluating someone else or a team is probably the most uncomfortable and disquieting thing anyone has to do. It is an integral part of the software project manager's job. I have provided means of achieving this in more accurate and less difficult ways both at the individual and the team level. As you've seen, if this evaluation is done fairly and with care, it can boost productivity, improve the bottom line for the corporation, and represent a positive force within the software organization. By tying several variables together, we are able to improve the performance of individuals and the entire team in multiple dimensions. Remember, people are your most important resource—treat them like it, and you won't be disappointed.

References

(Crandall, 2001)   Crandall, R. E. "Keys to Better Performance Management," *IEEE Management Review* **30**(3), pp. 58–63, 2001.

(Peters, 2002)   Peters, L. J. *Software Engineers and Their Managers,* doctoral dissertation, California Coast University, Santa Ana, CA, 2002.

(Kaplan and Norton, 1996a)   Kaplan, R. S., and D. P. Norton. "Linking the Balanced Scorecard to Strategy," *California Management Review* **39**, pp. 53–79, 1996.

(Kaplan and Norton, 1996b)   Kaplan, R. S., and D. P. Norton. *The Balanced Scorecard.* Boston: Harvard Business School Press, 1996.

(Peters private communications, 1985–1995)   Peters, L. J. Private communications with software project managers in several Fortune 500 companies, U.S. Government agencies, and Canadian Government agencies as part of the author's consulting practice, 1985 through 1995.

(McKenzie private communications, 2000)   McKenzie, R. M., author of *The Relationship-Based Enterprise* (Toronto: McGraw-Hill Ryerson, 2000), private communications, 2000.

(Paulk et al., 1993)   Paulk, M., B. Curtis, M. B. Chrissis, and C. Weber. "Capability Maturity Model for Software, Version 1.1" Technical Report CMU/SEI-93-TR-024, ESC-TR-93-177. Pittsburgh, PA: Software Engineering Institute, Carnegie Mellon University, 1993.

(Weinberg, 1971)   Weinberg, G. *The Psychology of Computer Programming.* New York: Van Nostrand Reinhold, 1971.

(Weick, 2001)   Weick, K. *Making Sense of the Organization.* Ames, IA: Blackwell Publishing, 2001.

(Thamhain, 2008)   Thamhain, H. J. "Team Leadership Effectiveness in Technology-Based Project Environments," *IEEE Engineering Management Review* **36**(1), pp. 165–180, 2008.

(Napier and McDonald, 2006)   Napier, R., and R. McDonald. *Measuring What Matters: Simplified Tools for Aligning Teams and Their Stakeholders.* Washington, DC: Consulting Psychologists Press, 2006.

Index

team building (*continued*)
  key factors in team effectiveness, 32-33
  leadership impact on developing desired
    team characteristics, 248-249
  and member incompatibilities, 36
  and Myers-Briggs model, 34-36
  as process, 32-36, 56-58
  as project-by-project exercise, 59
  role of DISC model, 45-46
  staffing as key factor, 253
  studying Apollo teams, 46-47
Telcordia, 11-12, 251
Thamhein, Hans J., 235-237, 248-249, 252,
  271-272, 274
themes, in SEM process, 264-265
thinking personality, as Myers-Briggs Type
  Indicator, 34, 35-36
3-D function point estimation method, 166-168

U

use cases, 116, 117, 141-144, 161

V

variability, in estimates, 152-154
von Neumann, John, 74

W

waterfall SDLC model, 108-109, 121
WBS. *See* Work Breakdown Structure (WBS)
"wicked" problems, 20-21
Work Breakdown Structure (WBS)
  absence, 131
  Analysis/Software Requirements phase
    example, 73
  comparison with Gantt chart, 195
  developing, 73-74
  Gantt chart information in simple table
    format, 79-80
  improving by using Design Structure Matrix,
    80-88
  introduction, 71-73
  project plan example, 195
  role of flowcharts, 74-77
  role of Gantt charts, 76
  role of PERT networks, 76-77
  role of Rummler-Brache diagrams, 77-78
  as tool for person loading, 78-80
  ways of depicting project plans, 74-78
workplace, impact on productivity, 240-243
Workplace Preference Profile, 40-42

Lawrence J. Peters

Dr. Peters is currently at the Boeing Company as a Project Management Specialist, and is President of Software Consultants International Limited, Kent, Washington. He has more than 40 years of experience in the software engineering field as a developer, analyst, manager, consultant, and instructor. As a software project manager, he has delivered more than a dozen multimillion-dollar software projects on time, within budget, and exceeding client expectations. He has consulted with and trained more than 9,000 software professionals worldwide at firms including IBM, Xerox, CSC, Fujitsu, the United States Department of Defense, and the Canadian Ministry of Defense. He has published three previous textbooks and several dozen papers on software engineering management and related topics. He authored the first Master of Science in Software Engineering curriculum in the industry, which was adopted at Seattle University; he has taught at Seattle University, UCLA, St. Martin's College, and St. Louis University in Madrid; and he currently teaches project management at the University of Washington. In keeping with his belief in the importance of lifelong learning, he received a Ph.D. in Engineering Management in 2002 and a Certificate in Executive Leadership and Management from the University of Notre Dame in 2008. He also holds an IEEE Certified Software Development Professional (CSDP) credential. He is a member of the IEEE Software Engineering Society, the Project Management Institute, and the IEEE Engineering Management Society.

What do you think of this book?

We want to hear from you!

Do you have a few minutes to participate in a brief online survey?

Microsoft is interested in hearing your feedback so we can continually improve our books and learning resources for you.

To participate in our survey, please visit:

www.microsoft.com/learning/booksurvey/

...and enter this book's ISBN-10 or ISBN-13 number (located above barcode on back cover*). As a thank-you to survey participants in the United States and Canada, each month we'll randomly select five respondents to win one of five $100 gift certificates from a leading online merchant. At the conclusion of the survey, you can enter the drawing by providing your e-mail address, which will be used for prize notification only.

Thanks in advance for your input. Your opinion counts!

* Where to find the ISBN on back cover

ISBN-13: 000-0-0000-0000-0
ISBN-10: 0-0000-0000-0

00000

0 000000 000000

Example only. Each book has unique ISBN.

Microsoft®
Press

No purchase necessary. Void where prohibited. Open only to residents of the 50 United States (includes District of Columbia) and Canada (void in Quebec). For official rules and entry dates see:

www.microsoft.com/learning/booksurvey/